Anonymous

Trial of Warren Hastings

Vol. II

Anonymous

Trial of Warren Hastings
Vol. II

ISBN/EAN: 9783337208752

Printed in Europe, USA, Canada, Australia, Japan

Cover: Foto ©Suzi / pixelio.de

More available books at **www.hansebooks.com**

TRIAL

OF

WARREN HASTINGS, ESQ.

COMPLETE

FROM FEBRUARY 1788, TO JUNE 1794;

WITH A

PREFACE,

CONTAINING THE

HISTORY OF THE ORIGIN OF THE IMPEACHMENT,

A LIST OF THE CHANGES

IN

THE HIGH COURT OF JUSTICE,

PENDING THE TRIAL,

AND THE

DEBATE IN THE HOUSE OF COMMONS,

ON THE

MOTION OF THANKS TO THE MANAGERS.

Journals of the House of Commons, 26th *February* 1701-2.—" Resolved,
" That it is the undoubted Right of every Subject of England, under
" any Accusation, either by Impeachment or otherwise, *to be brought*
" *to a speedy Trial,* in order to be *acquitted* or condemned."

VOL. II.

LONDON:

PRINTED FOR J. OWEN, Nº 168, PICCADILLY.

1794.

EIGHTY-SECOND DAY, May 15.

BEFORE the Court assembled, it was generally rumoured, that his Majesty's Ministers had received an account of the capture of Seringapatam, and the defeat of Tippoo. Amidst the joy and satisfaction which this intelligence gave, we believe that every man beheld the scene now acting in Westminster Hall with regret—where they saw the man to whom great Britain owes all that she possesses, and all that she hereafter looks forward to enjoy in Indostan, suffering under a six years prosecution, which no common mortal could have endured—the man who laid the foundation of those alliances, and procured those resources, which have enabled Lord Cornwallis to do all that he has done against the tyrant who has oppressed our countrymen in India. The eulogium which Mr. Pitt and Mr. Dundas has so often pronounced upon his exertions, when all India and all Europe were combined against him, were generally admitted to be well merited; and we believe there were few present in the Court who did not remember an observation made some time ago, " That some of the gentlemen who conduct the

present

present prosecution, have never once been right, even by accident, in their assertions and opinions relative to India."

Major Osborne was called, and continued nearly two hours under a cross-examination by Mr. Burke, the design and drift of which, to common capacities, was totally lost; since not one question appeared to be relevant to the business of Benares, or to any other point that can have a reference to Mr. Hastings: but this sort of examination was much more amusing to the auditors than reading documents.

Major Osborne was extremely clear and collected, and closed his evidence by a reply to two very important questions proposed to him by a noble Lord: The first, " Whether there ever appeared any thing in the conduct of Mr. Hastings to Cheyt Sing that indicated malice towards the latter?" The answer, " Certainly not." The next question was, " Whether the conduct of Mr. Hastings indicated partiality towards him?" The answer, " Certainly—Mr. Hastings was partial to Cheyt Sing, and it was his universal character to all the natives, as was very well known to all who had been in India."

Mr. Markham was then called, and his examination continued from three until five; during which time he went through a great variety of most interesting and important particulars, each
directly

direƈly contradiƈting some one of the positive
assertions in the article. He spoke of the disobedience of Cheyt Sing; the bad police of his
country; the forbearance. of Mr. Hastings, and
ultimately of the desperate resistance made by his
troops, regular forces—not in rabble or populace,
as stated in the article.

At this point, the examination closed.

EIGHTY-THIRD DAY, May 19.

THE Court met about twenty minutes before
two. The counsel of Mr. Hastings went through
their examination of Mr. Markham. That gentleman delivered his evidence with a perspicuity
and candour which did equal credit to his head
and heart. In speaking of Ally Ibrahim Cawn,
(a man whom Mr. Burke had mentioned with
every circumstance of opprobium, in some of his
printed speeches, and as a man whose appointment to the office of the chief magistrate of Benares had occasioned general disgust) Mr. Markham said, perhaps he was as well calculated to fill
that high office, as any chief justice in any country: that his appointment had given universal
satisfaƈion, and he believed that the police of
no city upon earth was so well regulated as Benares,

nares, from the time that officer was appointed, unto this day, for he still filled the office: That Mr. Hastings had abolished oppressive exactions; and that his arrangements had tended to the encouragement of pilgrims to resort to Benares, from all parts of Indostan; and to the general happiness of the people. There were very many other important points in his evidence, each tending totally to cut up the article as presented by the House of Commons.

He finished about half an hour past three, when, to the astonishment of all persons (Lords, Commons, Managers, and spectators) Mr. Burke got up, and said, he was not ready for the cross-examination; that he was himself exhausted; that he supposed the witness was fatigued too, and he wished the Lords to adjourn.—There was instantly a cry of—*Go on*—*Go on*—not without some marks of surprize and indignation in the galleries.—Mr. Burke hesitated, and then said, if the Lords *insisted upon it*, he would proceed—and then he put a question to Mr. Markham.

The Earl of Derby was sitting close to the Managers box, and went from thence to the table, and spoke to the Lord Chancellor, who desired Mr. Law to proceed with written evidence, if he had any.

Mr. Dallas said all was given in, except one paper.—Mr. Law stated the substance of that

paper,

paper, and called Mr. Wright to substantiate it, who was not present.

The Lord Chancellor then said, he did not see how the Court could proceed, with the civility due to the Managers, if they were not ready. Mr. Burke made no reply, and a motion was made to adjourn. To this Mr. Burke submitted, and the business ended.

EIGHTY-FOURTH DAY, *May* 22.

INFINITE ingenuity has been used by senators, lawyers, and even one General, to discover the improprieties of Mr. Hastings's conduct; but, it should be recollected, that in one month a very considerable province was in general rebellion, that Cheyt Sing's success was great and rapid at the onset of the rebellion, and that in the next month the province was restored to peace and tranquillity; that it has continued in that state ever since, with an increase of two hundred thousand pounds a year to the annual profit of the Company.

The gentleman pitched upon to cross-examine Mr. Markham, was John Anstruther, Esquire;

z   and

and here an additional proof is afforded us of the astonishing versatility of British politicians.

This case of Benares promises to last almost the life of man; nearly ten years ago it was just as well known as it is now.—At that time the conduct of Mr. Hastings, at Benares, was attacked by the King's Ministers, and their friends in Leadenhall-street, and most powerfully, ably, and successfully defended by Mr. Anstruther; who displayed almost as much oriental learning in his defence, as Mr. Pitt did a few years after in the House of Commons, but as the fashion of the world passeth away more in politics than in morals, Mr. Anstruther cannot allow Mr. Hastings to have been right in any respect at Benares; and accordingly he kept Mr. Markham at the bar, under a cross-examination of three hours and a half.

Mr. Anstruther put a great variety of questions to Mr. Markham relative to the conversation which passed between Cheyt Sing and Mr. Hastings, at Baxar. Mr. Markham's answers were very explicit; but at last he discovered that the Manager had taken his ideas of this conversation from a forged paper, which had been circulated in India some ten years ago, under the false name of Cheyt Sing's manifesto. Mr. Markham treated this paper with much contempt, and positively

positively declared his own conviction, that it was a forgery. Such we understand to be the opinion of every gentleman, in any degree conversant in the affairs of India.—Mr. Markham, however, gave it a death's blow.

Soon after five, the Court broke up; and here we must lament the premature adjournment of the former day; for not one question put by Mr. Anstruther had a connection with the examination of Mr. Markham in chief; consequently an hour and a half was actually lost: for, why are twenty Managers appointed by Parliament, and those Managers allowed, at a great expence, five counsel, and two solicitors? We suppose, that justice may not be delayed; yet the Court did adjourn on Wednesday last, because Mr. Burke said he was exhausted; and to-day, *not* Mr. Burke, but Mr. Anstruther, was the cross-examiner.

EIGHTY-FIFTH DAY, May 23.

From the difficulty of making a House of Commons this day, the Court did not assemble until a quarter before two o'clock; and the whole day was consumed in the cross-examination of Mr. Markham. There is a sort of anecdote in the polite circles relative to this cross-examination,

z 2

which

which may not be uninteresting to the generality of our readers.

In an earlier period of Mr. Burke's life, he was exceedingly intimate with the Archbishop of York, who, as we are told, is godfather to his son. When people in general were shocked and disgusted at the premature adjournment of Wednesday last, it was said that Mr. Burke, in consideration of the footing on which he had been for many years with the Archbishop, did not chuse to cross-examine Mr. Markham; and accordingly, Mr. Anstruther undertook the office. We are inclined to believe that this was a contemptible idle report, because those who saw Mr. Markham at the bar the first day, must have been convinced, that any species of cross-examination which either ingenuity or malevolence (if malevolence could have been presumed) had dictated, would in the end have tended to the honour, and not to the disgrace of that gentleman.

Again we disbelieve this report, because though Mr. Burke did not examine Mr. Markham on this day, he was at the elbow of Mr. Anstruther, and was his adviser throughout the whole examination.

It happened this day Mr. Anstruther was engaged; the cross-examination for the first hour therefore fell upon Mr. Burke. We do not chuse to enter into particulars, but we appeal to the

common

common sense of mankind, to determine, whether, in the two whole days consumed in the cross-examination, any one point was made, which tended in the slightest degree to support the article as voted by the last House of Commons. On the contrary, every answer served still more strongly to shew the merit of Mr. Hastings, and to place the firmness and integrity of Mr. Markham in the strongest possible point of view. To detail the questions would be tedious and uninteresting: to detect the blunders of those who put the questions, would be to expose the people of Great Britain, in whose names they were put.

We wish here to speak of the impression made upon men of common understandings. The Managers and their counsel are all able men; of course, they mean that this cross-examination should answer some great end; but we confess ourselves to be too stupid to discover it.

The Court broke up at half past five, and we understand that Lord Rawdon complained of the mode in which Mr. Burke had addressed him, and declared his intention of desiring a conference with the House of Commons, if such a circumstance should again occur.

The Court adjourned.

EIGHTY-

EIGHTY-SIXTH DAY, *May* 30,

At two o'clock, this day, the Commons were enabled to form a House, by the assistance principally of gentlemen who had been pleased to attend, on the pressing and earnest solicitation of Mr. Hastings himself.

We wish, once more, to call the fair and candid attention of every Englishman to the circumstances of this cause.

In the first year, 1788, the Managers, twenty in number, attended in a body; a House was always formed by twelve o'clock, generally earlier, and the Court sat from that time until five, and sometimes later; it sat also thirty-five days in that year.

At present, in the year 1792, it is with the utmost difficulty a House can be made before two, and though we are now in the last day of May, the Court has only sat in this year sixteen days, but in fact not a third the number of hours that it sat in the first year. Two, three, or four dressed Managers are all that attend—very few of the Commons—and of the Lords, originally

one

one hundred and eighty-six, there are now not more than from thirty to forty.

These circumstances are not detailed with a view of casting blame upon any of the parties, because what is passed cannot be remedied, but it will not appear extraordinary, that Mr. Hastings, subject to a trial of indefinite length, should take every possible means for bringing the trial in this year to a close. Some officers have been detained in England to give evidence—others are come up from distant parts of the kingdom—and the universal voice of mankind deprecates this protracted cause, as the most fatal stab that could be given to public justice and national honour. Mr. Hastings undoubtedly has many reasons for solid and heart-felt satisfaction under so long a trial:

The King's Ministers, and Parliament, his prosecutors, have adopted all his systems, and are now receiving the fruits of what the articles deem his crimes. The countries which he governed continue to produce the same revenues, to pay the same obedience, and enjoy the same laws as when he was in Bengal.

Not a ship arrives from India without bringing some gentleman of character, who proclaims it aloud, that the natives in India, of all ranks, sects, and descriptions, unite in expressing their astonishment on hearing that Mr. Hastings is under a

pro-

prosecution for desolating their country, for cruelty, injustice, and corruption.—Our own countrymen are equally astonished; and unversed in the mazes of British politics, cannot possibly conceive how those acts shall be highly merito-rious in Mr. Dundas, which are the subjects of censure in Mr. Hastings.

Mr. Markham was again called to the bar, and his cross examination was compleatly finished on this day, but attended with some peculiar circumstances.

Before he replied to Mr. Burke's first question, he informed the Lords, that a few minutes before the Court assembled, he had received a letter from Mr. Burke, informing him that Mr. Mark-ham had written to his father, the Archbishop of York, above ten years before.—It appeared, that in consequence of the very close intimacy and friendship which had subsisted between the Arch-bishop and Mr. Burke in former times, his Grace had, upon the receipt of this letter from his son, given it to Mr. Burke at Court in the year 1782, immediately after the receipt of it; that Mr. Burke had kept it ever since that time, and returned it to Mr. Markam with a polite note just before they went into Court yesterday.

Mr. Markham, with the openness and sincerity which ever marks a man of real character and honour, and has nothing to conceal, begged that

1

his

his letter to his father might be read. It was read, and in every point of any importance agreed *exactly* with the evidence that he had given, though it was singular enough that Mr. Burke had cross-examined him for two days, just as a man would have done who had studied the letter to the Archbishop, which letter Mr. Burke had never seen, as he assured the Court, from July, 1782, until he found it, in May, 1792, by accident.

Mr. Markham went through a very long cross-examination, the longest, perhaps, ever known or heard of; but each answer served to fix his former testimony the more strongly, and to confirm every assertion made by Mr. Pitt, in his speech upon this article in the House of Commons.

The close of his examination was singular and striking, and appeared to affect the Court and the auditors, as much as it did Mr. Markham himself. He was asked if there was any part of Mr. Hastings's conduct to Cheyt Sing that appeared to him as resulting from vindictive, malicious, or interested motives? He replied, that he had known Mr. Hastings for many years, most intimately, and was convinced, that in no part of his public conduct was he biassed by vindictive, malicious, or interested motives; that he was convinced he had ever made the public good, and the honour and advantage of his country, his first object; that of himself or his

own

own interest, he never bestowed a thought : and, with a voice scarcely audible, (probably from the reflection that such a man should have been so treated by a combination of parties against him), laying his hand upon his heart at the time, he added, " I am convinced, my Lords, he is the " most virtuous man of the age in which he " lives."

After this evidence Mr. Burke, with evident marks in his countenance of a man who felt that Mr. Markham was *believed* by every gentleman present, proceeded to a few questions, none of them of any consequence, and then Mr. Markham was dismissed—having sustained his character as a gentleman, a man of honour, and information, through three long days of cross questions, in which many points were enforced by Mr. Burke's cross-examination, which were not stated with such force in the examination in charge.

The Court, at half past five, adjourned.

EIGHTY-

EIGHTY-SEVENTH DAY, June 6.

THE Court met this day at half-past one o'clock, having been detained some time in the expectation that a few Managers might arrive. Mr. Burke was the only one present when the House was made; and the particular and earnest application of Mr. Hastings to individual gentlemen, procured a House about one o'clock.

Four gentlemen were examined, viz. Lieutenant Birrell, Colonel Blair, Charles Greene, Esq. and Lieutenant Wade. The evidence of these gentlemen was decisive as to several points of the utmost moment in the two important articles, Benares and the Begum.

They all stated the delinquency of Cheyt Sing, his state of preparation, and his apparent determination to assert his independence at the first favourable moment.

These gentlemen also spoke of the assistance afforded to Cheyt Sing, by the Begum, as a matter of which no doubt was ever entertained in India; that they believed it then, and believed it now.

Mr.

Mr. Birrell and Mr. Wade spoke of *Nujeebs*, taken prisoners at Patiete, who declared they were sent from Fyzabad by the Begum.

They also spoke of the universal estimation in which Mr. Hastings's character was held throughout India, by natives and Europeans, both before and since this prosecution commenced. In short, the pointed evidence of these gentlemen, the general voice of India, the improved and improving state of Bengal, as exemplified in Mr. Dundas's Budget, furnish such a mass of strong evidence on the side of Mr. Hastings, that with all our respect for the last Parliament, we cannot but wonder, how such a volume of unsupported criminatory allegations should have appeared on their Journals.

At half after five, Mr. Wade withdrew from the bar; and just as the Court was about to rise,

Mr. Hastings earnestly entreated their Lordships' attention for a few minutes; and as the matter he had to state, appeared to him to be extremely important, he begged to address them from his notes; which the Lords readily agreed to, and then he spoke as follows:

" I have, already, upon former occasions, ventured to state to your Lordships the hardships which I sustained by the unexampled length of this trial, even in the more early periods of it. I mean not now to repeat them; nor will it be

necessary

necessary to shew to your Lordships, how much they must be all aggravated by their subsequent extension. I merely allude to them for the purpose, and for that only, of bespeaking your pardon for the liberty I now take, in praying your Lordships to allow me as much time as you can afford during this session to hear the remainder of my defence. I should not so anxiously press this upon your Lordships, were I not assured that your Lordships have no longer any call for your attention to matters of greater importance, if any matter can exceed in its importance the course of a criminal trial protracted to such a length of years as mine has been.

" For my defence on the article now in evidence before your Lordships, my counsel will desire only to call two more witnesses, selected from the survivors of a much larger number, whom we forbear to call, from a respect to your Lordships time, and a consideration of the uncertainty of my life, or theirs, enduring to the end of a more complete refutation of the charge which the Commons have preferred against me. The examination in chief of these witnesses (for I cannot limit the time of the cross-examination, or answer for that which may be lost by interruptions will not take up the compass of two, or, at most three hours.

" Two

" Two more articles will then remain. On one only will it be necessary to call any parole evidence; and for that only three witnesses; one, a gentleman of very infirm health, who was settled with his family in the south of France, but came to England in the first year of this long trial, and has remained here to this time, in yearly expectation of giving his evidence at your Lordships' bar.

" Among the gentlemen whom I hope to be allowed to produce in evidence to the articles now under examination, there is one, who having given his attendance through a considerable part of the first year, when it became evident that he could not be called till the next, informed me that his means of subsistence, though not his patience, were exhausted; and requested me to dispense with his evidence, that he might return to his service in India. I without hesitation, cheerfully consented. That gentleman accordingly went to India, served with credit two campaigns under Lord Cornwallis, is again returned to England, and again in attendance to give his evidence in my defence. Your Lordships will not be surprized, if I should feel a more than common anxiety not to lose a witness whom I have recovered in so singular a manner, from so many obstacles which threatened to deprive me of the benefit

nefit of his testimony, nor to lose so impressive a memorial of the extraordinary charaĝer of this impeachment.

" It is hard, with so near a prospeĝt of a close, to see it vanish into darkness, and another year, or perhaps other yea/s, if I shou'd live to see them, destined for the continuation of this trial.

" Let me beseech your Lordships to recolleĝt, that more than five years are already past since I first appeared at your Lordships bar; and I am sure, that if any one of the noble Lords who were then living, and saw me there, had been told (if human wisdom. which is the result of experience, could have suggested such a conclusion) that more than five years must pass, ere I could obtain a judgment, he would have pronounced it against the course of nature to expect it, and have resented the supposition, as an unmerited reflection on the justice and dignity of this great kingdom.

" In the first year, which was the year 1788, the Court which your Lordships now compose, sat thirty-five days, generally assembling at twelve o'clock, sometimes earlier, and sitting until five, and occasionally later. This year, your Lordships have sat within a week of the same period of time, only sixteen days, and have seldom been able to open the Court much earlier than two o'clock. I should be as ungrateiul as unreason-

able

able, if I could insinuate that these delays were
in any respect imputable to your Lordships; neither is it my wish to impute blame to any: it is
the effect, and not the cause of which I complain. Yet, my Lords, if I might be allowed to
expostulate with those, whose zeal (animating
them to exertions, and to a perseverance, of
which even in that body there are few examples)
brought me to the situation in which I now stand,
I might plead, and surely without offence, that
the rights and interest of the people of this kingdom, and the honour of its Crown, which were
the great inducements stated by the Commons of
Great Britain, for calling together its highest
Court of Judicature to sit in trial upon me, are
at least as much concerned in their using the same
exertions to promote the course of that trial, and
to bring it to an issue.

" My respect forbids me to say more on the
subject, nor should I have said so much, but to
make it evident to your Lordships, that, whatever
causes of delay have occurred, or may in future
occur, in the course of this trial (if it can be supposed that I would willingly be instrumental to
my own wrong) neither have been, nor shall be,
in anywise imputable to me: in proof of this, I
may allude to, but need not specify, the many
constitutional, and even personal means, to which
I have had recourse, to accelerate the progress of
the trial, and remove every obstruction to it.

" That

" That I might not again urge a request to your Lordships, which it might not be in your Lordships power to grant, I have profited by the error which I have been told I committed in the petition which I last year presented to your Lordships, and have addressed an humble petition to his Majesty, praying that he would be graciously pleased to permit your Lordships to continue to sit till the close of the trial.

" I rely with a perfect confidence on his Majesty's gracious disposition to grant my prayer; and in that case I do assure your Lordships, that every possible means shall be used by me, and by the gentlemen whom you have given me for my counsel, to bring my defence to a speedy conclusion.

" If, which I reluctantly suppose, it shall be deemed unreasonable, or for causes which cannot fall within the scope of my limited comprehension, improper, I do most humbly and earnestly entreat your Lordships, in that case, that you will afford me as many days as may be necessary to bring the present article to a close, and to allow my counsel to sum up the evidence while it is yet recent in your Lordships' recollection."

EIGHTY.

EIGHTY-EIGHTH DAY, *June* 7.

THE Court met this day, at twenty minutes after one, and immediately proceeded to the examination of Lieutenant Grey, an officer in his Majesty's service, who gave a very clear and satisfactory evidence in favour of Mr. Hastings. He said, he was an officer in the Chasseurs, at the time of the insurrection of Cheyt Sing. He spoke of his disaffection—of the state of his preparation, and fully confirmed every material point in the evidence of Captain Wade, on the preceding day. He stated the assistance afforded to Cheyt Sing by the Begum, as a matter of universal notoriety, never, as he believed, doubted at the time, nor since: that he remained in the country many years after Mr. Hastings's departure, and could safely swear, that there never was a man more universally esteemed and beloved by the natives than Mr. Hastings was: that the affection the officers of the army felt for him, might be known by their letter to him, signed by many hundred officers, on his quitting the country, when it was impossible they could have been actuated by interested motives. A very long cross-

cross-examination was continued by Mr. Burke, in which every answer only tended to fix more strongly the evidence given in chief.

Colonel Popham then was called to the bar, and in a very distinct and impressive manner he stated the military force of Cheyt Sing, far different from what was necessary for him as a Zemindar. His state of preparation, the general opinion of his disaffection, the operations of the war, and the restoration of general tranquillity.

He spoke most pointedly and fully to the share the Begum had in the rebellion; that independent of its being a fact, of which no officer in his camp ever entertained a doubt, he had himself conversed with a wounded *Nugeeb*, whom he saw in the town of *Pateita*, after the storm of that place. That the man declared he was one of the corps entertained by the Begum—that he had received two rupees in advance—had arrived two days in Cheyt Sing's army—and had received two wounds —that the Colonel sent him to the hospital, where he was cured, and then discharged—that he made no report of this to Mr. Hastings, because the fact was so universally talked of, and in his opinion so clear, as to render any communication totally unnecessary. In fact, that no person could doubt of the disaffection of the Begum—That he had been a great number of years in India—that Mr. Hastings was beloved and revered by the people of India—was better calculated to govern them

than

than any man he knew, and the man of all others whom he would. wish to serve under.

The Colonel underwent a very long, and a most tedious cross-examination by Mr. Burke, chiefly from letters and papers, both printed, which Mr. Burke had before him.

Mr. Law once or twice interrupted Mr. Burke; but finding the interruption to lead only to speeches, he declared, that he would not object to any thing, of any kind, the Manager could say. — The Chancellor's patience appeared at length to be exhausted, and he said the sort of line taken by Mr. Burke might prolong the trial *to eternity.*—Earl Stanhope also objected, and said, that such proceedings *were insufferable.*

About five, Colonel Popham was released, and then Captain Symes was called. This gentleman is also an officer in his Majesty's service, and was Aid-de-Camp to General Musgrave during the present war. He was the officer mentioned by Mr. Hastings, who had gone to India since this trial began, and, after very active service in India, was now returned, to mark to future ages the peculiar character of this impeachment.

He stated, that he went through Cheyt Sing's country, the beginning of 1781, and was very ill treated, and insulted—that the report of his disaffection was then general. That he was with the army at *Cawnpore* when Cheyt Sing rebelled —that it was the universal report in the camp, that

that the Begum was disaffected, and had offered
military aid to Cheyt Sing--that nothing he had
heard to the time of his leaving India last January
tended to make him disbelieve the report; but,
on the contrary, much to fix it, as perfectly true.
That he had heard the opening of this trial before
he went last to India; that the trial was a subject
of general notoriety, and that, so far from effect-
ing a change of opinion as to Mr. Hastings, addresses, as he heard in India, were sent from all
ranks of people in his favour :—that he believed
there never had been a man in a high station so
universally esteemed and beloved as Mr. Hastings, and that the same opinions prevailed down
to January 1792, when he left India.—That he
had conversed with several persons of the highest
rank in that country, who all entertained the
same opinions of him; and that his prosecution
in England had not in any degree lessened the
attachment of the people of India.

Mr. Burke did not chuse to ask Captain Symes
one single question; but said, with a pleasantry
which was very ill received by all who heard him
—that he left Mr. Hastings to enjoy the full effect of the bounty of Providence, in having preserved Captain Symes to give evidence in his
favour.

Some documents were then read—the charge
closed—and Mr. Dallas gave notice, that he
should sum up on the next sitting day.

A A 3 *EIGHTY-*

EIGHTY-NINTH DAY, June 10.

MR. DALLAS began his summary of the evidence, at half-past one this day. From a speech, which for clearness of arrangement, fluency and elegance of language, and soundness of argument throughout, has never been excelled; it is difficult to select particular passages, without doing injustice to Mr. Dallas, by omitting others.

The Benares cause being so very well known, Mr. Dallas passed slightly over all the immaterial allegations, proving, however, by a reference to evidence, that each was false, unfounded, and unsupported by any testimony of any kind. He was pointedly severe on the Managers, for their mode of drawing out and supporting their article; pointing out a variety of evidence introduced by the counsel of Mr. Hastings, which must have been perused by the Managers' counsel, and which, upon every principle of honour and justice, they ought not to have suppressed. He declined, he said, the task of following Mr. Burke through a long dissertation upon arbitrary power; but he laid it down as an incontrovertible fact, that power, whether in the hands of one man, in

a few,

a few, or in many persons, was still a trust, for the benefit of the governed; and, if abused, the man or men who so abused it ought to be punished.

Upon this fair and manly ground, it was his pride and his glory to say, he wished the cause of his client to stand, and he was sure of a decision in his favour. Had he employed the great and extraordinary powers vested in him for thirteen years by Great Britain, to promote the happiness of the people whom he governed, and for the honour and advantage of his native country?—Facts of the most public notoriety, and the applauding voice of mankind, declared that he had done both. As to the particular charge before their Lordships, it must turn upon two points: the first, as to the right of the Company to make any demands upon Cheyt Sing beyond his annual rent; the second, whether Mr. Hastings, in making and enforcing the demands, was actuated by malice? He might, indeed, in one moment, make that sort of defence for his client, which he defied any power on earth to overturn. The demand was publicly made by Mr. Hastings and his counsel, transmitted by him to the Directors in 1778, by the Directors to his Majesty's Ministers; and those Ministers and the Legislature, had in 1781, for a fourth time, re-appointed Mr. Hastings Governor General of Bengal, and for

ten

ten years. If a crime there was, all these parties, Directors, Ministers, Parliament, and the people of Great Britain, in whose name Mr. Hastings was at the bar, were accessaries to the injustice, and had received all the advantages of it. He might well ask them, with what semblance of justice they could come at the end of fifteen years, and call upon Mr. Hastings to answer for his conduct to Cheyt Sing? He would, however, scorn to have recourse to this mode of defence. The honour of Mr. Hastings, and the honour of Great Britain, required that he should meet the charge boldly and fully, and he would shew the world that it was hastily, inconsiderately, and unjustly made, and had no foundation whatever to rest upon.

Mr. Dallas, then, by a variety of evidence, proved, that Cheyt Sing was a subject, and owed the Company every duty due from a subject to his Sovereign. He proved from history, at different periods of the Mogul empire, that Zemindars invariably afforded military assistance in war. He exposed, in very severe terms, the flimsy, mutilated, and garbled evidence given by the Managers, in order to shew, that in 1775 Mr. Hastings engaged to make no demands of any kind upon Cheyt Sing, beyond his annual rent. He wondered how a charge so strange could have been made, and, looking round to the Managers, asked,

asked, who could have drawn up such an article? He proved, incontrovertibly, that every settlement made with Cheyt Sing, applied to his annual rent only, and that he was not released from any one of those duties due from subject to sovereign; that he had taken an oath of fealty and allegiance on his investiture, and was proclaimed throughout the Zemindary of Benares, as the subject of the Company.

Having fixed the right incontrovertibly, and having exposed the unfairness of the article, in taking a partial expression of one of Mr. Hastings's minutes, for the express purpose of fixing a sense upon it, totally different from the real meaning, had the sentence been taken together, he said, that, for the sake of argument, he would make a concession, most wild and extravagant in itself: he would suppose it had been proved, that Mr. Hastings had no right to demand military aid from Cheyt Sing, still the Managers would not advance one step, unless they could prove that malice, which they had so boldy charged.

The state received and enjoyed the benefit of the annual subsidies, and had, in truth, given them their approbation, when the Legislature re-appointed Mr. Hastings, in 1781, to be Governor General. It remained then to examine what ground there was for this extraordinary charge of malice.

After

After using all the industry in his power, he found its origin to be a solitary passage in Mr. Hastings's narrative, who mentions, that on General Clavering's supposed accession to the Chair in Bengal, Cheyt Sing deputed a Vakeel to compliment him. This act of the Rajah's excited such mortal and deadly hate in the mind of Mr. Hastings, that, from that moment, he determined to ruin the Rajah. Such is the idea, monstrous and incredible, undoubtedly, and supported by evidence well worthy such a charge. The event happened in June 1777. No trace of enmity is discovered, until the 9th of July 1778, more than a compleat year after the offence, and then, to be sure it breaks out in a very curious manner.

It was in evidence before their Lordships, that his Majesty's Ambassador at the Court of France (Lord Stormont) had in June 1777 transmitted to Mr. Hastings an account of a design formed by the French Ministry, to attack the British possessions in India. In July 1778, an account arrived in Bengal, that war was actually declared between France and England—Every man knew that war with Spain must follow, and we had then been three years engaged in an unsuccessful war with America. What was Mr. Hastings to do in Bengal? Could he expect an union of two great powers in India, in his favour against France, with whom it was known they were then closely in alliance?

liance? Could he expect, that instead of receiving those returns of wealth from India, which were to uphold a sinking country, Great Britain would pour her treasures with a liberal hand into the lap of Bengal? Could he believe, that overmatched as she was in Europe, in America, and in the West Indies, Great Britain could afford to send ten British regiments, and a fleet, to India? He certainly could not; he must depend upon his own resources; he did depend upon them, and he succeeded, against the most powerful combination ever formed for the overthrow of an empire.

He entreated their Lordships to consider what Mr. Hastings did; and whether the imagination of man, or the malignity of man's nature, could have been supposed capable of so perverting his acts, until that perversion appeared in the name of the Commons of Great Britain. On the first news of the war, he proposed to increase the army —the Council unanimously approved the measure; —to capture all the French settlements in Bengal, and all their ships—the Council agreed;—to recommend to Madras, instantly to commence the siege of Pondicherry—the Council agreed; to fit out a naval force, to reinforce Sir Edward Vernon, the British Commodore—the Council agreed. Yet are these acts of the greatest public merit, involving in them very great personal responsibility, supposed all to be done with a view to harrass, oppress, and finally, to ruin Cheyt Sing;

because

because he was, on the same day, called upon to contribute his share to the additional expence that these measures would bring upon the public. Their Lordships would see, he said, that all these steps were taken upon an idea that Bengal might have been invaded, and with the public belief in all the Council, that France would make, in the course of the war, (as in fact she did) great efforts to recover her lost consequence in India. He then begged their Lordships to consider, how a charge so wild and strange was supported.

The motion for calling upon Cheyt Sing is made, as all the others were, on the same day, by Mr. Hastings. Mr. Francis says he acquiesces, but thinks Cheyt Sing should be told, that the demand will only be continued while the war lasts. Mr. Hastings says, he means so; and adds, that as there seemed to be some difference of opinion, *as to the right*, he wishes to leave the decision on that point to their superiors; stating his own opinion, which was, that we were precluded by no engagements from calling on Cheyt Sing for extraordinary aids on extraordinary emergencies. Mr. Dallas was as convincing as eloquent in this part of this speech.

He said, it was impossible that Mr. Hastings or Mr. Francis could have been actuated by malice in their conduct to Cheyt Sing; but notwithstanding the Managers had attributed to Mr. Francis

every

every virtue under Heaven, and had made him more an angel than a man, he must allow, that the charge of malice applied, with infinitely more force, to Mr. Francis than to Mr. Hastings. The latter makes a demand, and states, that he has a right to make it: the former, with doubts in his mind, *as to the right*, agrees with Mr. Hastings, without even expressing his doubts, for the information of his superiors; but Mr. Hastings, to whom he had mentioned them in conversation, fairly brings the subject forward, and, as there was a doubt as to the right, leaves his superiors to decide. Is there any thing like malice in this proceeding? or, if such a charge would apply at all, it must be to Mr. Francis, and not to Mr. Hastings. But, said Mr. Dallas, it applies to neither.

In the same manly, intelligible, and common-sense style of argument, Mr. Dallas continued, having displayed a complete knowledge of his subject, and a perfect acquaintance with the laws and constitution of India. He often turned round to the Managers' box—few were present. Mr. Burke, who went away at one time, sometimes coloured, and looked grave at other times; he had that sort of smile upon his countenance which is not to be described, but which struck all who saw him. The lawyers of the people, Messrs. Douglas, Pigot, Burke, and Lawrence, (to whom we suppose Mr. Burke alluded, when he said—

" *Superflua*

" *Superflua non nocent*") were also present when Mr. Dallas so emphatically asked, who *could* have drawn up the article so incorrectly and unfairly.

At a quarter past five, Mr. Dallas closed.

NINETIETH DAY, *June* 11.

THIS day the Court assembled at half-past one, and Mr. Dallas proceeded with the same fluency and clearnesss as before, to remark upon the charge and the evidence, from the point where he left off, down to Mr. Hastings's departure from Calcutta, in July 1781.

The first striking passage was, where he came to answer that part of the charge which alledges that Mr. Hastings under *pretence* of a war, of which he had received no authentic intelligence, called upon Cheyt Sing for military aid, but *really* with a view to harrass, oppress, and, finally, to ruin him. He bestowed upon this charge the epithets *futile, frivolous,* and *absurd.* He stated in the clearest manner, the intelligence that Mr. Hastings had received from Lord Stormont, that war was likely soon to happen, and also of the measures France would pursue until it should break out. He paid Lord Stormont the highest compliments

compliments for his zeal in the service of his country, which induced him to communicate this important information to Mr. Hastings, though he had no authority from his own Court so to do. He next stated the communication from Mr. Baldwyn at Cairo, that war had actually been declared between France and England, and he emphatically asked their Lordships, what would Mr. Hastings have merited, had he paid no sort of attention to this communication? Undoubtedly he would have merited the severest censures from his country; and what was his *return* for a conduct so much the reverse?—The Commons of Great Britain had brought him to their Lordships' bar, because, despising all personal consequences, he had acted upon the authority of Lord Stormont and Mr. Baldwyn, and had looked upon war to be actually declared, though he had received no official advice of the fact. A charge like this, Mr. Dallas said, was unworthy the dignity, the justice, or the common-sense of a great nation, and would operate in all future times as a dreadful lesson to Generals, Admirals, and Governors, who were entrusted by Great Britain with the care of her interests in the distant quarters of the globe.

Having exposed the absurdity of the article in this view of it, he next took it up most ingeniously in another. Under the *pretence* of a war in Europe,

rope, Mr. Hastings had not only made every defensive preparation in Bengal, of which the demand upon Cheyt Sing was a part, but he had also taken all the French settlements, and all the French ships in Bengal. Yet this act—an act against the law of nations—was not charged at all; but if there was any foundation for the article, all these measures he took merely to furnish a ground for harrassing, oppressing, and finally, ruining Cheyt Sing.

Mr. Dallas next proceeded to consider the various circumstances that attended the several demands made upon Cheyt Sing for military aid. He went through the part which Mr. Francis had in each of these transactions—He proved most clearly, that he was a party in every transaction; yet, strange to tell, he had heard a Manager lament it as a great public misfortune, that Mr. Francis was not a Manager on this impeachment. Mr. Dallas pushed this argument to the conviction of every gentleman present. He went very fully into the distressed state of India at the commencement of the late war, and we believe he left no doubts in the breast of any one who heard him, of the sole object Mr. Hastings had in view—namely, the preservation of the British empire in India, against the most powerful combination ever formed against it.

After

After having gone through all this part of his subject most completely and satisfactorily, he next came to consider the conduct of Cheyt Sing, in efusing to obey the orders of the government of Bengal. He exposed the falsehood of all his excuses, and established the right of the Company to make the several demands, by the most convincing arguments. He proved, by the evidence, the actual design formed by Cheyt Sing, to seize the first favourable opportunity to render himself independent; and, at a quarter after four, being a good deal exhausted, he prayed leave to close for the day, saying, that he would conclude all he had to offer to their Lordships on the next meeting of the Court.

The Lords adjourned accordingly.

NINETY-FIRST DAY, *June* 12.

Mr. Dallas began, by exposing in very strong and almost indignant language, the injustice of making that a charge against Mr. Hastings, of which the Court of Directors, the King's Ministers, and former Parliaments, had approved; but the charge having been made, he never would fly from it; and he proved, by reference to evidence, that every part of the charge was futile, ridiculous, and absurd.

B B

He

He next came to a subject, which he touched
with an ability that must command universal
approbation, while he preserved throughout the
language of a gentleman, and the deference due
to the person whom his Majesty has placed in the
first situation in the country—we mean the fun-
damental difference between Mr. Pitt and Mr.
Fox, on the only points on which the merit or
demerit of Mr. Hastings's conduct to Cheyt Sing
must turn.

He paid Mr. Fox the highest compliments;
declared that he looked upon him as the ablest
debater this country ever possessed; and as a
man, who scorning any appeal, but to the reason and good sense of his auditors, had fairly and
openly put this charge upon its true ground. He
had opened it in the last Parliament: he had held
this plain and intelligible language, that Mr. Hastings was under such engagements to Cheyt Sing;
that under no possible circumstances, could he
demand more of him, than his annual rent; consequently every extra demand was a crime; and
an intention to punish Cheyt Sing, for not immediately obeying these demands, was an aggravation of that crime.

All Mr. Fox's eloquence, could not, as he himself confessed to their Lordships (and that alone
entitled Mr. Dallas, as he said, to go into this
subject at all), induce another right honourable
gentleman (described by Mr. Fox as a person

of

of the first abilities, and the first integrity) to concur with him.

That gentleman (Mr. Pitt) had strenuously contended, that Mr. Hastings had an undoubted right to demand extra aids from Cheyt Sing, in war—that the Rajah was criminal in disobeying; that his disobedience merited punishment, but that Mr. Hastings had gone beyond the proper line, and therein the crime consisted. After stating the singular, unprecedented hardships of Mr. Hastings's case, he said it was impossible to prove that to be criminal, to which Mr. Pitt objected, namely, the intention to impose a fine.

All this part Mr. Dallas argued most ably, and to the conviction of every man who heard him; and concluded by observing, that whatever Mr. Pitt's opinion might be, the Commons of Great Britain had charged it as a crime, that Mr. Hastings called upon Cheyt Sing to contribute to the expences of the war; and therefore, as was his duty, he had fully, and he hoped completely, refuted the charge.

He next went into a clear detail of Mr. Markham's evidence, which totally destroyed every allegation in the articles.—Of Mr. Markham he spoke, as of a man whose character was far above his praise, who had stood a cross examination of four days from one of the most indefatigable examiners upon earth, and that every reply had

only

only served the more strongly to fix his former testimony.

He then mentioned that singular circumstance of the letter found by Mr. Burke on a Sunday, after having been in his possession ten years, and sent to Mr. Markham, just as he was going into Westminster Hall. He noticed the wonderful agreement between all the material facts in that letter, and the evidence given by Mr. Markham; though the one was written when the subjects were fresh in his memory, and the other given at the distance of ten years. It was an event most fortunate for the honour both of Mr. Markham and Mr. Hastings. He particularly remarked upon an expression in Mr. Burke's letter to Mr. Markham, that the facts he had stated, differed very little from those he had heard from *other channels;* and after this *confession,* Mr. Dallas said, he was indeed astonished how the charge of *malice* could have been preferred against Mr. Hastings.

After a most critical examination of Mr. Markham's, Colonel Popham's, and Mr. Burrell's evidence, and applying each to the total destruction of every allegation in the article, appealing as he did to the reason and common sense of the Court, and of all the auditors, Mr. Dallas came to his close, which contained some points that will be remembered as long as Great Britain is a nation; for so long will the eighteenth century

be

be celebrated for an impeachment, unexampled in the annals of the world.

He observed, that those whom the Commons employed, had expressed no concern for the British blood that was spilt at the massacre at Benares, nor for the general order issued by Cheyt Sing, to put all the Englishmen to death, as well as their dependants, wherever they could be found; but that Cheyt Sing was the object of compassion and commisseration.

Wishing, as he did, he said, to meet the Managers boldly and in front, he would admit, that there had been a consistency *in their conduct*, which he looked for in vain from *other quarters*.

They had asserted, and they had attempted to prove that Mr. Hastings had no right whatever to demand any military aid from Cheyt Sing. The Managers acted for the Commons, and the Commons were the representatives of the people of Great Britain.

Here then he would consider what that *British justice* was, which an honourable Manager had so eloquently described. From *British justice* it might be expected, that she would first relieve the *oppressed*, and then proceed to punish the *oppressor*. Was this the case? Was Cheyt Sing seated on the throne of his ancestors, as it was called by the Managers, or was he at this time a wanderer upon the face of the earth?

It

It was charged as a crime against Mr. Hastings
—strange, absurd, futile, and ridiculous indeed
was the charge—that after Cheyt Sing's expulsion,
he had raised the revenue of Benares from two
hundred and thirty thousand pounds to four hundred thousand pounds a year. Could it be believed possible, that a House of Commons, who
had made *such a charge*, had for ten years concurred in *receiving* that additional revenue for
the public? There was not a step he could stir,
he said, without finding the subject involved *in
the grossest absurdity*.

In a most animated and captivating stile, he
went through this line of argument, never de-
parting from that respect due from him to the
House of Commons, but leaving an *impression*
upon the minds of all who heard him, of the
unexampled *injustice* and *cruelty* with which Mr.
Hastings had been treated, *that time cannot
efface*.

He contrasted in a most happy stile the different treatment that Cheyt Sing and Mr. Hastings had experienced; the former, who in cold
blood had murdered our officers and soldiers;
who had notoriously been guilty of every crime
of which Mr. Hastings had charged him was an
object of pity to the Managers, who wept over
his hard fate, but suffered him to wander over
the

the face of the globe, and quietly accepted for the public the additional revenue arising from his expulsion: Mr. Hastings was brought to the bar of a Court of Justice, kept there for years, for having expelled Cheyt Sing.

Having pushed this in a style of argument which could not be answered, he spoke more generally of the wildness and absurdity of the accusation against Mr. Hastings. If it could be supposed, he said, that the character of any man could be fixed, Mr. Hastings's was established when the Benares revolution happened. The Commons of Great Britain had imputed motives to him contrary to the universal tenor of his life. No man was better known than Mr. Hastings, and what had resulted from his prosecution? His friends in England gathered round him, and all India rose up in his favour. Could this have happened, if there had been a shadow of truth in an assertion of one of the Managers, " that Ben- " gal felt relieved from a burthen under which she " had long groaned when he left India"? The as- sertion was wild and foolish. His cause, Mr. Dallas said, was the cause of truth and common sense. He chearfully submitted the honour of Mr. Hastings to their Lordships decision, and what was more, the honour and character of the British nation.

This

This is indeed a very faint and imperfect account of a few heads of Mr. Dallas's speech. We but echo the voice of the auditors, when we say, he far excelled Mr. Sheridan, and left Mr. Burke at a great distance behind him. This, however, may be owing in some degree to the subject, which gave him great advantages. He never stepped an inch beyond his evidence. He made no appeal but to the good sense of his audience, and in the sublimest part of the whole, when he exposed, in the most gentlemanly language, the mortal stab that British justice had received, by the mode in which this prosecution was conducted, he said not one word which the House of Commons could controvert, or at which they could fairly take offence.

The Court was unusually crouded, and there was that feeling on the whole, resulting from reason *convinced*—not that burst of theatrical applause which followed upon the close of Mr. Sheridan's speech, when men were pleased with splendid passages, which might have been applied with much more propriety to tales of chivalry in the middle ages, than to any one transaction in which Mr. Hastings bore a part.

In one passage, Mr. Dallas was most eloquent, when he commented upon a private letter, written by Mr. Hastings to Colonel Popham, recommending every kindness and attention to Cheyt Sing.

Sing.   This he compared to the Manager's speeches, delivered in a full Court, carefully revised, in order to be transmitted to posterity, and drew the parallel between the ostentatious *display* of *humanity* in a parliamentary oration, and the silent *exercise* of that quality in Mr. Hastings.

The Court adjourned until the second Tuesday in the next session of parliament.

SIXTH

SIXTH YEAR, 1793.

NINETY-SECOND DAY, February 25.

THIS day the trial of Mr. Hastings was recommenced, being the sixth year of the proceedings in Westminster Hall, and the seventh of the impeachment.

Mr. Law opened the case, and complained in terms of great force and feeling, of the hard and unexampled sufferings of his client; and he expressed his hopes and his wishes, that this might be the *last*, as it was the first instance of the extension of a criminal trial beyond the probable duration of the life of man.

Mr. Law then proceeded to remark upon the several allegations in the article of the Princess of Oude; and with very great ability and apparent knowledge of his subject, refuted them as he went along, observing the instances in which the allegations were utterly unsupported by evidence of any kind, and justifying in other points what Mr. Hastings had done, and avowed.

This

This cause is already so well known, that, in the present momentous and important situation of public affairs, a long detail is unnecessary.

· Mr. Law stated, what the whole world knows to be true, the critical and dangerous state of India in the last war; when it was actually preserved by the adoption of those very measures for which Mr. Hastings has been so long impeached. He justified him completely from the charges of cruelty or severity, and he stated various instances of the Begum's disaffection.

At five o'clock the Court adjourned.

NINETY-THIRD DAY, *February* 18.

THE Court on this day was fuller than on the preceding, though few of the prosecutors appeared. Mr. Law proceeded in his opening of the defence on the Begum article; and in very forcible language, and with his matter admirably arranged, went through the remainder of the article. He pointed out, that in almost every instance, the charges were refuted by the evidence called by the Managers themselves; and in a most pointed manner, alluded to the unjustifiable means resorted to by the Managers in examining their

wit-

witnesses. Amidst an infinite variety. of matter, highly interesting. to Mr. Hastings to have explained to the Court, which is to pronounce judgment upon him, he stated some that came home to the feelings and common-sense of every man in England. In the Benares article it had been stated by the House of Commons, that Mr. Hastings did certain acts under the *pretence* of a war. On so wild an allegation, Mr. Law commented with great force: he asked, if that was a *pretended war*, which all India knew to be true? which this country, to its cost, knew to be true; since she had expended above a hundred millions in it, and lost half her foreign dominions; in which, in India alone, she was successful under Mr. Hastings? In like manner he was accused, on this article, of taking from the Begum five hundred and fifty thousand pounds, in order to pay a *pretended debt*, due from the Vizier to the Company. Could such a charge be endured for a moment? Was it a *pretended debt?* Why then had not the House of Commons ordered it to be paid back again years and years ago?—But the fact was, that it was a real, a fair, and a just debt; acknowledged to be so by all parties, and paid as such. But it were an endless task, to enumerate all the absurd and contradictory accusations that had been preferred against Mr. Hastings. Some years ago, on a very memorable occasion, it was admitted, that this was

a fair

a fair debt; but the recovery of it was stated to be impossible; and a great leading character (Mr. Fox) struck it out of the public accounts as desperate. Hence the persecuted situation to which his client had so long been subject. He had falsified every prediction of his enemies as to India. He had preserved it in war; he had left it in peace; he had improved its resources: he had proved, that those who pretended to some knowledge of that country, knew nothing about it. These were crimes not to be forgiven: he had fallen a victim and a martyr to the zeal, ability, and success, with which he had served his country.

Mr. Law then went rapidly through all that remained, and in a most admirable close, recapitulated the acknowledged services of Mr. Hastings; and added, that upon this, as on every other part of his case, he rested on the cool impartiality and steady justice of his enlightened judges.

The Court adjourned at four o'clock.

NINETY-

NINETY-FOURTH DAY, *February* 19.

THIS day was entirely spent in reading. The only remarkable circumstance was, that the name of Mr. Hastings seemed to operate as a charm in bringing about a temporary coalition between Mr. Burke and Mr. Sheridan—the latter, though in a great-coat, and unpowdered, coming to the assistance of Mr. Burke, on a point of order and form, relative to evidence. This took up some time; and Mr. Burke had almost called his associate, " My Honourable Friend ;" but, correcting himself, said, " My Honourable Fellow Manager."

The Court adjourned at five o'clock.

NINETY-FIFTH DAY, *February* 26.

THE Court met at half-past one. Captain Gordon was called by the Counsel of Mr. Hastings immediately. In one hour, or less, the examination was finished.

Mr. Burke began his counter-process, and continued it until near four, when Mr. Sheridan made his

his appearance. The evidence was full, clear, and distinct, applying most exactly to every point; and if Captain Gordon had not been settled in the South of France when the charge passed the Commons, and of course incapable of giving his evidence, there is some reason to think, sixty thousand pounds might have been saved to the nation, and a trial of every man's patience for six years.

About four o'clock, Mr. Burke said that he had finished with Captain Gordon for the present, but that he would call him again on the next day the Court met. Mr. Law instantly arose, and said he claimed *as a right*, what the laws of his country entitled him to expect, that the Managers should *finish* their cross-examination, before they called another witness.

Mr. Burke, Mr. Adam, and the Patriot Mr. Taylor, opposed this. Mr. Law, confiding in the justice of his objection, and in the *honour* of the Court, persisted, but without further loss of time, by urging arguments in support of an indelible truth. The Chancellor said, that if the counsel persisted, they had a right to do so; but that the Managers might consume the remaining time of the Court, by questions, and so have the privilege of pursuing their cross-examination on the next day.

Upon

Upon this, Lord Stanhope arose, and expressed his surprize at what had fallen from the learned Lord; adding, that he could not suspect the Managers to be capable of so scandalous a proceeding, as to ask frivolous questions for the sake of continuing an examination to the following day.

Mr. Burke, misunderstanding what was said, accused Lord Stanhope of attacking *the Commons,* by pronouncing their conduct to be *scandalous.* Lord Stanhope replied, by re-stating what he had said.

Mr. Burke and Mr. Adam began to re-argue the point; but the Lords, *with one voice,* desired them to go on, which they did, and finished with Captain Gordon.

Captain Williams was then called up; and, as his examination was likely to be long, the Court adjourned.

NINETY-SIXTH DAY, *February 27.*

CAPTAIN WILLIAMS, on the assembly of the Court, was called again to the bar, and the counsel were proceeding with all possible dispatch

in

in his examination; when first, Mr. Burke, and next, Mr. Sheridan, made observations as to the re-hearing of his evidence. They argued, and re-argued on the subject, until the Chancellor at last observed, that they had better permit the counsel to proceed. They took his Lordship's advice for a few minutes, and then again interrupted, and began an examination of their own. Some progress was made, and Captain Williams gave clear and pointed answers to such questions as were put to him by the Counsel, the Managers, and the Lords. The substance of his evidence went to prove the hostile acts of the Begum. Mr. Sheridan, contrary to all former practice, broke in upon the examination in chief. Objections were made, and the day nealy spent, when Mr. Hastings, with marks of agitation, mixed with something of impatience, rose, and addressed the Court. He began by professing the sincerest respect for his judges, and he trusted to their sense of honour, and their love of justice, to excuse the irregularity he was about to commit. He observed, that an intimation had been given to him, that this was the last day the Court were to meet prior to the circuits. If therefore, that intention, supposing their Lordships to have formed it, was to be changed, it must be by an application made before the rising of the Court. He called to their Lordships' recollection the unprecedented,

dangerous,

dangerous, and alarming length of the trial; that he was now in the sixth year of his appearance at their bar, and the eighth from the commencement of the process in the House of Commons; that no man's life could fairly be estimated to last so long, particularly a man at his age; that he had entertained a hope of its being the universal wish to bring the trial to a close in this session. By a close, he meant a conclusion of the process on both sides, and the judgment of the Court. To *any other* he never would consent, and therefore it was that he was anxious for a judgment, while he had a chance of living until it should take place.

Mr. Hastings next mentioned the steps he had taken to get an attendance—his petition to his Majesty; and he professed that he had hopes, from what was lately done in the House of Commons, which met the universal approbation of the country (alluding to Major Maitland's motion): all these hopes were now vanished; and he threw himself upon their Lordships, of whom he never had thought or spoken, but with the utmost respect and confidence.

His present prayer, he said, was, that the House would sit day by day, in order to finish the present charge before the circuits. His reason was, that several gentlemen, for whom he had a very sincere respect and affection, had attended year after

year

year in vain, but were now assembled in the fullest confidence, that their evidence would immediately be taken.

Some came from very distant countries.—One
gentleman, Major Lumsdaine, from the North of
Scotland; another officer, Colonel Duff, who was
waiting to do justice to his character, had actually been in the Hall, the second year of the
trial; had returned to India; had served with very
distinguished reputation in the war; came home a
few months ago, on the restoration of peace, and
was now ready to embark again.—Could it be
expected, that even private regard should induce
this officer to neglect his public duty? Another
gentleman, who had been waiting year after year,
whose name had been mentioned yesterday, was
Mr. John Pendred Scott; that gentleman pre-
paring to come over from Ireland, to give his
evidence, died about ten days ago.—With such
examples before him, Mr. Hastings said, he
implored, he entreated their Lordships to afford
him at least an opportunity of closing his evidence on this charge before the circuits, and
to take such steps as should insure a compleat
close and judgment in the course of this session. Mr. Hastings said much more. His speech
was not preconcerted, but made with infinite force
and effect.

Mr.

Mr. Burke declared, that it was the Commons' wish to expedite the trial, as much as that of Mr. Hastings.

Mr. Sheridan got up to speak, when the adjournment was moved.

NINETY-SEVENTH DAY, February 28.

MR. BURKE having declared the earnest anxiety of the Commons to finish this trial, and also that they were always in their place, we wish with great deference and respect to notice these assertions. In the first place, the Managers have been so far from being in their *places*, few of them have assisted for the *three last years*, even to make a House. Major Maitland has publicly affirmed, that it was made last year, in the trial days, by the exertions of Mr. Hastings himself. A love of *justice* may induce the Managers to finish the trial; but the *personal inconvenience* which they suffer, is of no moment; they may attend, or not, as they like—and though there was some *demur*, when only three thousand pounds were expended, sixty thousand pounds have since been paid without difficulty. As to the Counsel employed by the Managers, no gentlemen can be more at their ease.

case. Mr. Burke, Mr. Pigot, and Mr. Douglas, received one thousand and thirty guineas each, merely for attending in Westminster Hall, but without its breaking in upon any of their business. The Managers themselves being both pleaders and examiners of witnesses, nothing can be more comfortable than the situation of all the parties employed by the public. But far different is the case on the other side:—Mr. Hastings appears in the humiliating situation of a defendant, with bended knee, as Major Maitland well observed, year after year. His counsel, all men of eminence in their profession, must be most diligently and unceasingly employed in this cause, to the evident abandonment of much more business. The result is, that neither Mr. Hastings nor his counsel can have a wish but for a speedy close; while, on the other side, all parties are at their ease.

This day was productive of extraordinary events. The Lords assembled at twelve; but there was no House of Commons. After some time the Managers attended, and then Captain Williams was called to the bar, and examined at great length, by Mr. Burke. The Lords retired at twenty minutes past two, to receive his Majesty. Lord Stanhope, as we understand, lamented that the present Chancellor did not follow the example of the last, in himself putting the questions to the witness, as it would prevent such *rubbish* from appearing on their

Journals;

Journals; and he lamented, in very strong terms, the intolerable delay on the trial.

At four o'clock, the Lords returned to the Hall, and the examination of Captain Williams continued till half-past five; when Mr. Sheridan rose, and said he had a proposition to make to the counsel, which, if assented to might shorten the proceedings. He observed, that however his public duty led him to support the charges against Mr. Hastings, yet he must freely confess, that that gentleman had the fullest right to complain, in the strong terms he had done, of the intolerable injury which he had sustained by the unconstitutional duration of the trial. Nor was this all; the country, he was free to confess, would be completely disgraced in the eyes of all Europe, and there never would be a future impeachment. Having put this very strongly, and apparently much to the surprize of Mr. Burke, he proceeded to his proposition, which was at once rejected by the Counsel, and tolerably strongly remarked upon by the Chancellor. When this conversation ended, it was near six o'clock, and the Court adjourned.

NINETY-

NINETY-EIGHTH DAY, March 1.

To understand the drift of the evidence given this day, and to elucidate the cross-examination, it will be necessary to state some circumstances that occurred in the last Parliament. Amidst a very large mass of matter, framed into articles by the late House, and abandoned by them, there was a charge, that Captain Williams, or some British officer, had caused Rajah Mustapha Cawn to be put to death; and the same charge calls this execution a *cruel and atrocious murder.* Captain Williams petitioned the House, either to bring a direct charge against him, or to give him some satisfaction for so foul an injury. By an appeal to the journals of the House, it will appear, that this article was voted without the Members having had an opportunity of looking into it. Captain Williams could obtain no sort of satisfaction, and he represented the very peculiar hardship of his situation in a series of letters, addressed to Mr. Francis, who had taken an active part in this business. Here the matter rested, but Captain Williams had the pleasure to hear his Majesty's Attorney General express

in

in the House his sincere concern, that he, as a Member, should appear to call that " *a cruel and atrocious murder*," of which he never had heard one word.

To this business of Mustapha Cawn, Mr. Burke examined Captain Williams, who shewed all the eagerness an innocent man could do, to wipe off the foul reproach which the last Parliament had cast upon him; and it appeared by his evidence, that when he relieved Major Lumsdaine, early in 1781, in the command of Gorricpore, a man of the name of Mustapha Cawn, was delivered over to him a prisoner, and under sentence of death; that he received a positive order from his commanding officer, Colonel Hannay, to carry this sentence into execution, which he did; and he stated, that the man had for many years been a free-booter and a rebel; and that in the perilous situation in which he was, he found it absolutely necessary to obey the orders which he had received.

The whole day was expended by Mr. Burke and Mr. Sheridan, in questions and cross-questions upon this point, and relative to a letter which Captain Williams had found amongst some papers. In the midst of all this examination, it came out very clearly, that Captain Williams had received information, which left him no reason to doubt of the intrigues of the Begum; and that

that no man in India ever entertained a doubt upon the subject.

At half past five, the Court adjourned.

NINETY-NINTH DAY, March 2.

THE business on this day commenced by the Lord Chancellor's stating, that the House, observing the unfortunate delays which had occurred by the Managers interrupting the examination of Mr. Hastings's witnesses, and by observations, had determined, that in future, until the examination in chief was finished, the cross-examination should not begin; and that no remarks should be made, which were in their nature observations on the effect of evidence. The same rule was to be observed by the defendant's counsel.

Mr. Burke made a speech, in order to express his submission, and declared, that so extremely anxious were the Commons for a very speedy close to this unprecedented trial, that if the defendant's counsel wished it, and their Lordships chose so to determine, they were ready to go on during the circuits.

As soon as Mr. Burke sat down, Mr. Dallas called Lieutenant Shuldham, who, in reply to the
several

several questions put to him, said, that he had
been ten years in India, and returned about two
years; that at the time of Cheyt Sing's insurrection he was in Major Macpherson's regiment
at Cawnpore; that it was then currently reported,
and universally believed, that the Begums were
hostile to the British government, and had afforded military aid to Cheyt Sing; that he had
not then a shadow of doubt as to the truth of
those reports, nor has he now; that he remained
in India nine years after the event, and he could
safely swear that no one circumstance had come
to his knowledge, which led him to doubt it, nor
was it doubted by any one person of any description in India with whom he had ever conversed,
and he had conversed with great numbers of natives, as well as his brother officers, on the subject. That if any one were asked to bring strict
legal proof of the existence of a design some time
ago, to overturn this happy constitution, he might
not be able to do it, yet the fact was of such notoriety, that associations had been formed throughout the kingdom, to counteract the design. That
the battalion to which he belonged marched from
Lucknow to Fyzabad, and that the eunuchs Jewar
and Bahar Allly Cawn, were under their charge;
that he had often seen and conversed with them;
that they were attended by a great number of
their men servants, and sustained no hardships of
any

any kind, and complained of none; that in order to induce them to pay the balance of the sum they had agreed to pay, they had been for a short time in irons; that he was present when a smith was taking the irons from one of them, and that they were very little heavier than the gold or silver ornaments which the women of that country wear round their ancles. He was cross-examined by Mr. Burke and Mr. Sheridan, and gave his answers in the clearest terms. Mr. Sheridan asked, why there should be a necessity for a smith to take off the irons, if they were so extremely slight? To which Mr. Shuldham neatly replied, that unless they had been rivetted, slight as they were, they would themselves have taken them off.

Mr. Sheridan asked if it was not known in India that Mr. Hastings had been *many years* impeached on this article? Mr. Shuldham said, it certainly was universally known in India. This led Mr. Dallas to ask, if the circumstance of being impeached had hurt the character of Mr. Hastings in India? To this he replied, that when he spoke of Mr. Hastings, he spoke of a man with whom he was not personally acquainted; that he spoke from no sense of personal favours received, since none had been conferred; that he could say, with the utmost confidence, there never had been a man whose character stood higher

higher than that of Mr. Hastings; that as Governor there never was a man more able, nor, as a private character, more amiable; and that this was the general opinion of India, both amongst the natives and his own countrymen, and that it was not at all shaken by the impeachment.

The next evidence called was Colonel Duff. This officer said he had been in India about thirty years; that he had returned to England since the commencement of this trial, stayed a short time, went back, commanded the artillery under Lord Cornwallis in the late war, and arrived again in England two months ago; that he was in India during the insurrection of Cheyt Sing; that the disaffection and hostility of the Begums was a fact at that time universally believed; that he himself had then no doubt of it, nor has one circumstance that he has since heard led him to doubt it, nor does he believe any man in India ever did doubt it; that in the years 1781 and 1782, the Company's situation in India was most dangerous and alarming, much more so than at any other period before or since; that the troops were many months in arrears, and that the most strenuous exertions were necessary to preserve India to Great Britain.

With respect to the bullock contract, Colonel Duff deposed, that this was a service on which the success of every operation in war depended;

that

that good bullocks never could be procured by
an annual contract given to the lowest bidder;
that under Mr. Croftc's contract, the bullocks
were excellent, the regulations highly proper, and
rigidly enforced; that six thousand seven hundred bullocks were by no means too large a
number; that so far from one driver being too
much for every two bullocks, he thought there
should be *two* to every *three bullocks;* that with
regard to Mr. Hastings, though he thought Mr.
Hastings had in his public character done him
no favour, but rather the contrary on one occasion—yet that circumstance should not prevent
him from doing justice. He had many years ago
concurred with some hundreds of his brother
officers in transmitting to Mr. Hastings the sense
that the army entertained of his great merits and
public services; that he knew the opinion of
India to be very highly in favour of Mr. Hastings, and that nothing which had happened during
this trial had changed that opinion; but quite the
reverse; that no man stood higher in the general
estimation, or had performed more important services; that the people of India, Europeans and
natives, looked upon Mr. Hastings to be a very
great and a very injured man; and, added Colonel
Duff, *this is my opinion too.*

In the cross-examination Colonel Duff was
very pointed. Mr. Sheridan asked him to what
mismanage-

mismanagement it was owing, that the army had been so much in arrears in 1781 and 1782? The Colonel replied, to no mismanagement at all, but owing to the very large sums sent by Mr. Hastings to support the war in the Carnatic, and on the Malabar Coast. He was asked, when he heard of the disaffection of the Begums? He said, as soon after the revolt of Cheyt Sing as the news could arrive—and that he heard it repeatedly since, and had not a shadow of doubt in his mind on the subject. In reply to Mr. Burke's questions, he said, that the bullock contract met the warm approbation of Sir Eyre Coote, the commander in chief in India, and of General Stibbert, the provincial commander in chief.

Major Lumsdaine was next called, and gave the same pointed evidence as to the existence of the Begum's disaffection, which he said was a fact universally believed in India, and never doubted but in England. He said, that nothing could be so alarming as the state of the British empire in India at the close of 1781, and in the first months of 1782; that it was his firm opinion the existence of our Indian dominion depended at that time on the life of Mr. Hastings; that the army with which he was acting was six and seven months in arrears; that he is confident the army must have been disbanded, without some assistance, in a very short time, their distresses were

arrived

arrived at so great a height; and that the brigade under the command of Colonel Sir J. Cumming could not move for want of pay; that in February 1782, they were relieved by the Vizier, having paid the Company a large sum of money, which, as he understood, was a part of his father's treasures, that he had taken from the Begum at Fyzabad; that without such a seasonable supply, the most ruinous effects would have followed; that he had served in India until the close of Mr. Hastings's administration; that no man ever stood higher in the opinion either of the natives or of his own countrymen, or was more esteemed either as a public or a private character. He said Mustapha Cawn, the man whose death was termed by the late House a cruel and atrocious murder, was sent a prisoner to him in May 1780, by order of the Nabob, and under sentence of death; that he received very strict directions for the guard of his person, and when he delivered over the command to Captain Williams in 1781, he reported Mustapha Cawn as a prisoner under sentence of death.

The cross-examination by Mr. Burke lasted above two hours, on points, apparently at least, foreign from any charge against Mr. Hastings, and the Lords seeing no prospect of a close, adjourned to the 12th of April.

HUNDREDTH

HUNDREDTH DAY, *April* 12.

———————

THE Court assembled, this day, at one o'clock. The cross-examination of one gentleman, (Major Lumsdaine), was finished about half past two, Mr. Burke being the only Manager who asked a question; and, to men of common conception, there was not one single point on the cross-examination which could, under any possible construction, apply to the case of Mr. Hastings.

Mr. Wombwell was the other gentleman called. Mr. Dallas asked him a very few questions, and his answers confirmed the evidence of many other respectable witnesses, as to the universal belief that obtained in India, of the disaffection of the Begums, and also of the general respect and affection which all ranks of people felt for Mr. Hastings.

Mr. Burke kept Mr. Wombwell two hours on a cross-examination as to salaries or pensions, that he had paid to English gentlemen in Oude, from the Nabob's treasury; and though Mr. Wombwell twenty times told him, that all his accounts were public, and at the India House; that he never had paid one rupee privately; that

he

he knew nothing of any money having been privately paid, either as a pension to a person in his
own name, or for the use of that person, *under
some other name*, yet question succeeded question,
until the patience of every human being present
appeared to be entirely exhausted; and Mr.
Wombwell himself, with some degree of impatience, said, he was ashamed to say he could not
recollect to whom he had paid money, but that
he had paid none which was not regularly entered
in the accounts at the India House, to which he
again and again referred Mr. Burke.

Many of the Lords shewed strong signs of impatience, and the Archbishop of York declared,
with a very strong and pointed emphasis, that the
conduct of Mr. Burke was *illiberal*. To this remark no reply was made; and Mr. Wombwell
being discharged, at half past five the Court adjourned.

HUNDRED-AND-FIRST DAY, *April* 18.

THE Court met at two, when Mr. Auriol was
called, and gave a very full and distinct evidence
in favor of the general measures of Mr. Hastings's
government.—Mr. Plumer particularly called the

attention

attention of the Lords to one purpose for which he had brought Mr. Auriol before them. Mr. Adam and Mr. Sheridan had adduced evidence to shew, that Mr. Hastings had dated a letter on the 29th of November 1781, which contained the first information of the rebellion of the Begums; no such letter appeared in the consultations until January 1782, consequently Mr. Hastings had put a *false date* to that letter, and this was Mr. Sheridan's strongest argument to prove his guilt.—— Mr. Auriol swore, that the letter in question was received *in due course*; that *Sir John Macpherson* took it from the Council table; that he *repeatedly* applied to Sir John for it, in order to enter it *upon the Records*, and to send it to England by the Swallow in December—that Sir John in reply said, it was not necessary to send it by the Swallow, and in January a *second copy* came down with Mr. Hastings's narrative, so that it became unnessary to get the original letter from Sir John Macpherson. This evidence effectually cleared Mr. Hastings from the strongest imputation that had been thrown on his character during the trial.

HUNDRED-AND-SECOND DAY, *April* 20.

THE Court on this day completed all the evidence on the Begum charge. The day was spent in producing a great number of letters, extracts from many of which had been read by the Managers

nagers, and the remainder was now given, that the Lords might have the subject complete and ungarbled before them.

Mr. Plumer very neatly opened the evidence he was offering, and observed upon the strange and unfounded assertion of the Managers, as it was entered on the minutes of evidence. He observed, that they had stated, that after the month of September, 1781, no state necessity existed in India.—Mr. Plumer said, he would produce evidence to prove, that for two years subsequent to this period, the distress was of the most serious nature; that Madras and Bombay, receiving no pecuniary assistance from England, as they had done in the late war, depended entirely on Bengal, and owed their preservation solely to the exertions of Mr. Hastings. Mr. Plumer then produced authentic documents, which completely justified his assertions. He next offered to the Court a minute written by Sir John Shore, on Jaghire tenures.

To this evidence, Mr. Burke objected.

Mr. Plumer replied, by saying, that in every point of view it was unobjectionable evidence, Sir John Shore being a man well versed in the laws and customs of India, and selected by the King's Ministers and the Court of Directors to fill the high office of Governor General of Bengal.

Mr.

Mr. Burke said, that the Commons had nothing to do with Sir John Shore's appointment,
but that the Managers knew that he was implicated in the crimes charged upon the prisoner
at the bar, under whom he had for many years
managed the revenues of Bengal; that the Managers had arraigned his conduct; that he had
written part of Mr. Hastings's defence, and that
he knew nothing of his knowledge of the constitution of India; that as to his being appointed
Governor General of Bengal, so had Mr. Hastings, four several times, by the Legislature,
though the Commons had since thought it right
to impeach him.—No answer was given.

The Chancellor said the evidence was proper,
and it was read accordingly.

Soon after five, Mr. Plumer finished all the
evidence on the Begum charge.

HUNDRED-AND-THIRD DAY, *April 20.*

MR. PLUMER on this day began to sum up the
evidence on the Begum charge, which he did as far
as he went, in a manner that tended to clear up
every doubt that had been thrown on the subject.

He

He began by reminding the Lords, that nearly
eight years were elapsed since the charge was first
brought forward. He quoted those strong, forcible, and, as they now appear, those strange expressions of Mr. Sheridan, describing Mr. Hastings as the most cruel, faithless, tyrannical, and
corrupt man, that any age, or any nation, had
produced. After remarking upon the great responsibility which Mr. Sheridan had incurred,
by his assertions, it should be his humble province, he said, to examine whether *facts* or *evidence* would in any degree justify such language.
He said, that if ever man's *general character* could
be known, Mr. Hastings's must be ; that the unprecedented, and alarming length of this trial, had
enabled the Managers to obtain every information of every kind from India ; that they were
themselves men of the highest talents, and infinite
industry ; that they were assisted by able and la-
borious counsel ; that they represented the whole
people of Great Britain, in whose name, and for
whom they prosecuted. Added to this, it was
well known, that *truth* was strengthened in its
operation in the human mind by time. But
would there be *a man* now found hardy enough
to subscribe to that character which one of the
Managers had given of Mr. Hastings?—He
would venture to answer, *No, not one.* Their
Lordships well knew the *opinion*, and the *voice*

of

of India. The proceedings daily held on the state of the East India Company sufficiently shewed the *sense* entertained *at home* of the advantages resulting from the long administration of the gentleman now under trial before their Lordships.

Mr. Plumer then went into a minute scrutiny of the evidence.—A question, he said, had been put by their Lordships to the Managers *six years ago,* as to the tenure by which the Begums held their Jaghires; to *which one of the Managers,* without any hesitation, replied, that the Begums, and their Ministers, *always* contended they were for life.

Mr. Plumer said, he never could suppose that the Managers, or their counsel, *intended* to deceive their Lordships; that he himself believed they spoke truth; but, after a most accurate search, he could not find that they had *at any one time* so contended. But, not satisfied with this, he had called the proper officer from the India House, who had expressly searched the records, and who deposed, *upon oath,* that he could not find *one single instance,* in which either the Begums, or their Ministers, contended that they were for life. In a most feeling manner Mr. Plumer then called to the recollection of their Lordships the *treatment* which Mr. Hastings had received from the Managers. Though the

the multiplicity of business that *he* had to transact was well known, yet if in the perusal of hundreds of volumes of important matter, a mistake of the most trivial nature was found to have been committed *by him*, no allowance was made—*False, false, false*, was repeated, and he was compelled, day after day, month after month, and year after year, to hear the foulest invectives uttered, because he had made, on some occasions, the most inconsiderable and unimportant mistakes, by gentlemen who had *roundly asserted*, in a Court of Justice, that certain declarations *always* were made, which, upon the fullest investigation, were, as it now appeared, *never made at all*.

Here Mr. Plumer said, he would leave this subject to the reflection of the Managers themselves.

The next point was, as to the nature of Jaghire tenures in general, which, he contended, had been totally *mistaken* by the Managers. After quoting several passages in the evidence, he laid particular stress on the opinion of Sir John Shore, formed from a very full consideration of the subject, which he had taken up by the express orders of the Court of Directors, and the Board of Controul.

To this evidence, he said, Mr. Burke had objected in that *ingenious* mode, which never failed him, when he wished to make an impres-

sion

sion *against any person at any time.* He had described Sir John Shore as the *fabricator* of Mr.
Hastings's defence, and the accomplice of his
crime.

Here Mr. Plumer most happily exposed the
futility of such objections. A charge, he said,
had been brought against Mr. Hastings, for forming a plan for collecting the revenues of Bengal.
That plan, as well as *all the plans* by which the
Company were to be benefited, and the public
to receive half a million a year, continued, with
very little variation, to the present moment.—
Sir John Shore having been so long employed
in the revenues under Mr. Hastings, was thought
the properest person to make some observations
on that particular charge. But then, said Mr.
Burke, he was *the accomplice* of Mr. Hastings.
The fact was, that Sir John Shore's skill and
ability in the revenue line had induced Ministers
twice to call him from his retreat in England :
the first time, to go out as an associate to Lord
Cornwallis, and *now* as the successor to that noble
Marquis. So that this *accomplice* of Mr. Hastings
was selected and solicited to fill the first office in
the British empire. Possessing, as Sir John Shore
did, the highest character for ability, integrity,
and honour, distinguished by the gracious favour of his Sovereign, who had conferred the
rank of Baronet upon him, and enjoying the

good

good opinion of his confidential Ministers, he trusted that no observation of the sort made by Mr. Burke would in any degree impeach the credit of his evidence, important as it was to this point, and to another, namely, the general estimation in which Mr. Hastings's name and character were held, amongst the natives of India.

Mr. Plumer proceeded with very great precision, and appealing often to the evidence adduced by the Managers themselves, sometimes to the elucidating evidence which he had himself called, he cleared the ground as he went, and proved, that the allegations in the articles were founded on the grossest ignorance of the manners and customs of India, and a complete misrepresentation of the right of the Begum to any treasures left by Sujah Dowlah, prior to that treaty to which the English were the guarantees in 1775.

On the next day, when he meant to close, he said, he trusted he should prove to their Lordships, that the right which the Begum enjoyed under our guarantee, was wholly done away by her conduct during the revolt of Cheyt Sing; and, as to the idea of *distress* sustained by her, it rested only on the *imagination* of the Managers, since it was a certain fact, that she was left in

posses-

possession of above one million sterling, even after the seizure in 1781.

The Court was very full of company; and from twenty to thirty Lords were present.

The Court adjourned.

HUNDRED-AND-FOURTH DAY, May 2.

The Court did not assemble this day until half-past two o'clock, which prevented Mr. Plumer from going completely through his summary of the evidence, being obliged, as he was, to take some time in refuting and exposing the assertions made by Mr. Sheridan, in the course of his long speech in the prosecution on this charge.

Mr. Plumer opened, by calling to the particular recollection of the Lords the position laid down by the Managers; namely, that this was a *plot* invented by Mr. Hastings, for the purpose of ruining the Begums, who, so far from having been hostile to the British nation, were really friendly —who could have no motive whatever for entertaining the designs imputed to them; that to suppose them to have entertained such designs, was to suppose them weak, foolish, and absurd, and consequently the whole was *an afterthought of* Mr.
Hastings,

Hastings, adopted when his attempt to procure money from Cheyt Sing had failed. This assertion, the most extraordinary ever made by man, and which is the more serious, because it is really made in the name *of all the people of Great Britain,* Mr. Plumer proved, by direct and positive evidence, to be totally void of foundation. He might rest his proofs, he said, upon the evidence adduced by the Manager himself, who had entered, as part of his case, a variety of affidavits, all stating important information as to the hostile acts of the Begums in the month of September 1781. Extracts from these Mr. Plumer read, and seemed to carry with him the fullest conviction of his auditors. But if to these was added the evidence offered by the counsel *on the defence,* then Mr. Sheridan, to make out his proposition, must prove, that a great number of very respectable witnesses had been guilty of the foulest perjury ever attributed to man.

Mr. Plumer here read a number of letters written by Colonel Hannay, in September 1781. In these he mentions *positively,* that the Begums took an active part in favour of Cheyt Sing. He mentions being credibly informed, that a body of troops had marched from Fyzabad, to reinforce Cheyt Sing, in September 1781.

Mr. Plumer read next the evidence of Captain Wade, Captain Burrell, Captain Grey, and Colonel

nel Popham. These gentlemen all swore, that at the action of Pateeta, some of these troops were wounded and taken prisoners; that they had conversed with them, and had been expressly told by them, that they were entertained by the Begum's orders, who sent them to Cheyt Sing, where they had arrived the day before, having each received two rupees advance for their services before they left Fyzabad; that what they stated in their evidence was matter of public conversation in camp, and of universal notoriety; that Mr. Hastings must have heard it, and, as Colonel Popham deposed, had repeatedly talked of the Begum's disaffection in the month of September. Colonel Blair also swore to the notoriety of the fact; that in India no doubt ever was entertained of the truth of it; nor had he, or any of the other gentlemen, ever heard a doubt of it until they came to England, where *alone* a doubt had existed.

He next adverted to the strong evidence of Captain Williams and Captain Gordon, and to the pointed affidavit of Major Macdonald, who, being in India, could not be examined at their Lordships' bar; not contented with these evidences, they had called gentlemen of great respectability, who had lately returned from India. Colonel Duff, an officer of very high rank, who had not arrived from India above three months, had solemnly sworn, that he heard of the hostile acts

of

of the Begums at the time they happened; that he was sure the fact of their disaffection was never doubted in India.

To oppose to the strongest possible evidence that the nature of the case would admit of, *nothing* had been offered—nothing *could be offered*, but a bold unfounded assertion of Mr. Sheridan, that Mr. Hastings *invented* this tale *above two months after all the facts were known*, to which so many gentlemen had positively sworn; and his observation, that it would be so *weak*, *absurd*, and *foolish*, in the Begums to think of resisting the English, that it could not be credited for a moment.

Mr. Plumer said, that it was not his business to prove, that all men always acted with prudence and propriety. He had stated *facts* which were indisputable, and proved the falsehood of the charge. But he confessed that one of the Managers had, upon being *hard pressed*, recourse to an argument of a very singular nature. He said, that the *Commons* were obliged to go into the *enemy's camp* for witnesses, and therefore were entitled to indulgence; a declaration in the highest degree *honourable* to Mr. Hastings, while it shewed to what *distress* his accusers were driven.

The voice of India was undoubtedly on the side of Mr. Hastings. Even the Begums themselves remained silent and quiet spectators of this cause. No one information *of any kind* had been received

from

from the *natives* of India, that tended to support *a single assertion* made by a single Manager. The Tyrant, the *Oppressor*, the Captain General of Iniquity, as Mr. Hastings had so often been called, was the object of the love and veneration of the people of India. His countrymen joined *as one man*, in repelling the unjust attack that had been made upon him. Except, therefore, the Managers could persuade their Lordships, that more *knowledge* of India was contained in that box, than those possessed who had spent the best part of their lives in India; or except they could shew, that gentlemen of the most irreproachable characters had perjured themselves, they had no ground to stand upon.

The leading Manager in this cause (Mr. Sheridan) would not believe a syllable as to the existence *of a plot* here, to undermine the Constitution. It was a mere aristocratical trick; but India was the true centre of all plots, and Mr. Hastings the inventor of them.

After exposing the inconsistency and artifice displayed in the prosecution of this article, Mr. Plumer said there were but two points more to touch upon, but those he was afraid would take up more time than the Lords could give him to-day; but that he would go through them at the next sitting.

The

The Lords shewed an unremitting attention, and appeared to feel as the audience did, in the detection of the many misrepresentations.

HUNDRED-AND-FIFTH DAY, May 6.

Mr. Plumer began by thanking their Lordships for their patient attention. He said, that what remained to be discussed was rather appendant matter, than important as charge; yet it concerned the honour of Mr. Hastings that it should be completely refuted.

The first absurdity he would point out, was this: That in one part of the article, Mr. Hastings was accused of *compelling* the Nabob to seize the treasures and the jaghires: In another, that the Nabob *bribed* Mr. Hastings, to allow him, the Nabob, to do those acts. Another strange and absurd assertion of the Manager (Mr. Sheridan) was, that whatever the *necessity* might have been, previous to the 19th of September 1781, no necessity existed subsequent to that period, on which the measures of seizing the treasures could be defended.

Mr. Plumer, in the strongest terms, expressed his astonishment either at the gross ignorance, or the

the *artful misrepresentation* of the Manager. There was not a boy, he said, in India or in England, who pretended to the slightest knowledge of the History of India, who did not know that the distress of the Company's affairs was considerably *increased* after 1781. To put this matter out of all doubt, Mr. Plumer read a variety of extracts from the Letters from Madras and Bombay, expressing the warmest acknowledgments to Mr. Hastings, for the great relief which he had afforded them, stating their *increased* distress from the continuance of the war, and their *sole reliance* on Mr. Hastings for their future support. Mr. Plumer put this so strong as to convince his hearers, that if the Manager was not *ignorant*, he was *something worse*.

He next exposed their gross ignorance, or misrepresentation, of the whole history of Oude, " But thank God," said Mr. Plumer, " *the hour* " *of delusion is gone by*. Their Lordships had now before them the whole history of that country, by which it was evident, that from the Nabob's accession in 1775, down to 1781, he experienced the greatest distress, owing to two causes; the one, because his mother withheld from him the treasures of the state—the other, as the Marquis Cornwallis has since said, " to the character of the Prince," whom he describes as careless, inattentive

attentive to business, swayed by favourites, and, exceedingly expensive. But such were the consequences of the Treaty of Chunar, that from Oude, a country, affirmed by Mr. Francis, in November 1781, *to be ruined beyond redemption,* a country from which Mr. Fox would not receive a balance of seven hundred and ninety thousand pounds, due to the Company in November 1783; yet, Mr. Plumer repeated, such were the consequences of Mr. Hastings's exactions, that between 1781, and 1785, as appeared *in evidence,* the sum of *four millions two hundred thousand pounds* had been received. This was one great resource, he said, which carried us successfully through a war, in which Great Britain could not, as she had done in the latter war, afford Mr. Hastings the assistance of a shilling.—After *exposing* the folly of the accusation in this instance, he proceeded to the bribes, in which he pointed out the contradictions between the *evidence* and the *charge.*

Mr. Plumer next proceeded to prove from evidence, that Mr. Sheridan might just as well have charged Mr. Hastings with being the author of the dreadful massacres in Paris, on the first and second of September, as of the distresses of the Khord Mahal, in 1782. He pointed out the gross inconsistency and falsehood of the charge, and laid open such a scene of villainy and fraud, in the mode of wording the article, as ought to cover

those

those who drew it up with *perpetual infamy*, provided Mr. Plumer quoted fairly, but which, on
the other hand, ought to ruin his *own chara&er*, if
his statement was not corre&.

With infinite ability Mr. Plumer next exposed
the incorrigible prejudices of the Managers,
who had opened and fummed up the evidence on
this charge—One of them, Mr. Adam, had boldly
affirmed that Mr. Hastings, by putting a false date
to a letter, had written *a lye*—and Mr. Sheridan
had first assumed *as a fa&*, that a false date was put
to the letter; and had then concluded, that it was
a proof the *most convincing* that could be offered of
the guilt of the defendant. Mr. Auriol had proved
that the letter was written and dispatched *on the day
of its date*, but that Sir John M'Pherfon had taken
it from the Council Board. This circumftánce
the Manager might have known both from Sir
John and Mr. Auriol in the year 1788, if their
anxiety to discover *truth*, had equalled their eagerness *to condemn*.

He next proved, that the Dire&ors had sent no
orders for an enquiry into the fa& of the Begum's
rebellion; and it being now five o'clock, and a
great number of members of the House of Commons, with Mr. Dundas, coming down, he took
the opportunity of placing the inconsistency, absurdity, and injustice of the Impeachment, in
terms so strong, that he excited the attention of
all

all his auditors. He said, that Great Britain was a nation famed for her regard to justice throughout the world ;—but the *nation* and Mr. Hastings were both upon their trial, and that both must rise or fall together. Their Lordships had in *proof* before them, what India thought of this long persecution. *Twelve years* had elapsed since Cheyt Sing was expelled from Benares, and since the Begums were deprived of a part of Sujah Dowlah's treasures. The nation had *enjoyed* the benefits of both—it had taken the money, and *exposed* them by Impeachment. There was no end of the absurdity and injustice of Great Britain, provided the articles against Mr. Hastings were *founded in truth.* But, thank God, the honour of the country was in no danger; a *six years trial* had had no other effect than this, to shew to the whole world the gross ignorance of those who first set the prosecution on foot—to call forth the testimony of all India in favour of the accused, and to induce the prosecutors reluctantly to confess, that in all their ideas as to India, they had been mistaken. Mr. Plumer put this in every possible point of view, and left this impression *strong* in the minds of those who were prejudiced against Mr. Hastings (if any such there be) that the nation participated in any *infamy* which might attach upon him; but he again and again repeated, that he was confident the judgment of their Lordships would vindicate

the

the honour of the nation, and of Mr. Hastings, both embarked in a common cause.

HUNDRED-AND-SIXTH DAY, *May* 9.

THE Court did not assemble on this day until a quarter *before three o'clock*; to this late hour is the meeting now commenced, though during the prosecution the Court generally met at twelve, and always before one, when the Commons could make a House in time.

Mr. Dallas immediately rose, and arrested the attention of the Court for two hours and a half, by one of the first speeches ever uttered in a public assembly—never *once* deviating from the subject before him, nor venturing to make one single assertion which he did not prove, either by evidence already adduced by the Managers, or by documents which he read, and proposed to enter hereafter.

He reminded their Lordships, that he was now about to answer a charge or charges, which had employed *two whole years* in the prosecution, and upon which the Managers had spoke *seven days* in the opening and the close. The charge was a corrupt receipt of money—and in return for such receipt,

receipt, the forming such arrangements for the collection of the revenues, as brought *oppression, ruin,* and *destruction* on the natives of Bengal. To every part of this charge, Mr. Dallas said he would give that full and complete answer, which should satisfy the mind of every free and candid man. After placing the previous matter in the clearest point of view, he proceeded to examine the several allegations in the article; and he entreated their Lordships to go along with him in examining the immense extent of the charge made by the *Commons of Great Britain,* and the poverty of the proof by which the charge was supported. No man would say, that *time enough* had not been given to procure evidence of the guilt of Mr. Hastings, if he had been guilty. No man would say, that *talents* and *perseverance* were wanting; for he was as ready as any man to do justice to the *abilities* and, to the *industy* of those who were opposed to him, as any gentleman could possibly be : yet, though armed as they were with all the *power* and authority of the country, he was ready to meet them boldly in front, and to shew, that from the first allegation to the last, their charge was utterly unfounded.

Mr. Dallas then stated, that they set out, by asserting as a *fact,* what a very little *attention* to the Company's Records would have proved to be totally unfounded; namely, that Mr. Hastings had

succeeded

succeeded to the Government of Bengal in 1772, determined to act corruptly, and therefore he had neglected to take that *oath*, which all his predecessors had taken. The falsehood, and the baseness of this allegation, Mr. Dallas exposed in the most clear and convincing manner; not by oratory, but by a reference to original documents, which, if they were *forged*, must *destroy his reputation for ever*, but which, *if true*, leaves it as a point to be settled between the *Managers* and the *Counsel* and Solicitors of Great Britain, on whom the *infamy* of such scandalous neglect ought to rest. Six years, and sixty thousand pounds, wasted in the name of the public, upon points which *common industry* would have prevented from having been agitated at all, fixes indelible disgrace *somewhere*; and Mr. Fox, who was present, appeared to *feel* for the situation he had been brought into. Such are the advantages of a *public trial*, that the *infamy*, as Mr. Burke truly said, must rest *somewhere*.

The next point in Mr. Dallas's speech, was the *discovery* and *detection* of such a mass of misrepresentation and abandoned profligacy, as never yet occurred in a public proceeding. Here he could not be mistaken, for he read faithful extracts from Mr. Burke's speeches, and compared them with the evidence that Mr. Burke produced.

From

From the speech it appeared, that Mr. Burke represented Mr. Hastings not only as the most *corrupt*, but as the most cruel and unprincipled of human beings. The date of all this corruption was supposed to be in the year 1772. As there was nothing *like evidence* to justify such wild expressions, Mr. Dallas said, it would be right to consider what Mr. Hastings *had been* up to that period. In the most chaste and modest language, he proceeded to state, that in 1749 Mr. Hastings went a writer to Bengal; that, after filling the highest situations there, that of Governor excepted, after having been concerned in all the important events which happened between 1749 and 1765, he returned in that year to England; that in 1769, he was appointed second in Council at Madras, and was removed, and succeeded to the Government of Bengal in April 1772. That much clamour had been raised in England, on account of the fortunes acquired in Bengal, and the various changes that had taken place between 1756 and 1765; that accounts had been published of the several sums gained by individuals in that period, but that amongst their names, that of Mr. Hastings was *not to be found*. That this circumstance, and the highest opinion entertained of his abilities by Lord North, induced him to propose, in 1773, that Mr. Hastings should be appointed Go-

vernor

vernor General of Bengal for five years, by the Legislature of Great Britain.

These circumstances, Mr. Dallas said, he did not mention as a *set-off* against any *proved fact*; but the Managers had proved *no facts*; it was therefore fair to oppose to the monstrous absurdities which they had ventured to utter, what was the established character of Mr. Hastings, up to 1772; and he would put it to any candid or honourable man to determine, whether, upon such *flimsy reasonings* as the Managers had offered, their Lordships would be induced to think, *that, in one moment*, Mr. Hastings should assume a character *totally new ?*—for to such *an absurd extent* did the charge go.

Mr. Dallas then proceeded to state the unexampled cruelty, the baseness, with which Mr. Hastings had been treated. He examined, and refuted, *point by point*, the allegations of the charge, as far as he went. He quoted several parts of Mr. Burke's speech, and sifted the evidence in support of it. He accused him of a most unwarrantable mis-statement of facts—of taking the beginning and the close of the sentence of letters, with a view of totally perverting the sense—of making assertions, that so far from having a shadow of foundation *in fact*, were contradicted by his own evidence; and, in short, of those acts which disgrace the Commons of Great Britain,

Britain, provided Mr. Dallas is well-founded, and he repeatedly *pledged his character*, well aware, as he said he was, of the sacredness of the pledge, for the truth of all he had advanced.

At five o'clock the Court adjourned.

HUNDRED-AND-SEVENTH DAY, *May* 16.

At two o'clock on this day the Court assembled, when Mr. Dallas proceeded in opening those articles which had employed the Managers *two complete years*. He apologized to the Lords for the time that he was taking up, but he entreated them to consider, that the part of the charge in which he was then proceeding, was a direct accusation of the receipt of a sum of money for an appointment to an office; and though he had *proved*, that this appointment was not only proper, but the best that could have been made, yet he was very ready to allow, that if Mr. Hastings had taken money for making it, the propriety of the appointment would in no degree lessen the corruptness of the act. He then stated the evidence as adduced by the Managers *themselves*, from which it clearly appeared, and was allowed by Colonel Monson, one of the Supreme Council opposed to Mr. Hastings, that it was an invariable custom

custom at the Courts of Eastern Princes, to allow
a specific sum in lieu of table expences. Such
sum *all the predecessors* of Mr. Hastings had re-
received while at *Moorshedabad.* Such sum the
Nabob received when in *Calcutta;* and he affirmed, that to call this receipt a corrupt receipt
for an appointment to office, was wild and absurd
in the highest degree, since the receipt had no
sort of connection with Munny Begum's appointment.

After clearing this matter completely, he called
the attention of the Lords most particularly to the
period of time when the transaction happened, in
order to shew *the justice and gratitude of the late
House of Commons* (which Mr. Burke had *sometimes*
called *a House elected by a corrupt Indian interest.)*
The transaction happened in 1772, now *twenty-one
years ago.* Since that period, Mr. Hastings had
four several times been appointed Governor Go-
neral of Bengal, by the Legislature of Great Britain. It could not be said, that *time* had thrown
any *new light* upon this subject, to authorize a
departure from every *principle of justice ;* because
the fact was, that *every circumstance* was as well
known in 1775, as at this hour. Yet *those* who
now supported this Impeachment, were *then* the
friends of Mr. Hastings. Every effort was made
by the Minister of that day 1775) to remove him
from his office. That Minister, when the danger
pressed,

pressed, when Great Britain was sinking in Europe, Africa, and America, had three several times, with the unanimous concurrence of the Legislature, *re-appointed* Mr. Hastings Governor General of Bengal, and Mr. Hastings had preserved India to Great Britain. The credit of so preserving it was given to him by those who *voted for his prosecution*; yet such *was the gratitude of the Commons of Great Britain*, that *sixteen years* after this transaction of Munny Begum, and subsequent to *four Parliamentary appointments*, they had made it the subject of a criminal charge; and *now*, *twenty-one years after it happened*, was he, Mr. Dallas, defending Mr. Hastings from that accusation.

Mr. Dallas said, that, after having *completely refuted the charge*, he could with propriety expose the baseness and ingratitude of it. He next exposed a great number of most wicked and audacious misrepresentations in the charge, and in the evidence; some not having, as he said, a shadow of foundation *in truth*; some so *marked*, that Charity itself could not impute them to hurry or mistake, but evidently resulting from design. He pointed particularly at Mr. Burke here; and he read a quotation from his speech, in which Mr. Burke gave *his* character of Nundcomar. This Mr. Dallas finely commented upon, and, in return, described what really Nundcomar *was*, so as to convey

convey to every person, that he meant to describe *another great man* under his description of Nund-comar.

Having effectually done away all the early part of the charge, he next came to consider those pre-sents, the receipt of which Mr. Hastings avowed, and for which there was no evidence *of any kind*, but the declaration of Mr. Hastings himself. He said, that if he could have the good fortune to convey to their Lordships that distinct idea which he had formed, he was sure that he should clear up every circumstance, and convince their Lord-ships, that when Mr. Hastings thought the British empire in India at stake, no thought for *himself* ever occurred to him. He then went completely through the present of Cheyt Sing, and made it clear, even from the Managers' evidence, that there was not a shadow of a ground to suppose, that Mr. Hastings ever intended to appropriate that money to his own use, and he entered into a full discussion of the Act of 1773, in order to prove, that the laws never meant to preclude the receipt of money for the public.

After a number of very pertinent observations, the Court adjourned at a quarter after five o'clock.

HUNDRED-

HUNDRED-AND-EIGHTH DAY, May 17.

THE Court on this day assembled soon after two. o'clock. Mr. Dallas immediately proceeded in his summary, and desired their Lordships would have the goodness always to bear in mind, that upon this case of the *avowed presents*, as the Managers termed them, there was no evidence of any kind except what Mr. Hastings had himself furnished; and that no doubt did exist but that every rupee received by Mr. Hastings, as a present, was expended in the public service.

Having already shewn, that the two lacks of rupees received from Cheyt Sing's Buxey were publicly applied, he would now take up the sums for which bonds had been granted to Mr. Hastings in the years 1780 and 1781. He proved, most satisfactorily, from a reference to dates and circumstances, that Mr. Hastings never could have had the most distant idea of applying any part of this money to its own use.

He next took up the present of one hundred thousand pounds sterling from the Nabob of Oude and his Ministers, and proved, that every rupee of this present also was applied to the

public

public service, at a time when our very existence depended on the realization of every rupee that could be procured.

After having very fully gone into this transaction, and effectually repelled the insinuation of the Managers, that Mr. Hastings had instructed Major Scott either to avow or conceal the receipt of this present, as parties might be at the time, Mr. Dallas most eloquently stated the services performed by the appropriation of these several sums to the public. He then went into a full consideration of the letters of Mr. Hastings and Mr. Larkins, and desired to put it seriously to the honour of every noble Lord present, whether a man, who, from all the proceedings before them, never had a thought but for preserving the great and important empire committed to his charge, should have practised those mean and contemptible arts which he must have done, if any part of this accusation was founded in truth.

At five, the Court adjourned.

HUNDRED-AND-NINTH DAY, *May* 24.

Mr. DALLAS on this day closed his opening of the presents, and the revenue articles. If he astonished his auditors upon former occasions, he excited in their breasts on this day every sentiment of admiration of his talents, and conviction of the justice of his cause. The remaining points, he said, were, a present received from Rajah Nobkessin, and applied to the payment of certain public expences incurred by Mr. Hastings; and a present of one hundred thousand pounds offered by the Nabob of Oude, but not accepted. He stated, in the most clear manner, the circumstances of the first transaction, and proved, that the expences incurred and charged to the Company were equally charged by Lord Cornwallis as they had been by the predecessors of Mr. Hastings. As to the next charge, he knew not how to treat it seriously, because *all the evidence* adduced by the Managers proved the facts to be directly *the reverse* of those described in the charge. The only remaining article then was, the revenue—a charge most important indeed,

if

if it were *true* in any of its parts, since it accused Mr. Hastings of overturning all the establishments of the country, of violating private
property, and of *oppressing* and *destroying* the
natives of Bengal. The Managers, however, had
abandoned all the *material* parts of the article,
and had confined themselves to three points: the
sending Aumeens to the provinces, abolishing the
Provincial Councils, and establishing a Committee of Revenue in February 1781.

A very few words, he trusted, would be sufficient to do away every evidence that had been
offered on these points—and as to the first, he had
to shew their Lordships, the most monstrous absurdity that ever disgraced a proceeding offered
to a Court of Justice. The criminality in appointing Aumeens, was stated in the charge to
consist of the dangerous powers granted *by their
instructions,* which gave them liberty to treat with
oppression and cruelty every native who should
presume to disobey their arbitrary orders. Yet,
strange to tell, *these instructions were not to be
found in evidence,* though they were the very
ground of the charge; after exposing, as it deserved, this scandalous neglect in those who have
been so liberally paid by the public, Mr. Dallas
said, that neither the instructions, which he would
produce, nor any one document could in any,
the slightest degree, justify the allegations in the
charge.

As

As to the abolition of the Provincial Councils, he proved that all men of all descriptions approved the abolition, and the subsequent appointment of the Committee of Revenue. He then took the same ground that Mr. Pitt had taken in the House of Commons, who voted against this monstrous charge *in toto*—the *most monstrous*, by Mr. Fox's account, of all the charges—namely, that it was in the highest degree absurd to impute criminality to difference of opinion. After being most eloquent and convincing on this subject, he called the attention of the Court to the evidence of Mr. Anderson, Sir John Shore, the public accounts, and the known state of Bengal; and he put it in so forcible a manner, that Mr. Burke and his counsel hung down their heads, apparently with shame and remorse.

He read the allegations in the charge, one by one, as they were put to Sir John Shore, in the shape of questions. He read his answers, which proved that each allegation *was false*. He put it most forcibly to the Lords, to decide which they would believe—the Managers, who had no local knowledge, or Sir John Shore? The Managers said, that Mr. Hastings had *plundered, oppressed,* and *destroyed* the people of Bengal.

Sir John Shore swore, that during the whole period of Mr. Hastings's administration, Bengal had improved in agriculture and population, and

that

that the people were happier than under their native governments. But, said Mr. Dallas, I am aware of the answer that will be given, because it has already been said—your Lordships are not to believe Sir John Shore upon his oath, because *he is an accomplice in the crimes of* Mr. Hastings. Strange inconsistency!—whimsical caprice of fortune! The accomplice of the crimes of Mr. Hastings, was called forth from his retreat—solicited to accept of the highest office which this country could bestow—Lord of a mighty empire, with millions of men submissive to his authority. But if he *was* the accomplice of Mr. Hastings's crimes, why does not Mr. Burke move to recal him? Why does he not impeach him? Why does he stop here? Society in pain and pleasure is grateful—let the bar be taken down, and add to the list of delinquents the whole Court of Directors, and his Majesty's Ministers, to whom the right honourable gentleman had insinuated the impropriety of Sir John Shore's appointment.

If he were content merely to defend Mr. Hastings from the charge, he should now close; but he demanded much more. His client stood before their Lordships as the most injured man that any age or any nation had produced. His services were great, important, and *acknowledged,*

and

and the judgment of their Lordships would, he was *confident*, establish his fame to the latest posterity. Ask Sir John Shore what *all India* thought of him? Sir John Shore had been asked, and answered the question fully. It was for the Managers only to run counter to evidence, and to the common sense of mankind, and their Lordships must believe them to be *mistaken*, to use no harsher phrase, or they must believe every evidence *perjured*, and the *whole word* to be misled.

After a most eloquent close, Mr. Dallas sat down, and Mr. Hastings begged to detain their Lordships for a few minutes, and that he might not from hurry or confusion be mistaken in a point of great importance, he begged to read from a paper what he had to offer, which he did as follows:

" *My Lords*,

" I venture to solicit the attention of your Lordships, to the situation in which this trial at present stands.

" I hope, for your Lordships' indulgence, in requesting to be allowed such farther time, in the course of each day's sitting, as may enable me to bring the remainder of my defence, if no interruptions intervene, within the probable period of *three days*.

" I hope,

" I hope, by the means of such indulgence, to conclude my evidence, on the article now under consideration, within the compass of *one* day.

" I am informed that the observations of my counsel upon it, will only occupy another day; and the gentleman on my right hand (Mr. Law) is willing to wave any observations that the defence may be the sooner closed.—In that case, one day will be sufficient for this article. The abridged evidence with which I mean to trouble your Lordships, on the only remaining article, *that* of " Contracts," may be comprized within the space of *one day more*; I am willing to forego the benefit of a more detailed defence, in order to enable the Managers for the Commons fully to conclude their reply within the course of the present session—an expectation which, I trust I do not unreasonably entertain, in this advanced period of a trial that has been so many years depending. I am well aware of the disadvantages to which I subject my defence on this article, by leaving the evidence *unstated* and *unapplied* to make out its own effect; and it is with reluctance that I deprive myself of the benefit of those talents which have been so ably displayed on the former parts of my defence: for it is to those talents, aided by the zeal and cordial affection which have animated them to their best exertions, that I am now indebted for the hope and assu-

rance

rance I confidently entertain, that though *I should*. not live to receive the sanction of your Lordships acquittal, my name, at least, shall not descend blasted with infamy to posterity; but be recorded with those of the many other victims of false opinion, some of higher worth, none of better intentions, who have done service to the states which employed them, *and been requited with unthankfulness and persecution.*

" My Lords, I consider the resolution which I have taken as a sacrifice, and I make it with the greater chearfulness, as it may, and must in some degree, prove no less an accommodation to your Lordships' time, than the means (if your Lordships shall *so* permit it) of obtaining my own deliverance from a state of suspence, which is become *almost insupportable.*"

Mr. Burke made some remarks on Mr. Hastings's attack, as he called it, *upon the Commons of Great Britain,* and talked of the influence of his fortune and connections, apparently in a very confused stile—but said Mr. Hastings must judge as to the wisdom of making his defence long or short.

HUNDRED-

HUNDRED-AND-TENTH DAY, May 25.

THE Lords met this day before eleven o'clock, and sat until half past past five.

The first part of the morning was taken up in reading a short variety of papers, stated by the counsel as necessary, to complete evidence which the managers had mutilated and garbled.

Mr. Auriol was then called, and examined as to the oaths taken by Mr. Hastings, when he succeeded to the government of Bengal in 1772. He said he was pretty certain, that he had seen Mr. Hastings's name subscribed to these oaths, in a book kept by himself as secretary, and left in his office to his successor just as he received it from his predecessor.

As to the restrictive oath proposed by Lord Clive in 1766, taken by himself, and by his successor, Mr. Verelst, in the Town-hall of Calcutta, before all the inhabitants, that was a totally different oath, and had become *obsolete* before Mr. Auriol's arrival, and had not been taken by Mr. Cartier the predecessor of Mr. Hastings. This was also proved by Mr. Hudson, fully fixing
upon

upon the Managers, or their counsel, the charges
preferred against them by Mr. Dallas, of the most
atrocious, and wicked deception.

Mr. Burke cross-examined Mr. Auriol for
nearly two hours complete, asking him an infinite variety of questions, apparently of little
consequence, but to which he received the clearest answers. To one involved and complicated
question, Mr. Auriol replied, by desiring it might
be divided, and then he would answer it, which
he did; upon which Mr. Burke made some reflection, so very offensive, that the Archbishop of
York started up with much feeling, and said it
was impossible for him silently to listen to the
illiberal conduct of the Manager; that he examined the witness as if he were examining, not
a gentleman, but a pick-pocket; that the *illiberality* and the *inhumanity* of the Managers in
the course of this long trial, could not be *exceeded* by Marat and Roberspierre, had the conduct of the trial been committed to them.

Mr. Burke seemed much confounded, but said,
in reply, *that he had not heard one word of what
had been spoken*, and that he should act as if he
had not. He then pursued his examination;
and, in the course of it, Lord Stanhope, Lord
Moreton, and Lord Somers, expressed their belief that the trial never could come to a close, if
a gentleman was to be examined so long upon the

rumour

rumour of *rumours.*—Mr. Burke then began to talk
about the Begums, but was called to order; and,
about half past four, the counsel closed their evidence on the sixth, seventh, and fourteenth articles—taking *five days only*, for what had occupied
the Managers *thirty-four* on the prosecution.

Mr. Plumer then observed, that, agreeably to
Mr. Hastings's engagement of yesterday, they
should not sum up, nor expend any time in
opening the only remaining charge, the contracts,
but proceed *directly* to the evidence. The first
was the opium contract; and here he should supply what, in *candour* and *justice*, the Managers
ought not to have left deficient. He said, the
evidence he should produce would prove:

First, That until the government of Mr. Hastings, opium was no branch of revenue to the
Company, but a monopoly in the hands of individuals.

Second, That Mr. Hastings took it from those
individuals, and made it a productive article of
revenue for the Company.

Third, That in 1775, it was put up to public
contract, and the contract given to the lowest of
fifteen bidders, that is, to the man who offered
the best terms for the Company.

Fourth, That in 1777 it was given to Mr. Mackenzie *for three* years, on the same terms that the
lowest bidder had it in 1775.

Fifth,

Fifth, Which the Managers had *tota'ly sunk*, That in the year 1780 it was granted to Mr. Mackenzie *for one year longer*, by Mr. Francis, Mr. Wheeler, and Mr. Hastings—the two first being a *majority* of the Board. This omission was the more unpardonable, because *the jett* of the charge against Mr. Hastings was his neglect of the Company's orders, who in December 1778 disapproved of the grant of the contract to Mr. Mackenzie in 1777, because it had not been advertized.—Now, as this letter arrived in Bengal in 1779, and the contract was *again* given to Mr. Mackenzie in 1780, when the disapprobation was *fresh* in the recollection of Mr. Francis and Mr. Hastings, it was *partial* and *unfair* to *sink this transaction*, and to go on to the grant to Mr. Sullivan in 1781, who had it precisely on the same terms with Mr. Mackenzie.

Sixth, He should give a minute of Mr. Francis, in which he said he thought, and he thought truly, that it would be bad policy to give the opium contract on too low terms to any contractor, for very valid reasons, and which undoubtedly induced the Board not to think this a contract, which every adventurer in India might speculate upon.

Seventh, He should examine a gentleman who had been one of the council at Patna, and accordingly Mr. Law was called to the bar, who said,

that

that from the time he came into the service in 1765, until 1773, opium was a monopoly for the advantage of the Company's servants at Patna; that they bought it at two hundred Sicca rupees a chest, and generally sold it from four hundred and fifty to five hundred rupees a chest; that Mr. Hastings took it from them and gave it to the Company.

It appeared, that from 1775 to 1785, the contract price was one hundred and ninety rupees a chest, for a large quantity as large as was in most years procured, and an advance of fifty rupees a chest upon all manufactured beyond that quantity.

Mr. Plumer then gave in all his evidence to substantiate these facts, which it did *most completely*, and then the Court adjourned.

Mr. Fox came into the Manager's box soon after the Archbishop of York had spoke, but did not stay long.

Mr. Michael Angelo Taylor was the *only Manager* who supported Mr. Burke, though he had declared, some time ago, that he would no more be seen in the box with him. The Lords seemed as if their patience was nearly exhausted, but we hope and trust, that a very few days more, will end this tedious enquiry.

Mr. Law in the course of the day gave in a very material and important piece of evidence.

The

The Managers had in the year 1790, called Mr. Wright from the India House, to prove *the amount of* Mr. Hastings's *fortune* by a statement of the remittances *made in his name*. These, in bills, and in diamonds turned out to be *two hundred* and *thirty-eight thousand pounds*, from which the inference drawn by the Managers was that that was his fortune. Mr. Law therefore called Mr. Woodman, who in conjunction with Mr. Francis Sykes, and a Mr. Waller, were his attornies in England. Mr. Woodman swore, that *above eighty thousand pounds of this money* never came into their hands, but was indorsed over to other persons; that bills were drawn upon them for other sums, which they paid away; and that the state of Mr. Hastings's fortune, from 1778 down to 1786, when it was finally delivered over to him, was from seventy-three to sixty-five thousand pounds; the particulars being each year respectively stated; that he never knew, nor did he believe that Mr. Hastings ever employed any other persons in money transactions, nor did he believe, that he ever remitted money, except to the three gentlemen who had the management of his affairs. Mr. Burke did not chuse to put any question to Mr. Woodman.

HUNDRED-

HUNDRED-AND-ELEVENTH DAY, May 27.

THE Court met this day soon after eleven, when Mr. Plumer proceeded to complete his evidence on the opium contract; and he proved the great addition to the public revenues, which resulted from Mr. Hastings's having made opium a branch of revenue for the Company, in 1773. He proved also, that the plan of sending opium to China was a very wise plan for the year it took place in; but that in fact it was not the plan of Mr. Hastings, but a scheme adopted by Mr. Wheeler, on the recommendation of a very ingenious and industrious officer, Colonel Watson.

He then proceeded to the bullock contract, a subject which had been much expatiated upon, by men grossly and foolishly ignorant; and he proved the following facts by evidence.

First, That so far from its being *true*, as the charge *affirmed*, that Mr. Hastings, in the year 1779, abolished a contract, without any complaint from the army of its inefficacy—*the truth was, that* complaints *of the most serious nature* had been transmitted from several corps of the army, to the Commander in Chief, and by *him* to Mr. Hastings.

Second,

Second, That no *possible remedy*, for so dangerous an evil, could be applied, unless by giving
a contract on such terms as should insure a faithful discharge of so important a service.

Third, That upon *this principle*, Sir Eyre Coote
recommended in July 1779; and the Board agreed
to that contract, which is the subject of the present charge.

Fourth, That by the evidence of Colonel Duff,
and by various authentic documents, it appeared,
that the contract was not improvident, either as
to terms or numbers.

Fifth, That when it was converted into an
agency, the same checks and regulations were
kept up.

Sixth, That the experience *of the last war* fully
evinced the necessity of attending most diligently
to this, the most important branch of military service.

The next contract was that of Mr. Auriol, or,
more properly speaking, the agency for supplying
the Carnatic with provisions, in the last *general
war*. This agency Mr. Pitt most strenuously *defended*, giving the *highest praise* both to Mr. Hastings and Mr. Auriol, for having saved *a whole
people* from perishing by famine, and that too *on
the most economical plan ;* but Mr. Burke beat Mr.
Pitt in a division on this charge, in the House of
Commons, *that is dead and gone ;* and *this day*
Mr.

Mr. Hastings answered *to the charge of having saved a nation*, and he did it *most completely* through Mr. Dallas.

So much time was expended in the examination of Mr. Auriol, and in arguments, and in an adjournment to the Chamber of Parliament, that at six o'clock Mr. Dallas said they should take an hour and a half, or two hours more; in consequence of which the Court adjourned.

────────────

HUNDRED-AND-TWELFTH DAY, *May* 28.

On this day the case of Mr. Hastings was totally closed. The Lords met at half-past two, and, in a very short time, Mr. Dallas put in the whole of the evidence necessary to elucidate Mr. Belli's agency: that agency which Mr. Pitt defended most strenuously in the House of Commons. After having finished, Mr. Law desired to introduce the several testimonials which had been sent from India in favour of Mr. Hastings, by the Marquis Cornwallis, as the best reply that could be given to that sort of *general abuse* which had been so plentifully heaped upon Mr. Hastings.

To this Mr. Burke made some sort of objection; but on Mr. Law reading to him a quotation *from his own speech*, in which he stood *pledged*
himself

himself to introduce this evidence, it passed, as also the addresses to Mr. Hastings, from the civil servants of the Company, and from the officers of the army, and also the unanimous thanks of the Court of Directors and Proprietors, *approved by* Mr. Dundas, Mr. (now Lord) Grenville, Lord Walsingham, and Lord Mulgrave, the members of the Board of Controul, for his *long, faithful,* and *able services,* and with this *mass of evidence* to rebut the charge of having *oppressed, ruined,* and *destroyed the natives of India,* of having *materially affected the interests of the Company,* and *disgraced* and *degraded* the British name and character, did the counsel of Mr. Hastings conclude.

Mr. Hastings, when all the evidence was closed, addressed the Court to the following effect:

MY LORDS,

My evidence is now brought to its close.

Sufficient has, I trust, been already done for every immediate purpose of necessary justification; and it is not, my Lords, from any apprehension which I entertain, lest any defects of this kind should exist, or from a vain opinion that they could be supplied by me, that I present myself once more to your Lordships' attention. No, my Lords, I leave the proof which I have offered to its just and effective operation, without any degree of doubtful anxiety for the issue. But, my Lords,

I rise

I rise for a purpose, which no external testimony can adequately supply, to convey to your Lordships' minds a satisfaction which honourable minds may possibly expect, and which the solemn asseverations of a man, impressed with a due sense of the sacred obligations of religion and honour, can alone adequately convey.

I know that the actual motives of human conduct are often dark and mysterious, and sometimes inscrutable. As far as the subject is capable of further ascertainment, and the truth can be sealed by a still more solemn attestation, it is a duty which innocence owes to itself to afford it.

In the presence, therefore, of that Being from whom no secrets are hid, I do, upon a full review and scrutiny of my past life, unequivocally and conscientiously declare, that, in the administration of that trust of Government, which was during so many years confided to me, I did, in no instance, intentionally sacrifice the interest of my country to any private views of my own personal advantage; that, according to my best skill and judgment, I invariably promoted the essential interests of my employers, the happiness and prosperity of the people committed to my charge, and the welfare and honour of my country, and at no time with more entire devotion of mind and purpose to these objects, than, during that period, in which my accusers have endeavoured to represent

me

me as occupied and engrossed by the base pursuit of·low, sordid, and interdicted emolument.

It may be expected of me to say something in addition to what you have heard from Mr. Woodman, respecting the actual state and extent of my fortune.

He has proved the total amount of my remittances from India, during the period of my Government; and that the balance of my fortune, when last adjusted, shortly after my return to England in 1785, amounted to little more than sixty-five thousand pounds.

I protest, in the name of Almighty God, that I made no remittances to England during that period, which were not made to him, and my other attornies joined in trust with him; that I had no other persons in England or Europe, in trust of my pecuniary concerns; and that his account of those remittances is accurately true, according to my best means of knowledge and belief upon the subject; and that, including those remittances, I at no time possessed a fortune which exceeded, at its most extended amount, the sum of one hundred thousand pounds; and in this calculation I would be understood to comprehend every kind and description of property whatsoever. That, at the period of my return to England, my fortune did not exceed the balance already mentioned to have been then in the hands of my attornies, by

more

more than the sum of twenty-five thousand pounds;
amounting, on the largest calculation, to an aggregate sum of between eighty and ninety thousand
pounds; and all the property which I possess
stands pledged at the present moment for the discharge of such debts as I have contracted since
the commencement of this long depending trial.

These are the enormous fruits of thirteen years
of imputed rapacity and peculation, and of upwards of thirty years of active and important service!!!

My Lords, I know not how I can more fully
and explicitly disavow every purpose of appro-
priating to my own benefit any of the various
sums received, and applied by me to the Company's service in moments of extreme peril and exigency, than in the very terms in which I expressed such disavowal at your Lordships' bar, in the
month of June 1791. I again repeat, that " I solemnly, and with a pure conscience, affirm, that I
never did harbour such a thought for a single
instant."

If, in addition to the proof upon your Lordships' table, of the justice and necessity of the
measures which are the subjects of the two first articles of the charge, it can be required of me, by
an act of solemn and sacred attestation on my
part, to vouch the truth of my defence in these
particulars, and to vindicate my character from

the

the unfounded charge of malice alledged to have
been entertained by me against the immediate objects of those measures, I once more call God to
witness, that no motive of personal *enmity*, no
views of personal *advantage* to myself, or others,
induced the adoption, on my part, of any of those
measures, for which I am at this day criminally
questioned; but that, in every instance, I acted
under the immediate and urgent sense of public
duty, in obedience to the irresistible demands of
public safety, and to vindicate the just rights of
the empire committed to my care against those
who, in a moment of its greatest peril, were engaged in hostile confederacy to destroy it.

I have no doubts, but that upon a fair review
of all the existing circumstances, and the means
of information then before me, no lavish or improper expenditure of public money will be found
to have taken place in respect to the contracts
formed during my administration.

For the prudence and success of the regulations
adopted and pursued in respect to the controul
and management of the public revenue, I trust I
may be allowed to appeal to the flourishing condition which the Company's provinces enjoyed
during the period of my government, and which
has been, from the continued operation of the
same cause, in a course of progressive improve-
ment to the present hour.

I know

I know that your Lordships will, in your own en‑lightened and impartial wisdom, justly estimate the difficulties by which I was surrounded, during a long and arduous period of public service; that you will allow for all the embarrassments arising from the long counteraction of my associates in the government;—for errors resulting from the honest imperfection of my own judgment, from occasional deference to the counsels of *others*, and from the varying sense of expediency which at different periods governed my *own*.

Your Lordships well know, that the imperious exigencies of public affairs often present to the servants of the state no alternative but the painful choice of contending evils.

The transcendent and peremptory duty of my situation, was to devise and to procure the neces‑sary means of public safety. Feeling, as I did, the exigencies of the government as my own, and every pressure upon them resting with equal weight upon my mind;—besieged, as at some times I was, by the hourly and clamorous impor‑tunities of every department of the military ser‑vice; goaded at others with the cries of our then famished settlements on the coast of Coromandel —should I have deserved well, I do not say of my country, but of the common cause of suffering humanity, if I had punctiliously stood aloof from those means of supply, which gratitude or expecta‑
tion

tion enabled me to appropriate to the instant relief of such distresses?

The whole tenor and conduct of my public life
is now, my Lords, before you: it has undergone
a scrutiny of such extent and severity, as can find
no parallel in former times, and, I trust, will, in
many of the peculiar circumstances which have
characterized and distinguished this trial, leave no
example to the future.

My Lords, I have now performed the most solemn duty of my life, and with this I close my defence.

I may now, I trust, assuredly consider myself as
arrived at the threshold of my deliverance; at that
period, when no delay or procrastination can prevent the speedy and final termination of the proceedings now depending before your Lordships.

After such recent and acceptable proof on the
part of your Lordships, of your earnest disposition
to accelerate the conclusion of this trial, it would
betray an unwarranted and unbecoming distrust of
your justice, to offer any request to your Lordships on this subject, had I not other causes of
apprehension. At this momentous and awful crisis,
ignorant of what may be in the minds of others,
I am compelled to obviate every possible, even
though improbable, danger.

In the short address which I made to your Lordships on Friday last, I stated, that I should wave

the

the observations of my counsel on the evidence of the article then before the Court, and both the opening and application of the evidence on the next; and that I made these sacrifices, well aware of their importance, for the express purpose of affording ample time to my prosecutors, during what remained of the probable term of this session, to make their reply.

If the Managers for the Commons·had been equally desirous of accelerating the close of this trial, and I had a right to suppose that they were so, from their repeated declarations to that effect, what I had said might have been construed an offer of mutual accommodation; but, my Lords, it was received with resentment, and answered with reproach, and worse insinuation.   •

What other conclusion can I put upon this conduct, but that which is conveyed to my ears from every quarter; that they mean to endeavour to prevail on your Lordships to adjourn over this trial to its *seventh* year, that one more may be given them to prepare their replies. I do not know that this is their intention; but I may be allowed to suppose it; and though impressed with the firmest confidence of the just and favourable disposition of your Lordships, I cannot but dread the event of a question in which my rights may be at issue, with such opponents as the Managers of this prosecution, speaking in the name of the House of Com-

Commons, and of all the Commons of Great Britain.

To meet such an attempt, if made, I humbly offer to your Lordships the following arguments, most anxiously recommending them to your consideration.

In an address to a Court of British Peers, I cannot offend by pleading the rights which I possess as a British subject—rights, which are assured to me in common with all my fellow-subjects of this realm, by the pledges of ancient charters, and the sanction of an oath, the most solemn that can be tendered, or taken by man. My Lords, I claim the performance of that sacred promise, in all its implied obligations, that justice be administered to me, and that it be administered now.

In the long period of another year, I may be numbered with those of my Noble Judges whom I have, with sorrow, seen drop off year after year; and in aggravation of the loss which I have sustained by their deaths, I may thus lose the judgment of their survivors by my own.

To the *precepts* and *sanctions* of the law, I join the rights which are derived from the *practice* of it.

In the other courts of this kingdom their criminal process is limited in its duration, by express and positive regulations.

On this High Court, charged with other various

H R   and

and important duties, the wisdom of our ancestors has imposed no restraint, but the rule of honour; and to that honour I make this, my last, appeal; humbly praying, that if in the course of this hard, and long extended trial, I have conducted myself with the most patient and respectful submission, and borne all the aggravating circumstances of it with a tranquillity of mind, which nothing but a consciousness of integrity, and an equal reliance on your ultimate justice could have supported, I may obtain from your Lordships this only grace, that your Lordships will order the trial, now past its legal process, to continue to its final conclusion during the present session.

After Mr. Hastings had finished, both Mr. Fox and Mr. Burke remarked upon the very great freedom which he had taken with the Managers, and solemnly denied that they had the least wish for a further delay of this most enormously long trial: and that no part of the delay could fairly be attributed to them. Mr. Fox felt the charge so strongly, that he said he should appeal to *facts*, to shew that the Managers were not to blame; so that we may hope that it will not be deemed *libellous*, if a friend to the freedom of the press should meet Mr. Fox *openly* and *fairly* on this ground.

SEVENTH

SEVENTH YEAR, 1794.

ONE HUNDRED AND TWENTY-FIRST DAY*, February 18.

THE Court being assembled this day at half past twelve o'clock, Lord Kenyon sitting for the Lord Chancellor, as he was indisposed; after the customary formalities, Mr. Law rose, and said, that in the hope of bringing this tedious trial to a close in the last year, Mr. Hastings had very much shortened his defence, but he had been disappointed, and that the trial had been adjourned over to this year, even before the Managers had commenced their reply. Whatever reason he had had at the time to complain of the delay, it was in one respect highly fortunate to him, as it had enabled him to have the benefit of the evidence of the noble Marquis, who was so lately returned from Bengal, after acting with so much credit to himself, and so much advantage to the public in the situation which Mr. Hastings had so

---

* We begin this year with the 121st day, because that day is marked on the tickets. The Court was appointed for some days, when it did not meet, or if it did meet, when no business was done.

long

so long held.   But, as he understood his Lordship would not be able to attend in his place for
some days, he now laid in his claim to examine
him as soon as he had taken his seat in the
House.

Mr. Grey said, that without admitting what the
learned counsel had contended for, a right in the
defendant to examine the Marquis Cornwallis, he
was very ready to declare that the Managers
would give their assent to the examination of his
Lordship, and they would go further, however
favourable the noble Marquis's evidence might
be, he could only speak to the general character
which the defendant bore in India, and to the
general success of his measures, but there was
another gentleman, Mr. Larkins, who had for
many years been confidentially employed by Mr.
Hastings, and they had no objection to his being
called also.

Mr. Law rose again, and said that he disclaimed every idea of receiving as an indulgence the
evidence of Lord Cornwallis, that the Managers
not having commenced their reply, and it being
known that Mr. Hastings closed his defence last
year in the manner he had done, was with a hope
of bringing in that year this intolerably tedious
trial to a close, he claimed it as a right to examine
the noble Marquis, whose testimony he conceived
would

would be extremely impórtan ; but with his evidence Mr. Hastings would close his case.

Mr. Grey declined opening the reply until Lord Cornwallis had been examined, and the Court adjourned to Wednesday the 19th inftant, and afterwards to Tuesday the 25th.

———

ONE HUNDRED AND TWENTY-SECOND DAY, *February* 25.

The Court met this day at half past one, when the Lord Chancellor informed the Managers that Mr. Hastings, owing to the continued indisposition of the Marquis Cornwallis, had waved the privilege of calling his Lordship. The Managers would therefore proceed in their reply.

Mr. Grey immediately rose, and said, that as they had already consented to the calling of Lord Cornwallis, so they were willing still to allow Mr. Hastings the benefit of that examination, if his Lordship should be well enough to be examined before the Managers had completed their reply. Mr. Grey said they had also offered another evidence, Mr. Larkins, whom Mr. Hastings's counsel might call, if they pleased. That this

gentleman

gentleman was in India during the whole of Mr. Hastings's administration, whereas Lord Cornwallis could only speak as to the general effect of his measures, and his general character throughout the country.

Mr. Law, in reply to Mr. Grey, said, that he disclaimed every idea of receiving from the Managers any indulgence as to the intended examination of the Marquis Cornwallis. That as soon as his client had heard of the arrival of that noble person in England, he had expressed an anxious wish to have the benefit of his evidence on many most essential and important points. That with the hope of obtaining it, their Lordships had made two adjournments of the Court— a favor from their Lordships which Mr. Hastings would ever hold in grateful remembrance; but as, from the precarious state of Lord Cornwallis's health, it was uncertain at what period he would be enabled to attend in the Court, Mr. Hastings was reduced to the painful necessity of a protraction to an eighth year of a trial which was now in its seventh year, or of giving up the advantage which he was confident he would receive from the testimony of the noble Marquis. In this situation, the anxiety of Mr. Hastings to bring this long depending trial to a close, and his confidence that he had already laid ample testimony before their Lordships, as to the important advantages

vantages derived by the public from his successful exertions in India, and his evidence on every
material head of the accusation that had been
preferred against him by a for███ House of Commons, had induced him now to declare that his
evidence was closed: That he did so with pain,
he confessed; but he did not do it while a hope
remained that the state of Lord Cornwallis's
health would allow him to appear at any definite
period, so as to allow of time sufficient to close
the trial in this year.

Mr. Grey then proceeded to state that as Mr.
Law did not mean to accept their offer of calling
Mr. Larkins, the Managers would do it in the
course of their evidence in the reply. He then
read some documents, and proposed to call Mr.
Francis. That gentleman accordingly entered
the box, and Mr. Grey said, that as the council
had affirmed that Mr. Francis had approved of the
extra demand made upon Cheyt Sing, they would
shew that in conversation at the Council he had
mentioned his disapprobation of that measure.
The question was, therefore, put to Mr. Francis
whether any thing had passed in debate on the
subject on the 9th of July, 1778---and whether
he had approved of that measure?

To this question Mr. Law pointedly objected,
as leading in its consequences to another seven

years

years trial. That if the Managers were competent now to give evidence, which they might have
given seven years ago, the life of man would not
be of length enough for the close of this trial.
The law of evidence, he said, was so clear that
no doubt could remain on the subject.

Mr. Fox and Mr. Grey replied, and contended,
that as the council had laid a stress on Mr. Francis's consent to the demands that were made on
Cheyt Sing, they had a right to shew the nature
of the debate that took place when the demand
was made. Mr. Fox said, he lamented as much
any man could do the enormous length of this
trial, but he affirmed that the fault lay neither
with the House of Commons nor the Managers.

To this speech, Mr. Plumer made a full and
most able reply. He denied that, under any possible circumstances, the Managers could be entitled to examine Mr. Francis.

The evidence adduced was brought by the
Managers themselves.

Mr. Plumer went through the different years,
and referred to the pages in the evidence; by
which it appeared, that when the war broke
out Mr. Hastings proposed, on the 9th of July,
1778, to call on Cheyt Sing to contribute his
proportion to the expence of it. That Mr.
Francis agreed, though he expressed some doubts

as

as to the right. That Mr. Hastings was convinced of his having the right, inherent in every state, to call upon the subjects in cases of emergency to contribute to the defence of the state: but that if the right was not clear the Company would determine it. That in the next year, 1779. Mr. Francis agreed to the demand without any reservation. That in the next year, 1780, he also agreed; that he further agreed, to demand the assistance of a corps of cavalry from Cheyt Sing, for the service of the war. That Cheyt Sing having demurred to the payment of the subsidy in 1780, Mr. Hastings proposed to fine him for his disobedience.

To this Mr. Francis also agreed, though professing a hope that the threat would be sufficient. All these facts, said Mr. Plumer, were given by the Managers themselves in evidence, and surely the counsel had a right to avail themselves of them in argument; nor had they stopped there, they hoped they had stated what had a considerable effect on their Lordships and the public, and they saw where it pinched the Managers. Mr. Hastings was prosecuted for measures in which Mr. Francis had concurred, which neither the Directors nor the King's Ministers had disapproved, of which the public had received the benefit, and do still receive in the receipt of an additional revenue of two hundred thousand pounds a-year.

On

On all these grounds, Mr. Plumer denied that there was any thing like a reason to justify the demand of the Managers, and that if it were not resisted, the trial would be perpetual.

Mr. Grey again expressed his anxious wish for a very early end to so tedious a trial—that the public expected, and the Managers anxiously wished it. Some time was spent in framing the question, and just as it was about to be put

Mr. Burke rose, though he said there was no necessity for him to rise, his respectable fellow Manager having said all that was necessary, but as he had seen, by the arguments of this day, the use that had been made of the word acquiescence, he rose to declare that he did not acquiesce in any of the arguments used by Mr. Hastings's counsel, nor in any of the rules of law they had adduced: as to rules of law and evidence, he did not know what they meant: he and his friends had searched for them in vain; that the character that properly belonged to a Member of the House of Commons was that of a plain, ignorant layman; that it was true something had been written on the Law of Evidence, but very general, very abstract, and comprised in so small a compass, that a parrot that he had known might get them by rote in one half hour, and repeat them in five minutes. These rules, such as they were,

might

might serve for rules to the Courts below, but were not to shackle the House of Commons, nor that High Court, who in their great national prosecutions claimed a right to obtain by whatever means they could acquire it, an entirety of their evidence. Unlearned laymen, as they were, they could produce, in support of their right to examine Mr. Francis, precedents from trials by Impeachment.

Mr. Burke continued to speak for a considerable time to the same effect.

After some further discussion, the Lords adjourned, put the question to the Judges, and meet again on Thursday.

The most remarkable circumstance of the day was, the declaration of Mr. Fox, that the delay which he allowed to be most grievous, was not the fault of the House of Commons, nor of the Managers.

Of delay, no man accuses the present House of Commons—but that the delay in this article was occasioned by the last House of Commons, is a fact that cannot admit of a doubt; because it is well known that to this hour no man knows what the opinion of the last House was upon this very article. Mr. Grey has invariably argued, that the crime of Mr. Hastings was in demanding a subsidy from Cheyt Sing, which he had no right

to

to demand; and he deduces all the subsequent
acts from this original crime. Here Mr. Grey
speaks intelligibly at least---Mr. Pitt has invariably affirmed that Mr. Hastings had a right to
make that demand; that Cheyt Sing was criminal
in resisting it; that he deserved punishment;
but that Mr. Hastings's crime was in proposing to fine Cheyt Sing in the sum of
fifty lacks of rupees, a fine beyond the offence.
Now is there any one man in this kingdom
who will agree with Mr. Fox, that it was not a
fault in the last House of Commons, to send so
material an article to the House of Lords without
coming to a specific vote on the various allegations in it? The probability is, that if Mr. Pitt's
avowed opinion had ever been put into the form
of a question, he would have left the Managers
in a minority, and then the Benares article could
not have taken three days to try. The nation
would have saved the many thousand pounds that
the prosecution of this article has cost them, and
the trial might have been over long ago. The
facts we state are of universal notoriety, and as
often as they occur to honourable men, must
strike them with astonishment. They were fully
detailed by the counsel of Mr. Hastings, one of
whom said, with great propriety, that if Mr.
Hastings were guilty, the bar that inclosed him
should

should be taken down, and the space enlarged so as to take in the Court of Directors, the Board of Controul, the King's Ministers, and Parliament itself, which had taken all that Mr. Hastings had acquired, and had loudly boasted of the value of the acquisition. Whatever delay may now be occasioned by settling the principle on which evidence can be produced in reply, we trust it will have the effect when the rule is established, of bringing to a very speedy close, a trial, the end of which all parties seem anxiously to look for. The Managers complain of the delay —Mr. Hastings remonstrates—and the Treasury, alarmed at the enormity of the demands made upon it for the expences of this trial, has lately sent the Solicitor's bills to two Masters in Chancery, and one of the Clerks of the House of Commons to be examined. We may venture to say that one hundred thousand pounds will not defray all the expence that the nation has been put to by the trial. Surely, then, it is time to bring it to a close, even if no consideration were due to a man who has received the thanks of his constituents, with the complete approbation of the King's Minifters, for his long, faithful, and important services, and of whose merits there is hardly a dissenting opinion.

ONE

ONE HUNDRED AND TWENTY-THIRD
DAY, February 27,

The Court assembled this morning at half past one, when the Lord Chancellor informed the Managers that the question proposed to Mr. Francis could not be put. Upon this, Mr. Burke immediately rose, and made a very long and violent speech, in which he lamented that the Managers were ignorant of the principles on which so precipitate a determination was founded. That his respect to the Court forbad him to think what he otherwise would, namely, that to allow them to put the first question and to refuse the second, was a fraud and a cheat. That many calumnies had been spread abroad, accusing the Managers of being the cause of delay by their repeated attempts to introduce improper evidence, but that these and all other calumnies should be cleared up, and his character, and that of his fellow Managers should go down pure to posterity.

After continuing for some time, he was called to order by the Earl of Radnor, who begged the learned

learned Lord on the woolsack to stop so irregular a proceeding, and that the trial might be allowed to proceed. Mr. Burke replied, that any thing he could do with regularity he would not do irregularly. He then referred to the printed trials of the Earl of Stafford, in the reign of Charles the First—of Lord Viscount Stafford, in the reign of Charles the Second—and of the Earl of Macclesfield, in the reign of George the First.—He said, that in all these trials the Managers for the Commons contended that they had a right to ſtrengthen their case in reply, by supplemental proof, and that, in faĉt, no rules by which inferior Courts were bound ever had, or ever ought to bind the Lords and Commons, and in a trial by impeachment the Court had no guide, but its own diſcretion*. Mr. Burke then called Mr. Francis, and

---

* It is to the honour of the Lords, that they reprobate by their practice, this dangerous doĉtrine. " To leave it in the breast of the Judge (says Mr. Fearne) to relax, or supersede general reſtriĉtions and rules, whenever he shall think particular cases not within the reason of them, may, perhaps, by some be thought a more important absurdity, and a matter of greater mischief in its tendency and consequences, than that which is intended to be obviated by it ; for this is in faĉt, making the discretion of the Judge, the only law in such cases—an error, which our forefathers seem to have been illiberally studious to keep clear of For their creed seems to have been, what I have read, expressed in so much energy of terms, by a great Judge even of these times. The discretion of a Judge is the law

and asked him whether it was in his power, at any time during his refidence at Bengal, to put an end to the demand of subsidy made upon Cheyt Sing during war? To this question Mr. Law objeɛted, and with much feeling faid, he would not add to a delay which was intolerable, by offer'ng a single argument, to shew that consistent with law and justice, no such question could be put in this stage of the trial.

Mr. Fox, Mr. Burke, and Mr. Grey defended the propriety of this question, by repeating at very great length the arguments they had urged before, and Mr. Burke again affirming that no rules were to bind the House of Commons; but that under the title of supplemental proof, they had a right to ftrengthen their original case. He denied the soundness of the doɛtrine supported on the last day by the Counsel of Mr. Hastings, and added, that such a doɛtrine would be a complete cover slut. Much more was urged, and Earl Stanhope twice attempted to shorten the discussion, though in vain.

law of Tyrants; it is always unknown; it is different in different men; it is casual, and depends upon constitution, temper, and passion; in the best, it is oftentimes caprice; in the worst, it is every vice, folly, and passion, to which human nature is liable."

Vide Fearne on Contingent Remainders, p. 428 and 429, 3d edit. and Lord Camden's Argument in Doe v. Kersay, Eafter, 5 George III. 1675.

The

The Lord Chancellor applied to Mr. Law again, to know if he had any observations to make? who answered, that he had none; that this queſtion came completely within the rules already laid down by their Lordships, and that this day, like the last, had been uſelessly wasted; that he owed too much to his client, and to their Lordships, to offer a single argument in reply to all that had been asserted.

After this question was put, and when the Lords were about to adjourn to the Chamber of Parliament, Mr. Hastings rose, and said, he earnestly intreated their Lordships to address a few words to them; that he had put his thoughts on paper just as he was coming down to-day, and had made a small addition, in consequence of what he had heard on this day. Leave being very readily granted, Mr. Hastings addressed the Lords as follows:

" In the Petition which a noble Lord (Lord Hawkeſbury) had the goodness to present to your Lordships for me on Monday last, I informed your Lordships that I should forego the benefit which I had hoped to derive from the testimony of Marquis Cornwallis, whose ill state of health might probably diſable him from attending to deliver it, without the loss of so much time that might involve me in the peril of ſeeing my trial

ɟ ɟ adjourned

adjourned over to another year; and I prayed your
Lordships therefore to order that the trial should
proceed, and with that degree of acceleration
and dispatch which a due regard to the general
rights of justice, and the sufferings of an individual, now in the seventh year of his trial, might
induce your Lordships to adopt.

" The immediate cause of my troubling your
Lordships with that Address was a report conveyed to me, that your Lordships had been pleased,
in consideration of the noble Marquis's illness,
to adjourn the trial, which stood for Monday last,
to the following day, for the purpose of allowing
me to make my option in the mean time, and to
signify it to your Lordships, either that the proceedings in the trial should be stopped until the
noble Marquis's health should be sufficiently restored to enable him to attend in his place, or that
it should proceed without it.

" My Lords, if this information had been given
to me on grounds of certain authority, I should
not trouble your Lordships at this time, but rely
with implicit confidence on such a pledge as it
would be criminal to distrust; since it is impossible to admit, for an instant, the suppsition that
your Lordships would offer me an alternative
which included so great a sacrifice, with-

out

but the most absolute determination to fulfil the condition of it.

" But, my Lords, I neither know the terms on which that declaration of your Lordships was made, nor with certainty do I know that it was made at all; and when I see the time so very near in which it has been annually customary for your Lordships to adjourn the trial for many weeks, to allow for the absence of the Judges on their circuits, I cannot but feel the greatest alarm lest the same obstruction should be given to the trial even in this period of it, when the evidence on the part of the prosecution, and that of the defence, have been finally and declaredly closed, and almost a whole year elapsed, since the close of the latter.

" My Lords, I beg leave to remind you of the great sacrifices which I have made to cut off all possible cause of delay ; that I put my defence on two charges almost wholly to issue on the evidence adduced by my prosecutors, and I gave up the pleadings of my able advocates on both. This year, it is known to your Lordships with what earnestness and anxiety my Counsel solicited your Lordship's permission to call upon the House of Commons for his evidence, and that I have departed from the whole tenor of my conduct, by being myself the mover of delay to obtain it. Of

these

these delays, and these only, I am the cause, and I thank your Lordships for admitting them. My appeal to the noble Marquis was not made on slight grounds. When I first notified to him my intention of calling for his evidence, I had never had any communication with him respecting the subject. But I knew what was the truth, and I was confident he would declare it. I knew his heart and mind—I knew myself, and I therefore knew with the most absolute certainty what his testimony would be.

Yet I have made this great sacrifice added to the past—And surely, my Lords, I am not unreasonable in exacting this only requital, that my trial may suffer no further delay.

" I do therefore most earnestly supplicate your Lordships to grant me the indulgence of a continuation of your proceedings in this Court, without any adjournment for the Circuits, or any other delays than such as the business of Parliament may render unavoidable, and that you will have the goodness to afford me such an assurance of it, as shall immediately quiet my mind from its present apprehensions.

" My Lords, do not think this request presumptous, nor that it proceeds from an impertinent curiosity.

" My

" My Lords, it has more urgent motives, and pardon me if I once more repeat, as my plea for making it, that I am now in the seventh year of my prosecution in this Court, which has never before suffered any trial, even of the most criminal nature, except in the times of originating disorder and rebellion, to exceed the period of twenty-two days. That as I have been already subjected to a prosecution which has now endured six years, I may not (if I may trust to my understanding of all that I have heard this day) be the continued subject of it, during six years more."

As soon as Mr. Hastings sat down Mr. Burke rose, and said, that Mr. Hastings had merely repeated what he had said five years before; that the delay was not imputable to the Managers, but to the Counsel of Mr. Hastings, who had objected to evidence, and that in this instance Mr. Hastings allowed himself to be the author of the delay. It was very true that the Prisoner had been six years before the Court, but he had no right to complain on that account—had they not been employed in considering his Crimes? Crimes that he had been committing for fourteen years?

Mr. Burke proceeded for some time longer in a similar strain, when Mr. Hastings rose, and with a look in which indignation and contempt were strongly mixed, he said, " True, it is, my

Lords,

Lords, as the Manager has said, that I did complain five years ago, when my trial was on the point of being adjourned, as it had then lasted longer than any other trial in this Court. I repeated my complaint in every succeeding year, because every year was an aggravation of the hardship which I suffered. I complained of it, my Lords, as an abuse of justice, and I repeat, my Lords, that it was an abuse of justice, come from whom it may; but is it, my Lords, any argument, that, because I have suffered a prosecution of six years, I should endure it six years longer?"

To this speech, Mr. Fox replied, that he most anxiously joined with Mr. Hastings, in entreating the Lords to proceed with all possible expedition to the close of the trial.

The Court adjourned, and meet again on Saturday.

ONE HUNDRED AND TWENTY-FOURTH DAY. *March* 1.

FOURTH DAY OF THIS YEAR.

THE Court met this morning ten minutes before two. The delay was occasioned, as we were informed,

informed, by the time taken up by the Lord
Chief Justice of the Common Pleas, in deliver-
ing the unanimous opinion of the Judges, on the
last question referred to them, and by a most
excellent and constitutional speech of the Lord
Chancellor, who laid down with the utmost clearness and perspicuity the Law of Evidence, in
reply, in criminal cases. His Lordship went at
large into the several precedents quoted by Mr.
Burke, and by reference to these cases, proved
that they did not in any manner sustain the arguments offered by the manager. On the contrary,
that in each instance the managers on those trials,
had merely claimed what the Law allowed, a right
to support their own witnesses, whose credibility
had been impeached, and the right to reply to new
matter offered by the several noble prisoners,
whose cases were quoted. His Lordship concluded by moving, that the managers be informed, that it was not competent to them to put the
proposed question to Mr. Francis. On their
Lordships assembling in Westminster Hall, the
Chancellor declared this opinion.—Mr. Burke
said, that though the Commons submitted, they
did not acquiesce in the determination of their
Lordships.

Mr. Grey seemed to be desirous of adhering
very fairly to the rule laid down. He said, that

he

he offered with some doubt a piece of evidence, which he thought material. The managers had, by mistake, given in a triplicate of a letter, instead of the original; that to this triplicate the names of Mr. Hastings, Mr. Francis, and Mr. Wheeler were signed; that as the two latter formed a majority, the Counsel had argued that they had it in their power to revoke the demand of subsidy, had they thought it an improper one; but in truth and fact, the name of Mr. Barwell was signed to the original letter; of course, if the fact were cleared up, the argument of the Counsel would fall to the ground.

The Chancellor said, that this evidence was clearly inadmissible, and against the rules laid down by the Court; first, as tending to support their own evidence, and next, as it was not to rebut evidence, but argument. Mr. Law, however, removed the difficulty, by saying he had not the least objection to the managers correcting their own mistake.

This important point of evidence being settled, Mr. Grey said, that he would next propose to insert a Report of Mr. Duncan, the Resident at Benares, in 1788. The Counsel had cross-examined one of the manager's witnesses, who stated that the four hundred thousand pounds a-year, the rent settled by Mr. Hastings, had been fully paid,

paid, and that the country continued in a very flourishing state, well cultivated, and well peopled, during the whole of Mr. Hastings's administration, and for two years after—Mr. Markham had given similar evidence. The Counsel had also entered a Letter from Mr. Duncan, dated in 1790, who stated that the country was then very flourishing, and paid the full rent which Mr. Hastings had settled. The managers, therefore, proposed to read another letter from Mr. Duncan, dated in 1788, by which it would appear, that at that time parts of the country had fallen into decay, and were recovered by the exertions of Mr. Duncan. This evidence was admitted, and Mr. Burke chose to read detached extracts from it, with a view of shewing, that Mr. Duncan had been told, that certain parts of the Province of Benares had been badly cultivated since the expulsion of Cheyt Sing; and that above one lack of Rupees of additional Revenue had been imposed upon the Province by the present Rajah.

To save time, Mr. Law was content that this report, which is of great length, should be entered as read; but to this, Mr. Burke objected, saying, that he wished to select certain passages, because if they were then read, their Lordships must hear them; whereas if they were only entered on the minutes, they never might read them at

2   all.

all. A sentiment more extraordinary, undoubtedly, than is to be found, even in all the works of Thomas Paine. Mr. Burke has been the professed champion of the Aristocracy of Great-Britain; but in this single sentence he has said more to degrade it, in the opinion of the world, than any democratic writer could possibly do. 'We are confident, however, that every tittle of the evidence will be carefully read, and maturely weighed by every noble Lord, who commits his conscience and his honour to the issue, in this important cause.

Mr. Grey next proposed to read a letter from Mr. Hastings to Lord Macartney, dated in July, 1781.—It was not very easy to comprehend the drift of Mr. Grey in producing this evidence.— He said that it was to shew that there were other modes by which the distresses of the Carnatic might be relieved in 1781, better than by extorting money from Cheyt Sing. The extract proved, that in the opinion of Mr. Hastings, the Madras Government had acted wrong in not compelling the Rajah of Tangore to contribute largely to the support of the War in which the Sovereign State was engaged, and he advised Lord Macartney to furnish military stores and provisions, in future, to the utmost extent that the country could afford. Mr. Grey next wanted to prove,

that

that the Directors disapproved this advice. The latter evidence was rejected.

The last piece of evidence was so singular in its nature, and gave rise to so very animated a discussion, that we shall open it a little more at large than Mr. Grey did.

The account of Cheyt Sing's expulsion arrived in England in the early days of the Rockingham administration. It is well known that that ministry were anxious to seize any pretence to recal Mr. Hastings from Bengal—a select committee, of which Mr. Burke was the real leader, made a special report to the House of Commons on that revolution. Cheyt Sing was elevated to the rank of a Prince, and his expulsion was one of the grounds stated for the recal of Mr. Hastings in Parliament. Mr. Gregory and Sir Henry Fletcher were at that time the Chairman and Deputy and were afterwards nominated Commissioners under Mr. Fox's India Bill. Though these consistent gentlemen had known that Mr. Hastings, for three successive years had ordered Cheyt Sing to contribute 50,000l. a-year to the support of the War, and had never once disapproved of the subsidy, yet when the Rockingham administration took up the matter in Parliament, they passed a variety of Resolutions, condemning the conduct of Mr. Hastings. These Resolutions

were

were violently opposed by many of the Directors, and ultimately carried by very small majorities. The Resolutions arrived at Bengal in February 1783, and appeared to Mr. Hastings to be so dangerous in their tendency, that he wrote on the 23d of March 1783, a very strong, and possibly, in some points, an intemperate remonstrance from a public servant to his Masters. It may be said in excuse for Mr. Hastings, that he supposed, as any man would do who had then read the Resolutions, that it was intended to follow them by an order for restoring Cheyt Sing.

This letter arrived in England in the month of September 1783, when Mr. Fox and Mr. Burke were in office with the Coalition Ministry.

Sir Henry Fletcher, and the Deputy, ordered a gentleman in the India House to prepare observations upon this letter, which being approved by a majority of the Court of Directors, were published for the use of the Proprietors, in order to justify the Court from the supposed imputations thrown upon them by their servant Mr. Hastings. These Observations were published on the day, or near it, that Mr. Fox moved for leave to bring in his India Bill, and were highly extolled by Mr. Burke in the speech that he made in support of that Bill.

Mr.

Mr. Grey to the utter astonishment of every man who is at all conversant with the subject, offered these Observations as evidence on the following ground;—He said, that when Mr. Hastings arrived in England, in 1785, the Directors had returned him their thanks for his long, faithful, and able services. That these thanks were in evidence, and therefore the managers wished to enter the Observations, in order to prove, that however the Directors might generally approve the conduct of Mr. Hastings, they disapproved of it in this instance.

The Counsel declared that the evidence was utterly inadmissible. They opposed the introduction of it, because it was a mere Party Pamphlet, published for Party Principles, when the great body of the Proprietors were active in support of Mr. Hastings; and the gentleman who produced it, was acting in concert with those who wished to annihilate the East India Company. That it was neither more nor less than a defamatory libel, for which those who published it might have been liable to prosecution.

Mr. Burke took fire at this expression: talked wildly of prostituted Criminals, and prostituted audacity; with many other very intemperate expressions, which excited a general murmur of disapprobation in the Court.

While

While Mr. Burke was yet on his legs,

The Marquis Townshend spoke to order. He said, that such expressions were highly improper; and such language was not to be endured. It remained yet to be proved whether Mr. Hastings was a criminal or not; that to apply such an epithet to a gentleman under trial was contrary to the principle and the practice of the Law of England, which presumed every man to be innocent until he was legally pronounced to be guilty.

Mr. Burke rose again, and said, that he did not know the noble Lord who had called him to order. He then persisted in affirming, that the managers had a right to enter the observations, as containing the sentiments of the Court of Directors.

Mr. Hastings rose, and begged to inform their Lordships, that the observations which the managers wished to introduce had never been transmitted to him; that they appeared to be written not for the purpose of condemning him, but of justifying the Directors; that he could venture to assure their Lordships it was the first and only instance of an appeal made by the Directors to the public, relative to their conduct to one of their own servants. Such observations as these he was confident their Lordships would not admit in their minutes. He begged to remind their

3   Lordships,

Lordships, that he had been thirteen years at the head of the Government of Bengal. In so long a period many of his acts had been disapproved, as undoubtedly they must be; but no argument could fairly be urged against him, on account of these partial censures, since, on his return to England, when he conceived that he had entirely closed his public life, he had received the unanimous thanks of the Court of Directors, which certainly obliterated all partial censures.

Mr. Burke rose as soon as Mr. Hastings had concluded, and, in a speech replete with violence and invective, contended, that those observations were proper to be received, because they were an answer to a letter which the prisoner had dared to write to the Directors his masters, and to print and publish in Calcutta.

Mr. Hastings, with spirit and dignity, instantly rose, and said, " My Lords, I affirm that the assertion which your Lordships have just heard from the manager is false—I never did print or publish any letter in Calcutta that I wrote to the Court of Directors. I knew my duty better. This assertion is a libel; it is of a piece with every thing that I have heard uttered since the commencement of this trial, by that authorised, licensed—(and after a long pause, he added, turn-

ing

ing to Mr. Burke with infinite contempt in his countenance)—" manager!"

Mr. Burke continued to affirm, that Mr. Hastings had printed and published the letter in Calcutta. Mr. Hastings loudly called out him, it was not true—and the Counsel said to Mr. Burke, No! No!

When this altercation was over, Mr. Fox contended, that the observations were evidence in the view they offered them, and as to the allusion which the learned Counsel had made to the Bill, which he brought in many years ago, which the Commons passed, and the Lords threw out, he earnestly wished Mr. Law would diftinguish by the name of *his Bill* as often as he spoke of it. As to the secret History of " The Observations" he had nothing to do with it. What he wanted to enter was, an Act of the Court of Directors, by which it appeared they disapproved of the conduct of Mr. Hastings at Benares.

The managers persisting in their right to put the question, the Lords rose, Mr. Hastings having previously entreated them to proceed until his trial was closed, as the delay was more than he could bear. Mr. Fox expressed his readiness to go on, and Mr. Burke said, that Mr. Hastings had so often complained of delay, that it was absolutely necessary for the Commons to prove

to

to the world that they were not the authors of the delay. That in the year 1789 Mr. Haftings had made fimilar complaints; that they meant to examine the matter of his Petition* delivered at that time, and to falsify every assertion in it.

The

" * That your Petitioner was permitted by the Honourable
" Houfe of Commons to appear before their bar, on the 24th of
" April, 1786, to anfwer to certain charges which had been pre-
" ferred againft him in that Honourable Houfe. That your Peti-
" tioner, on the 14th of May, 1787, was impeached by the Ho-
" nourable Houfe of Commons of Great Britain, at the bar of your
" Lordfhips' Houfe, of High Crimes and Mifdemeanors—That
" your Lordfhips were pleafed to grant your Petitioner a Copy of
" the Articles of Impeachment, with leave to anfwer the fame.—
" That on the 25th of November, 1787, in the following Seffion
" of Parliament, your Petitioner, according to your Lordfhip's
" order, did deliver in his anfwer to the faid Articles, and the 13th
" of February, 1788, was appointed for the commencement of
" his trial, and it was accordingly commenced and continued by
" various adjournments, to the 15th of June of the fame year.
" That your Petitioner conceived an abundant confolation, when
" he faw himfelf brought before a Court, which was held in
" eftimation the moft juft, as it was the moft refpectable, from the
" high titles and dignities, and the noble characters of the Mem-
" bers compofing it: and impreffed at this time in an equal degree
" with the fame fentiments, and affuring himfelf, that your Lord-
" fhips will favourably receive any reprefentation which he may
" conceive himfelf under the neceffity of making to your Lordfhips,
" of the hardfhips which he has fuftained and may yet have caufe
" to apprehend, from the peculiar circumftances of the prefent trial,
" he humbly prefumes, in this ftage of it, to ftate the fame to your
" Lordfhips, and to pray for fuch redrefs and relief in the future
" procefs of it, as your Lordfhips' wifdom may be able to devife,
" and your juftice prefcribe.

K K   " An l

The Lords retired, and it was determined that
it was not competent to the Managers to read the
observations.   But it being then near five, and
the

" And your Petitioner humbly begs leave to obferve, that one
" year has elapfed fince the commencement of h's trial; and, in
" that interval, feven noble Lords, his Judges, have yielded to the
" courfe of nature; fome of the perfons, whofe evidence was re-
" quired for his defence, have returned to their duty in India, and
" many of thofe who remain are detained, to the injury of their
" fortunes and profpects, and to fome lofs of the fervice to which
" they belong.   That your Petitioner profeffes no means of indem-
" nifying them for their detention, nor does he prefume to eftimate
" his own right at fo high a price, as to exact from any man that
" he fhould devote the prime feafon of his l'fe to inaction.   That
" of fuch of the witneffes whofe conveniences may permit it,
" or whofe inclination may prompt them to remain, many muft, by
" death, or the variable accidents of life, be taken from him be-
" fore the time of his defence.   That his health, which a long re-
" fidente in an ungenial climate had impaired, has been precluded
" from receiving the only remedy which a foreign air could afford
" for its reftoration, and the only palliative which a ftate of eafe
" could afford it at home; his fortune wafted in the expences una-
" voidably incident to fo heavy a profecution, and his perfon thruft
" out from its place in common fociety; with other fufferings which,
" though moft fenfibly felt by him, may not be fpecified in an ad-
" drefs to your Lordfhips.
" And your Petitioner begs leave humbly to obferve to your
" Lordfhips, that although the profecution has yet been clofed upon
" two articles only of his impeachment, twenty articles were pre-
" ferred againft him by the Honourable Houfe of Commons, *that*
" *thefe comprifed in effect all the material tranfactions, civil,*
" *political, military, revenue, and financial of a Government*
" *of thirteen years;* that a confiderable portion of his time was a
" period of *great difficulty, danger and embarraffment, to every*
                              " *dependency*

the Lords conceiving it to be absolutely impossible to go on without the Judges, adjourned the Court to Monday, the 7th of April.

It

" *dependency of the British Empire, and more particularly to the*
" *extensive territories which were under the actual government*
" *of your petitioner, or which depends upon his exertions for*
" *subsistence and relief*; that your petitioner was therefore under
" the necessity, through his Counsel and Solicitors, of collecting
" and collating, from the voluminous records of the East India
" Company, *the whole history of his public life*, in order to form
" a complete defence to every allegation which the Honourable
" House of Commons has preferred against him ; for your Petitioner
" had no·, when your Lordships were pleased to grant him a copy
" of the articles, *neither has he now*, any means of knowing
" whether *any*, or what articles; *if any*, were meant to be *aban-*
" *doned* by the Honourable House of Commons. That it was not
" possible for your Petitioner to be prepared with the necessary ma-
" terials for such a defence, without incurring a very heavy and
" intolerable expence, the sums which have been actually paid,
" *and for which your Petitioner stands indebted*, amounting, ac-
" cording to the most accurate estimate which he could procure from
" the best authority, *to upwards of thirty thousand pounds*. That
" this is a subject of great and serious alarm to your Petitioner,
" who, in the indefinite prospect before him, sees himself, in dan-
" ger of wanting the means of defence, and even of subsistence,
" should his life, which is not yet probable, be continued to the
" close of a trial, *in which so small a progress has yet been made*,
" unless your Lordships' wisdom shall enable you to afford your
" Petitioner that relief which he humbly solicits, and confidently
" hopes to receive : that your Petitioner, with all sincerity of heart,
" craves leave to assure your Lordships that he does not presume to
" state his sense of the hardships to which he has been, and is sub-
" jected by the past events of the trial, as matters of complaint,
" being fully persuaded that they were unavoidably incident to the

K K 2　　　　　　　 " peculiar

It is with much pleasure we hear Mr. Burke pledge himself to examine fully into the charge of delay, which Mr. Hastings so often makes, and makes with so much juſtice : we trust that he will allow the discussion to be fully gone into.——He will be pleased to recollect, that he arraigned Mr. Hastings in the name of all the people of Great Britain, as far back as the month of May, 1787.—That, independent of four eminent Lawyers, Sir Gilbert Elliot, Mr. Anstruther, Mr. Adam, and Mr. Michael Angelo Taylor, he moved for two Solicitors, and he employed originally ſix Counsel, viz. Sir William Scott, Dr. Lawrence, Mr. Pigot, Mr. Mansfield, Mr. Douglas, and his own brother, Mr. Richard Burke.

" peculiar nature of ſuch a trial, *and to the peculiar character and*
" *circumſtances of the charge which was the ſubject of it.* That
" he has ſtated them with no other motive or view than to obtain
" from your Lordſhips a deliverance from the dreadful chance of his
" character being tranſmitted on the records of your Lordſhips high
" and auguſt Court, blaſted *with unrefuted criminations*, and an
" acceleration of the time in which he may be enabled to make
" his *innocence*, his *integrity*, and (may he be permitted in all hu-
" mility to add) *his deſerts* apparent to your Lordſhips.

   " Your Petitioner therefore moſt humbly prays, that your
    " Lordſhips will be pleaſed to order that the trial may pro-
    " ceed, according to your Lordſhips order upon the laſt ad-
    " journment, and that it may be continued to its cloſe, (if
    " it be poſſible) without interruption.

3*d. Feb.*   " WARREN HASTINGS."
1789.

                           Mr.

Mr. Mansfield, we believe, returned his retaining fee; Sir Wm. Scott retired after the firſt year; Mr. Douglas continued until he got a much better thing in Ireland, a few weeks ago; and Mr. Richard Burke, to the time of his decease: Mr. Pigot and Dr. Lawrence are still employed, and are each day drawn up in the rear of the managers.—Does Mr. Burke suppose the public has forgot the enormous amount of his Solicitor's Bill? Does he suppose that his saying that the Commons are unlearned Laymen will ſatisfy the world that there is to be no end to queſtions on evidence, which to common conceptions admit of no doubt?---Mr. Pigot is a man of eminence in his profession. Has he advised the managers to offer the evidence they have lately offered; or have the managers aɛted without advice?---When Mr. Pitt demurred at paying the first three thousand pounds for Counsel, he doubted whether they were really necessary. Every time he looks at the account now, what must he think of it?--- These and many, very many other points must be agitated when the subjeɛt comes forward.--- Mr. Burke complains of being calumniated. How, or by whom has he been calumniated?--- Does he suppose that people will not talk of so extraordinary a case as this, where a man, acknowledged by every man living, except those in

the

the Managers Box, to have performed great and important services, is kept for seven years on his trial---the Public enjoying, and the Minister loudly boasting of the value of the fruits of his supposed crimes?---The subject is indeed important, and will, we hope, be taken up with the attention that so important a subject deserves.

ONE HUNDRED AND TWENTY-FIFTH DAY. *April* 7.

THE Court met this day, after the adjournment for the Circuits, at two o'clock, when the Lord Chancellor informed the Managers, that the evidence which they had proposed to give on the last day, was inadmissible.

Upon this, Mr. Burke rose, and said, that tho' they might offer other reasons in addition to those which they had before offered, to induce their Lordships to consent to the admission of it, yet they would acquiesce in the decision; and he declared, that all the evidence in reply upon the Benares Article was closed.

As Mr. Sheridan was rising to speak, Mr. Plumer begged to be heard for a very few moments. He said, that when their Lordships adjourned last, the state of the health of the Noble

Marquis

Marquis Cornwallis, was such as to render it extremely doubtful at what period he would be enabled to give his attendance in Westminster Hall; that Mr. Hastings, from the anxiety he had invariably displayed to bring this intolerably tedious trial to a close, had informed their Lordships that he should forego the testimony of the Noble Marquis; but the adjournment of their Lordships was attended with this good effect: Lord Cornwallis, he was happy to say, was now restored to health, and as the Managers had expressed their concurrence to the Noble Marquis's examination at any period prior to the close of their own evidence, he hoped the Court would permit Mr. Hastings to call Lord Cornwallis on the first day that their Lordships should sit.

Mr. Sheridan said, that the Managers had expressed their willingness to give Mr. Hastings the benefit of Lord Cornwallis's testimony, and therefore they should make no objections. He then repeated what had before been said as to Mr. Larkins, whom they would also allow Mr. Hastings to call, if he chose.

Mr. Plumer said, he did not intend to call any further evidence than Lord Cornwallis, and if the Managers introduced further evidence, they would of course state the grounds on which they were entitled to call it, in reply.

After

After this point was settled, Mr. Sheridan commenced his evidence in reply, upon the Begum
Article. A conversation, rather than an argument, was continued between Mr. Sheridan and
Mr. Burke, on the one side, and Mr. Dallas and
Mr. Plumer, on the other, for two hours, relative
to the evidence which Mr. Sheridan produced,
and which in all instances was admitted. We do
not enter into any detail of this evidence, becaufe
not a line of it applied to the points on which the
charge rests, but was, as it was stated by Mr.
Sheridan, merely intended to fill up chasms which
were left in the evidence, by the Counsel having
followed the mode recommended him by Mr. Sheridan himfelf, namely, that each party fhould enter
such parts of letters and documents as each relied
on, to make good their case. They were all of
no consequence ; some related to events which
happened so far back as the years 1775 and
1776.

At half after four, Mr. Sheridan said that he
had completed all the evidence which he meant
to offer in reply on the Second Article. It was
then agreed that the Marquis Cornwallis should
be examined on Wednesday ; Mr. Burke adding,
that he did expe& Mr. Hastings would have proposed to examine Mr. Larkins, but that the Managers certainly would do it.

The

The Court after this conversation adjourned until Wednesday (to-morrow.)

We think we can now venture to congratulate the country, the Lords, and Mr. Hastings, on the approaching end of this Trial. The Managers have closed their evidence in reply to two Articles. Two only remain---the Presents and the Contracts. From our knowledge of the case, we do not see how the evidence in reply on these Articles can take up more than one day. All then that remains is the speeches of the Managers in summing up ; and when it is considered that the Managers spoke twenty-two days in the prosecution, and that the Reply is confined to certain points, we anxiously look forward to a speedy close of this unprecedented Trial--a Trial that has now lasted Seven Years, and which has cost the Nation more money than would pay for ever the Pensions settled on the posterity of Lord Chatham and Lord Rodney, for important public services.

ONE HUNDRED AND TWENTY-SIXTH DAY. *April* 9.

The impatience of all the world to hear the testimony of the Marquis Cornwallis, was such, that the

the Court was completely filled by twelve o'clock, and when the Lords met at two, the House of Commons appeared in numbers equal to those who attended in the brilliant days of the year 1788.

It is necessary to remind our readers, that the Impeachment which was voted seven years ago, was grounded upon strong declarations made by Mr. Burke, that under Mr. Hastings the most flourishing countries had became desolate ; that he was a man *hated* and *detested* through all India ; that he was a Captain General of Iniquity, at whose departure, the country felt relieved from a weight under which it had long groaned, with a variety of expressions of a similar nature. After having given evidences as to the *flourishing* and *improved* state of the resources of Bengal, during the administration of Mr. Hastings, and of the general esteem and regard in which he was held by the natives, it was earnestly wished that to the opinion of Sir John Shore, the *present Governor General of Bengal*, the opinion of the Marquis Cornwallis, who had so honourably filled that important office for many years, might be added.

The Noble Marquis was this day examined, and having stated the time of his departure from England, his knowledge of the accusation which was then preferred by Mr. Burke, and the date of his arrival in Bengal, the following questions in substance

stance were put to the Marquis, to which he gave the following answers :

Q. Whether it was known in India when **Lord** Cornwallis arrived there, and during the six years his Lordship governed Bengal, that he was then under accusation and trial ?

A. It was certainly very well known and generally.

Q. Whether it was not competent to any natives of India to prefer complaints to his Lordship and to the Council againſt Mr. Hastings?

A. Certainly, they might at any time.

Q. Whether in faɛt any one such complaint was made ?

A. None—No perſonal complaint against Mr. Hastings.

Q. In what estimation was the charaɛter of Mr. Hastings amongst the natives of India.

A. He believed Mr. Hastings was much esteemed and respeɛted by the inhabitants in general.

His Lordship then, in answer to more questions put to him, said, that he believed it was the custom of the Mogul Government to call upon their Zemindars to furnish military assistance in war; that the disaffeɛtion of the Begum's at the time of the rebellion of Cheyt Sing, was a faɛt of general report; that no steps had been taken, either for the restoration of Cheyt Sing, or to restore to the

Begum

Begum the money that was taken from her in 1782 ; that he does not believe, nor did he ever hear, that the Begum was at any time reduced to a state of pecuniary distress, in confequence of taking fifty lacks of rupees from her in 1782 ; that his Lordship never heard in India, nor did he believe, that the British name and character suffered in any degree by the expulsion of Cheyt Sing, or by the measure taken against the Begum. That he hoped, and believed, the inhabitants under the British Government were much happier, and their property better protected, than under any of the Native Governmnts.

There was a general and a marked Buz of pleasure and satisfaction expressed by the auditors, when the Marquis Cornwallis stated, that Mr. Hastings was much esteemed and respected by the natives of India.

Mr. Burke began the cross-examination by asking Lord Cornwallis, if he had read the Articles of Impeachment. His Lordship said, he had ; but after the lapse of so many years, he could not recollect the particular points in it.—That as he looked forward, he never made it his business to enquire as to the truth of the reports concerning the Begum's taking an active part against us during the revolt of Cheyt Sing—that he had never called on any Zemindars for military aid—though

1   he

he was not sure whether the Madras Government had not called on the Zemindars of the Northern Circars, and the Polygars.

Mr. Burke asked his Lordship whether it was from the natives or from Englifh Gentlemen, that he had heard that Mr. Hastings was much esteemed and respeĉted?

Lord Cornwallis replied, that as he did not speak the language, it certainly was delivered to him by English Gentlemen, in his conversation with different inhabitants of India.

Mr. Burke then read passages from letters and minutes of Lord Cornwallis, in which he faid, that mischievous consequences had resulted from the mode of letting the lands annually, and that the Zemindars were in general in a state of poverty, which, though partly owing to their own indolence and extravagance, was in a great degree to be attributed to the system of making the settlements annual.

Lord Cornwallis said he recolleĉted these letters, but, upon a question from Mr. Plumer, said, that he carried out the first orders which enabled the Government of Bengal to make a settlement for ten years, and ultimately to render that settlement perpetual.

Mr. Burke asked his Lordfhip whether he had heard of various sums of money said to have been received by Mr. Hastings?

Lord

Lord Cornwallis said he had—that he knew nothing of it, nor of a balance stated to remain in the hands of Gunga Gavend Sing.

Mr. Burke then asked his Lordship if Mr. Duncan was a gentleman of character?

Lord Cornwallis spoke very highly of him, and in the strongest terms of Sir John Shore, whom Mr. Burke had formerly described as the accomplice in the crimes of Mr. Hastings.

Two very strong concluding questions were put by Lord Hawke, whether the confederacy framed by the Native Powers in India, and assisted by the French in the last general war, did not require the utmost exertions on the part of Mr. Hastings to counteract it?

His Lordship answered, it certainly did.

Lord Cornwallis was asked, whether, by successfully counteracting those designs, and preserving the British empire entire, Mr. Hastings had not rendered essential services to his Country?

His Lordship replied, undoubtedly he had.

Here this important examination was closed, which we think we may venture to say, has put the seal upon the character of Mr. Hastings, since it fritters to atoms when combined with the former testimony, the very foundation on which the original accusation rested ; for how has Mr. Hastings been described? As a man hated, detested, and abhorred,

abhorred, except by the creatures whose fortunes he had made.

We had forgot one very singular circumstance: Lord Cornwallis had appointed Capt. Kirkpatrick to be Ambassador at the Court of Madagee, India, in 1787.—This Gentleman had written a letter to the Marquis, in Council, in which he stated that the Mahrattas, had so little confidence in our former moderation, that even our then conduct would not have the effect of perfuading them, that we might not, in future, wish to extend our dominion.

Lord Cornwallis was asked as to this point. He faid, that might be Capt. Kirkpatrick's opinion—and on being pressed by Mr. Grey, he said, he did not know how he could give any other anfwer. This opinion of *Mr. Kirkpatrick* was given in evidence seven years ago, to prove the *opinion of the Princes of India,* as to the moderation and good faith of the British Government.

Mr. Burke, on Lord Cornwallis stating so strongly the services of Mr. Hastings, in counteracting the designs of our enemies in the last general war, asked Lord Cornwallis, whether he was acquainted with the caufe of the late Mahratta war? The Chancellor faid that the question could not with propriety be put. Mr. Burke said it might, at least by any Lord, and Lord Stanhope said, that

3   he

he would put it, to prevent further argument.—
Lord Cornwallis answered, that their Lordships
all knew just as much of the matter as he did.

After this a long argument took place on the
propriety of calling Mr. Larkins. The Counsel
insisting upon it, that no period of time in the life
of man could close the Trial, if the law of the
land was not attended to.

Mr. Burke, though Lord Cornwallis had just sat
down, said, that Mr. Hastings had never shewn
compassion to man, woman, or infant!!! otherwise
he should pity the situation in which he stood, rejecting evidence that he never expressed a wish to
have.

Mr. Plumer and Mr. Dallas were clear, decisive, and firm. They left the matter entirely to
the Lords, to be determined as they chose.

The Court was adjourned to Monday, and the
question referred to the Judges—Whether Mr.
Larkins should be examined in the present stage
of the Trial?

Lord Cornwallis had said, in reply to a question
from Mr. Plumer, that he hoped and believed the
natives under the British Government were much
happier and their property better protected
than under the Princes of the country. Sir John
Shore, the present Governor General of Bengal,
had

had given exactly the same evidence in 1790, with this addition, which his residence in Bengal throughout the whole of the administration of Mr. Hastings enabled him to do, namely, culture, population, and commerce, in Bengal, under the British Administration, and that property was more secure, and the people happier, under our government, than under the Government of their own Sovereigns. " This," said Sir John Shore, " I speak with all the confidence conviction infpires." Mr. Burke's invariable assertion has been, that Bengal was eminently flourishing under its native Sovereigns, but that it had fallen to decay under the British Government.

In his cross-examination, therefore, he read extracts from minutes and letters of the Marquis Cornwallis, in which his Lordfhip, in the ftrongest terms, recommended the adoption of that fyftem which has now taken place, namely, letting the lands for ever, at a rent that is not to be altered, and he describes, in very strong terms, the mischievous consequences which had resulted from the system of letting the lands annually. The mischievous confequences of that system were alfo pointed out by Mr. Hastings, in the year 1780. In one letter, Lord Cornwallis affirmed, that one consequence of that system was, that a third of the lands were waste. Sir John Shore in reply to

this

this minute, very strenuously contended, that the
country had considerably improved under our
Government, and that during the period of it,
much waste land had been brought into culti-
vation.

Mr. Plumer, to rebut Mr. Burke's cross-examination, asked Lord Cornwallis's opinion of Sir
John Shore, and received an answer, that his Lordship had the highest opinion of his abilities and his
honour.

The next point was, the disgrace which the
conduct of Mr. Hastings had brought upon the
British character. It was asserted in the Articles,
and was by Mr. Burke and the Managers, affirmed,
that the character of Great Britain in India was
disgraced and degraded, by the expulsion of Cheyt
Sing, and the confiscation of the Begum's treasures.---Lord Cornwallis, very explicitly. answered, that he did not believe, nor did he ever
hear the British character had suffered in the opinion of the Princes of India, by either of those
acts.------On this head, Mr. Burke referred to a
piece of evidence given by the Managers in 1788,
for the purpose of shewing the opinion the Princes
of India entertained of the moderation and good
faith of the British Government. It was an
extract from a letter written to the Marquis Cornwallis, from Captain Kirkpatrick, the Ambassador

to

to the Court of Madrid Sinidia.—Lord Cornwallis said, it appeared to be Capt. Kirkpatrick's opinion, and the question being repeated, his Lordship said he did not see how he could give any other answer.

Of the several sums of money received by Mr. Hastings as presents, and carried to the Company's account, Lord Cornwallis could say nothing in reply to Mr. Burke—No complaints, as his Lordship observed, had been made, he thought it his business to look forward, and to improve the country all he could ; and here we cannot avoid joining our tribute of applause to that of the general voice.

After this evidence is added to the important testimony which had been given before on the same points, we think we may congratulate the country on the decision of the great and leading feature of the Impeachment. We think we may venture to say, that the character of Great Britain stands high in India ; that Mr. Hastings, who has been described as the most depraved of mankind, will stand high in the opinion of the world, and that the Empire which we have obtained in Asia, has been so managed, that our Government has been esteemed a blessing, and not a curse to the people.

ONE

ONE HUNDRED AND TWENTY-SE-
VENTH DAY. *April* 15.

THE Court did not meet this morning until two o'clock, and well indeed might Mr. Hastings exclaim against the evils of an eternal Trial. The Chancellor informed the Managers and the Counsel, that the question which the former proposed could not be put.

After this notification, Mr. Burke desired Mr. Larkins might again be called; and after one or two trifling questions, he proposed one similar to that which had been requested by the Lords.

Mr. Plumer upon this rose and said, that the question fell under the head of objection, the validity of which had already been established by their Lordships' decision; and added, " But perhaps, my Lords, I may be able to save your Lordships, and the Managers, from all further trouble on this subject."

When the objection was taken to the evidence of Mr. Larkins, it was in the confident hope that no doubt could prevail any where respecting the real, and the only reason for making it, considering the past proceedings of the Trial, and the present stage of it. But, my Lords, so much has been

been said, so often repeated, and so industriously
circulated, respecting the nature of Mr. Larkins's
testimony, if it were adduced, and of the motives
operating upon the mind of Mr. Hastings in resisting it, that any longer to forbear bringing these
bold assertions to that test which has hitherto, and
invariably proved so fatal to every accusation
against Mr. Hastings, namely, the test of proof,
would be to afford some colour for the aspersions
cast upon the Gentleman at your Bar, as if he
shrunk from this enquiry, because he dreaded the
result of it.

Under these circumstances, Mr. Hastings cannot for a moment hesitate what part he ought to
take.

Anxious as he is, for the close of this long
Trial, but still more anxious for the vindication
of his honour and character, from every possible
suspicion that can be thrown upon it, Mr. Hastings confidently hopes that the justice and humanity of your Lordships will prevent this or any
other proceeding from having the effect of carrying over the final termination of this proceeding
to another year; and in that hope, Mr. Hastings
consents to wave his objection to the testimony
of Mr. Larkins, and to allow to the prosecutors
all the full scope of examination to which they
would have been entitled at any period of the
Trial.

After

After this full permission granted to Mr. Burke, it was expected that he would have proceeded to expose that system of fraud, iniquity, swindling, thieving, cheating, &c. which he declared was to be fully proved, if he could but examine Mr. Larkins. This was far from being the case. He began by acknowledging, that any mischief which might accrue to Mr. Hastings from the examination of Mr. Larkins, must be less than the impression which would be made by not examining him at all, and then three quarters of an hour were expended, by Mr. Burke repeating over and over again, at least twenty times, that the Commons had a right to examine Mr. Larkins, under a precedent, established in 1641, on the Trial of Lord Strafford, the ancestor of the late Marquis of Rockingham. After all the arguments of Mr. Burke, he at last yielded up the point to the Lords, and then proceeded to examine Mr. Larkins, who gave answers the most clear and direct, but not one of which tended to establish any assertion that Mr. Burke had made. As the examination is not closed, we shall forbear to state the particulars until the day the Court meets again.

At half past five the Court was about to rise, when Mr. Hastings begged to say a few words. He conjured their Lordships to consider the state

of

of the Trial, and the season of the year. He had been much alarmed on this day by a report which it would be improper in him to state to their Lordships, (meaning the report of an early prorogation.) He therefore did earnestly pray their Lordships to take some steps to satisfy him that his Trial was to close, and that judgment would be given in this the seventh year of it. His future conduct would be regulated by what their Lordships should say. He meant no disrespect to them, but human patience could not sustain this eternal Trial. By the delays of this day he saw what he was to expect, and therefore he most earnestly prayed their Lordships to give him some assurance, that his Trial would be finished in this year.

The Court after this Address adjourned, and resolved to sit again on Wednesday.

A Committee is appointed to report the causes of the delay on the trial of Mr. Hastings. What the nature of this report will be, we do not presume to conjecture; but that the continuation of this trial---the slow progress that is made on it---the enormous expence attending it---the injustice done to the individual---and all the circumstances of the case, are such as make it to be the most flagrant abuse of justice ever known in a civilized country, is beyond all question. In that senti-

ment

ment all agree with Mr. Hastings. Where the fault may be, if there is a fault any where, we are not competent to determine.

―――――――

ONE HUNDRED AND TWENTY-EIGHTH DAY. *April* 16.

If doubts had remained in the breast of any human being, as to one cause of the delay on the Trial of Mr. Hastings, we think they must have been removed completely, by the extraordinary transactions of this day, on which the Court sat from two o'clock until half past six; and the greatest part of the time consumed by Mr. Burke, in going over and over again the very same points that he had over and over again enquired into on the last day of the meeting. To give the questions which were then and now put, and the clear, col- lected, and impartial answers of Mr. Larkins, would take up too much room. We shall therefore con- tent ourselves by a short statement of the case, and of the points proved on the examination, in chief, by Mr. Burke.

Mr Burke commenced a speech on the evidence given by Mr. Larkins yesterday. He was inter- rupted by Mr. Law, who said it was extremely irregular

regular to observe, in the midst of an examination on the evidence of a witness.

The Chancellor said, that what Mr. Burke was
about was perfectly regular and proper, on which
Mr. Law gave up his objection, and then Mr. Burke
proceeded on the nature of the evidence given
yesterday. That Mr. Hastings had invariably declared, that Mr. Larkins was privy to every process of the business of taking money privately,
and applying it to the public service; whereas it
appeared that he knew nothing of any of the transactions prior to May 1782—that he knew nothing
of the caborleats or obligations for money, nor of
the bond. Mr. Hastings called out, that he never
had stated the facts in the manner Mr. Burke
mentioned.

Mr. Burke fired at this interruption, and at a
remark of the Counsel. He said the Commons
were beyond all controul, and that the Counsel, if
they persisted to remark on his proceedings, must
be kept in order, or the Managers must take the
instructions of the House of Commons.

As there seems to be some strange confusion or
misunderstanding of this subject, we shall state it
as it appears upon evidence, and we shall give
the heads of Mr. Larkins's examination in another
day.

On the 22d of May 1782, Mr. Hastings sent a letter to the Directors, informing them that he had received one hundred and ninety thousand pounds sterling, privately, which he had carried to the Company's account, and that he had received these sums at the time the Company very much wanted them, and that the whole had been applied to the public service.

That if the Directors wished for further information he was ready to answer upon honour or upon oath to any questions that should be put to him. The Directors, in reply to this letter, desired to know at what periods the several sums were received.

This letter Mr. Hastings answered from Cheltenham, and said, that if they required further information, Mr. Larkins would give it to them; who, he believed, possessed the only copy of the paper he ever possessed. Mr. Hastings wrote to Mr. Larkins, who sent the account home, which has occasioned so much enquiry.

It appears upon the evidence, that of this one hundred and ninety thousand pounds, one hundred and fifty-five thousand is so entered upon the Public Accounts at the time, as to leave it out of all doubt, that it was really and truly Public Money.

But

But as Bonds were taken in the name of Mr. Hastings, for 35,000l. in Nov. 1780, and in Jan. 1781, and as those bonds were not indorsed until the 29th of May, 1782, the argument has been, that in that period Mr. Hastings meant to keep to himself that 35,000l.

Mr. Hastings, from a most thorough conviction in his own mind, that Mr. Larkins knew the Bonds not to have been his property in 1781; and further being convinced that a declaration upon each Bond, declaring it not to be his property, was written in July 1781, desired Mr. Larkins to transmit the Bonds to the Company, in order, by their appearance, to verify his assertion.

Mr. Larkins made a public application to Lord Cornwallis, desiring that these Bonds might be sent to the Company. He said, he made this application at the desire of Mr. Hastings, transmitted to him by Major Scott. The Bonds arrived, and, instead of bearing date in July 1781, the declaration at the back of each is dated on the 29th of May 1782. Here then, is the whole case, in which so much time has been spent.—Mr. Hastings eagerly furnished the evidence, to prove his own mistake, a strong proof, however, that he thought he was correct.

The next point is the Paper transmitted to the Directors, at the express desire of Mr. Hastings, from an anxiety to give the fullest answers to the

ques-

questions put to him, as to the period when the several sums were received.

This account was immediately sent by Mr. Larkins to the Directors; it arrived in April 1787, and the following facts appear from it:

1st. That two lacks of rupees were paid by Gunga Gavind Sing into the Treasury, from Dinagopore; and that a balance of one lack remained in the hands of Gunga Gavind Sing.

2d. That two lacks were received from Patna, and paid into the Treasury, as public money.

3d. That one lack and a half was received from Nuddea, and paid into the Treasury.

For the first and the last sums, bonds were taken in the name of Mr. Hastings, whose private property they appeared to be, until he voluntarily declared that these bonds were not his property, and that he had no right nor title to them. If therefore the changes were to be rung upon this subject for seven years longer, until One Hundred Thousand Pounds more are expended, we must still come back to the same point. That of the money received by Gunga Gavind Sing, he has not accounted for one lack; and that Mr. Larkins does not recollect his being informed that the three bonds given to Mr. Hastings in 1781 were for money the property of the Company prior to the 22d May 1782.

These

These are the only two points that Mr. Larkins' evidence or his letter have a reference to at all, though he has been examined so many hours in two days.

It is very material for those who feel an interest in this, as the most remarkable cause that ever was undertaken in a civilized country, to notice, that when the Counsel opposed the examination of Mr. Larkins, Mr. Burke boldly said, that if he were called, the Commons would prove by his teſtimony a system of swindling, cheating, thieving, &c. &c. Mr. Burke on this day changed his tone, and now merely professed to prove that Mr. Larkins was not privy to the receipt of thirty-five thousand pounds, out of one hundred and thirty thousand pounds, so easy as Mr. Hastings had supposed him to be acquainted with it. This point, and the information as to the jewels supposed to be given to Mr. Wheler, are the only two circumstances which this great examination has produced.

To one of the questions put by Mr. Burke, Mr. Law objected in a very pointed manner, as being merely a repetition of what had been so often asked before. Mr. Burke, in reply said, that the Counsel objected becauſe the answer would damnify their Client ; that they already had experience enough on this trial, to know, that any attempt to controul the Managers, only tended to

waste

waste time on Speeches; for that the Managers would have their way.

Mr. Law, with great feeling, and with much contempt of the remark, said, that their Lordships knew he had no motive whatever, but to endeavour, by confining the Managers to some sort of rule, to bring this Trial to a close in this year.

Mr. Hastings, when Mr. Law sat down, rose, and said, he wished to be heard for a few moments.—To the question then put by the Managers, or to any question of any kind that they might put in future, neither he nor his Counsel would object, provided their Lordships would sit, and close the Trial this year. Surely, as an Englishman, and claiming the Rights of a British Subject, this was not too much for him to ask. If their Lordships would only sit on this day and tomorrow, to finish this evidence; and if they would afterwards sit to finish this Trial, now in the Seventh Year of it, in this Session, the Manager had his full permission to say what he pleased, and to ask what questions he pleased, no one would interrupt him.

Mr. Hastings then, in a style of natural eloquence which no studied speech could equal, said, as nearly as we can recollect, as follows : " My Lords, I beg leave shortly to call to your recollection the sacrifices which I have made, merely to

get

get this eternal trial to an end. In the year 1791, now three years ago, I offered to wave my defence altogether, provided this Court would go to judgement on the case made by my Prosecutors. This was not agreed to. In the last year, 1793, the last Session, I gave up the advantage of the observations of my Counsel, in the evidence on one of the Articles, and waved both the opening and closing speeches of my Counsel on another Article, in order to leave time to the Managers to close their reply in the last session. Though three and twenty days were left to them for this purpose, they desired to postpone the reply to this session. Thus I lost the benefit of the observations of my learned Friends, and was deprived of the purpose for which alone I gave them up. In this session, for the first time on this trial, I was the cause of delay. I wished to avail myself of the advantage of Lord Cornwallis' testimony. His unexpected illness occasioned two adjournments of the Court; but when I found that it would be uncertain at what period the Noble Marquis would be well enough to attend, I even waved the benefit of his testimony, that the trial might be accelerated. The desire of the Managers to introduce evidence which your Lordships would not admit, occasioned the adjournment for the Circuits; and in that period Lord Cornwallis recovered.

covered. This was the only instance in which I
delayed the Trial for a single moment.

" The Managers then wished to call Mr. Larkins. My Counsel objected, merely to avoid further delay. To them I trusted the conduct of my
cause—I never instructed them to object to the
calling of Mr. Larkins. They wished, as I do,
that in some period of the life of man this cause
should be brought to a close. Was it to be expected, my Lords, after having made so many sacrifices for the acceleration of this Trial, that I
should consent to continue it to an indefinite period, to accommodate the Managers—But when I
heard him declare, that if Mr. Larkins was called,
such a scene of fraud, deception, and iniquity
would be discovered, that I should wish for mountains to cover me, (I think this was one of the
strange expressions) I earnestly intreated my learned Friend (Mr. Plumer) who sat next to me, to
allow him at once to be called; he thought the
expressions of less consequence, and your Lordships determined that he could not be examined ;
but my Counsel concurred with me in opinion,
that the best way to counteract the insinuations of
the Managers, was to consent to Mr. Larkins'
appearance. He has now been two days before
your Lordships, you have heard his testimony, and
you see how much of the time has been wasted,

by

by repeating the same questions to him so often over. 'I say, my Lords, that I will object to no question that can be put, but surely I do not ask too much in return, when I request that you will sit to-day and to-morrow, to close this examination, so that a sufficient time may remain in this Session to bring this trial to a close—that is all I am anxious about, and that secured neither I nor my Counsel will interrupt the Manager in any thing that he may say, however irregular it may be.''

This speech had a visible effect on all who heard it. Mr. Burke had begun a reply, but was desired to proceed with his evidence, which he did, twice saying he had done, and twice rallying again, but going back precisely to the questions that he had put on the last day the Court met.—At length Mr. Burke said he had done, and then

Mr. Dallas began his cross-examination; the material answer to his question was, that every Rupee received by Mr. Hastings had been expended in the public service. All the Lords being gone, except five or six, the Marquis of Townshend moved to adjourn.

The Court meets again on the 24th, the first day after the Easter adjournment, when, as we hear, the Lords determine to sit every day until this Trial is closed. We think it extraordinary

that,

that, in a civilized country, a criminal Trial should have lasted seven years, at an expence to the nation of one hundred thousand pounds, and, to the individual, of a larger sum than ever was imposed upon any individual as a fine, except in the reign of Charles the Second.

ONE HUNDRED AND TWENTY-NINTH DAY. *April* 24.

THE Court did not meet this day until the usual hour of two, when Mr. Dallas immediately proceeded in his cross-examination of Mr. Larkins, by which it appeared, that upon the bonds for three and a half lacks of rupees taken by Mr. Hastings in his own name, he never had received one rupee of interest. It further appeared, that though Mr. Larkins did not recollect being fully acquainted until the 22d of May, 1782, that these bonds were not the property of Mr. Hastings, but of the East-India Company, yet he thinks from circumstances, that he must have had some intimation upon the subject from Mr. Hastings, prior to that period, because the bonds were dated, two of them, 1ft and 2d of October, 1780, and the third on the 23d of November 1780, of course one year's interest would become due upon them

in

in October and November 1781. As Mr. Hastings was at that time up the country, and as Mr. Larkins had the charge of these bonds, he thought he could not have neglected to receive the interest upon them, unless he had received some directions on that head from Mr. Hastings. That no interest ever was received upon them, and that they never were entered upon the books of Mr. Hastings as his private property he was certain; but he cannot swear positively to being fully acquainted with the transaction relative to these bonds prior to the 22d of May, 1782. In like manner the present received from Sadanund, the Buxey of Cheyt Sing, stood upon the Company's books as the property of Mr. Hastings; but it was employed in the public service, and Mr. Hastings never made use of one rupee of it. That while these bonds, and this deposit, appeared apparently to belong to Mr. Hastings, he was under the necessity of borrowing money on his own private account from individuals, that necessity being created by the readiness always shewn by Mr. Hastings to assist those who wanted his assistance: that for the money so borrowed, he was obliged to pay an interest of 10 or 12 per cent. per annum, which he would not have done had he conceived the three bonds in question, or the deposit, to be his own property. That Mr. Hastings was a man

known

known to be perfectly careless as to the state of his own private fortune, and that it was with the greatest difficulty he (Mr. Larkins) could get Mr. Hastings to devote an hour to the consideration of the state of his private affairs, so very inattentive was he to every thing that concerned himself.

Mr. Larkins said, that he believed he had the entire management of every thing that had a relation to the private fortune of Mr. Hastings.--- That during the thirteen years in which Mr. Hastings was at the head of the government of India, he verily believed, that in no one instance, and he had full opportunities of making the observation, had Mr. Hastings done any one act, either with an immediate or a remote view to his own personal advantage; on the contrary, his known and fixed character was the very opposite to that which had been imputed to him, namely, of a man venal, corrupt, and oppressive, who, in all his acts, looked only to the accumulation of exorbitant wealth---the allegation in the charge preferred by the late House of Commons.

Mr. Dallas closed his examination, by asking Mr. Larkins, if he was the Accountant General at the time when Lord Cornwallis described him as a man, whose knowledge, abilities, and acknowledged integrity, entitled every thing that

came

came from him to the fullest consideration? apologizing for the mode in which he put the question.

Mr. Larkins answered, that he was. He asked him one question more, which was, Whether he was obliged to Mr. Hastings for the honourable station which he had so long filled in the Company's service? He replied, that he was not; that he entered into the Accountant's Office as the youngest assistant, that he rose regularly in the same office, till he came to be the head of it, in which he was confirmed by the Directors, and did not deem himself at all obligated to Mr. Hastings for his situation. This examination was completely finished in half an hour, when Mr. Burke began a cross-examination, which lasted until twenty minutes after five, and Mr. Burke convincing every person who heard him, that there was one cause of the duration of this trial, which the Managers had omitted to mention in their report.——— He began by asking Mr. Larkins whether he had communicated with the Counsel of Mr. Hastings? To which he replied, that he had; that he avowed himself to be the friend of Mr. Hastings; but friend as he was to him, he was what he had described himself to Mr. Burke to be, *magis amica veritas*, and therefore, without any consideration how it might affect Mr. Hastings, he was ready

to

to answer any question that could be put to him. This he had said to Mr. Burke, in the committee of managers, and this he now repeated. Mr. Burke then went through a very long examination, treading over and over again the same ground that he had gone through before, and drawing from Mr. Larkins a more complete confirmation of his former testimony, namely, that he the witness was convinced of the purity of Mr. Hastings's intentions, of his perfect indifference to every personal consideration, and of his invariable attention to the welfare of the East India Company. It appeared also on his re-examination, that the letter written by Mr. Larkins to the Company, on which so many comments were made, was not in consequence of any application from the Company to him, but at the requisition of Mr. Hastings; that he had every reason to believe the information which he had given was full and complete, because the Company never had called upon him for an explanation on any one of those points which now were said to have been so imperfectly stated. Mr. Burke rang the changes again and again upon the subject; and in one of the replies of Mr. Larkins, he observed that the witness must not attempt to give so impudent an answer.

At last the Lords began to grow impatient; and on Mr. Burke asking the witness to speak
from

from memory to the contents of written papers, Lord Hawke and Lord Stanhope, both remonstrated. At this time there were not above thirteen Lords present in the Court. Mr. Burke took fire, and after many personal allusions to the learning of the Lords, which appeared ignorance to ignorant men, he repeated the following lines :

" Turpe est difficiles, habere nugas,
" Et stultus labor est ineptiarum."

which may be truly translated, " You bafe fellows treat trifles as of importance, and like fools, you boggle at mere nonsense." How the admirers of Martial have translated this passage we do not know.

Mr. Burke continued the examination for two hours and a half, each answer bringing the points more clearly forward in favour of Mr. Hastings, as to those particular traits in his character which those who know him have described as the distinguifhing features in it. At last Mr. Burke touched again upon the balance of the lack of rupees, which was said to be left in the hands of Gunga Gavind Sing, and which he pretended to have given in jewels to Mr. Wheler. Mr. Burke asked Mr. Larkins if he had had any conversation on this subject with Mr. Hastings since his arrival

in

in England? He said he had, and since he had
been examined by the Managers---That when he
mentioned the circumstances to Mr. Hastings, he
told him that he had not the slightest recollection
of it, and could not think it possible he should
have said so ; but on Mr. Larkins telling him that
the fact, though happening so many years ago,
was so strongly imprinted in his memory that he
should be ready to swear to it before the Lords,
Mr. Hastings replied to him, " Then, Larkins, it
must be so."

At length, after repeating again and again the
questions which he had asked on the examination
in chief, and going through all the bonds and all
the presents, and asking whether Mr. Hastings
might not have received larger sums, of which
Mr. Larkins knew nothing? to which the answer
was, he did not know what he might have received, but that he did not believe he had received
any other sums---and asking Mr. Larkins from
whom Mr. Hastings had borrowed various sums,
and whether he had repaid those sums ? To which
the most satisfactory answers were given---Mr.
Burke said he had done, and Mr. Dallas saying
he had no further questions to ask, Mr. Larkins
withdrew, after undergoing an examination of
two very long days, in which he acquitted himself highly to his own honour, and to that of Mr.

Hastings's

Hastings's character, in the fullest and the most complete manner ; for it will be recollected, that at the time it was a matter of doubt, whether, according to the Law of the Land, Mr. Larkins could be called. Mr. Burke affirmed unequivocally, that if that witness were examined, he would expose such a system of thieving, cheating, swind. ling, and robbery, that Mr. Hastings would wish for mountains to cover him, and that if he (Mr. Hastings) had ever shewn compassion to man, woman, or infant, Mr. Burke would pity him for objecting to the examination of Mr. Larkins. What is the result ? As far as the evidence of a man can go, whom we may describe as covered over with the eulogiums of General Clavering, Colonel Monson, and Mr. Francis, Mr. Hastings, Sir John Macpherson, the Marquis Cornwallis and the Court of Directors, that evidence is most decidedly in favour of Mr. Hastings. He describes him as a man wholly regardless of his own interest, and whose mind was occupied by an attention to the interest of his constituents.

We trust we may now conclude the evidence upon this long and most expensive cause, as closed. That the Nation will cease to be called upon for thousands after thousands, in support of a prosecution of which every man is heartily sick. Do we want to know the result of the measures

of

of Mr. Hastings? Look at the amount of the re-sources—Three millions sterling a year when he came to the Government—Five millions two hundred thousand pounds when he left it—Five millions five hundred thousand pounds now. Do we want to know the character of Mr. Haftings, and the respect in which his name is held in India? Look at the evidence of the Marquis Cornwallis, Col. Blair, Col. Duff, Col. Popham, and of every gentleman who was examined. Look at the testimonials transmitted by the natives of India—the addresses of the inhabitants of Calcutta—the Officers of the army, and the thanks of the Directors and Proprietors approved by the King's Ministers, for his long, faithful, and able services. If we are told in reply, that his services were accidental, but that his object was as stated by the last House of Commons, to acquire exorbitant wealth. —Let us ask which one fact through the whole trial supports such a charge, and whether the evidence of Mr. Larkins does not totally do it away? After going through such an ordeal, Mr. Hastings may rest in security, his character is beyond the reach of fate, for the world will always remember that Mr. Hastings was not arraigned for petty crimes, but that he was charged with every atrocity that can disgrace and degrade human nature.——

nature.—In the end, we trust it will appear, that
Magna est veritas, et prevalebit, a quotation at least
as apt as Mr. Burke's, from Martial.

ONE HUNDRED AND THIRTIETH DAY.
April 25.

THE Court did not meet this day until twenty
minutes after two, although the Lord Chancellor
was down by half past one. It was hoped and
expected that the Managers would have proceeded
to deliver in what remained of their written evidence, and to make their speeches in reply, that
the public and the defendant might see an end to
this protracted and everlasting Trial; but, to the
astonishment of every one, Mr. Burke began by
saying, that he was going to open a new head of
evidence, in order to convict Mr. Hastings of
fraud, robbery, swindling, cheating, and forgery:
That it was the more necessary to do so, because
Mr. Larkins had attempted to palliate these crimes,
by stating that Mr. Hastings was negligent, inattentive, and laboured under a total want of
memory.

Mr. Law endeavoured, but in vain, to confine
Mr. Burke within reasonable bounds, but finding
that

that each interruption only led to further digressi-
ons, he suffered him to proceed as he pleased,
and, in a speech of one hour and eight minutes,
Mr. Burke went into the explanation of the most
singular evidence that ever was offered to be produced in a Court of Justice. It will tend to
clear this case to our readers, perhaps, if we state
what the cause was originally, and compare it with
the grounds now taken.

When the nation, eight sessions ago, agreed
with its representatives to impeach Mr. Hastings,
it was upon the idea, that through his measures
the welfare of the natives of India had been materially affected, the revenues of the East India
Company greatly diminished, and the British character disgraced and degraded in the opinion of
the whole world. No such opinions being fashion-
able at present, a new ground was taken, and it
was said that if Mr. Larkins could but be examined, Mr. Hastings would appear in his true
colours, and so apparent would be his guilt, that
he would wish for mountains to cover him. Mr.
Larkins has been examined fully and completely,
and he is now out of fashion with Mr. Burke.

The hero of this day is Rajah Nobkissen, whom
Mr. Burke described as a Jew, a Banyan, and an
Usurer—that they had to produce from a man of
this description, an allegation against Mr. Hastings,

ings, which must be true, because Mr. Hastings had refused to answer it.

Mr. Burke then went through the case as it appeared on his own evidence: that Mr. Hastings had borrowed three lacks of rupees from Nobkissen, which he had afterwards given to the Company, Nobkissen having desired Mr. Hastings to accept it ; that Nobkissen had since applied to have this money again, finding that Mr. Hastings had not taken it to himself, but given it to the Company; and in the course of his speech, he pitied the unfortunate situation of this banyan and usurer so much, that all the suffering millions in India, were for the time forgotten. Mr. Burke contended, that the bill filed in the name of Nobkissen on this subject ought to be received as evidence, in order to introduce the answer given by Mr. Hastings, which was, that as an impeachment upon this very subject was depending, he declined giving any answer at all to the bill filed against him. Mr. Burke argued, that the declining to give an answer was a confession of guilt.

Mr. Law very fully answered the argument of Mr. Burke. He said, that the Manager's arguments tended to make a trial perpetual; that there must be some period for closing proceedings, but
that

that in no stage of the trial could the evidence now offered be admissible.

Mr. Fox and Mr. Angelo Taylor contended for its admissibility, and were most fully and ably replied to by Mr. Law, Mr. Plumer and Mr. Dallas. The latter Gentleman said, broadly, that he believed Nobkissen was induced to enter his bill four years after the commencement of the Impeachment, by the efforts of those who were friendly to the Impeachment; and he said that under no possible circumstance could the evidence be admitted.

Mr. Law and Mr. Plumer reprobated the precedent of Lord Strafford's trial, that it happened almost at the commencement of a rebellion, when the Court and the Judges were panic struck, but that in better times no such doctrines as were supported in 1642 would be admitted.

Mr. Burke began his reply, by complaining of the length of the speeches of the Counsel, though their four speeches lasted one hour and seven minutes, and Mr. Burke spoke, in his first speech, one hour and eight minutes.—He then proceeded, in the strongest language, and with the utmost vehemence of manner, to contend for the admissibility of the evidence that he had offered. He said that he was addressing a body of Nobles, and he hoped they would act like Nobles, and not as

thieves

thieves in a night cellar ; that he could not suspect them of so foul a thing as to reject the evidence that he offered ; that the Law of Parliament was distinct from the Law of the Land ; that
the Judges had no right to guide the Lords, and
he trusted they would at all times follow the example of the Judges who were in office during
the Trial of Lord Strafford. He closed at six
o'clock, and the Lords adjourned, when, as we
are informed, it was instantly determined that
the evidence offered by Mr. Burke was inadmissible.

It is impossible to consider the singular proceedings of this day without reflecting very seriously on the state of this Impeachment. Either
Mr. Burke consults his Lawyers, or he does not.
If he does, what is their advice worth ? They receive an enormous sum from the public, and they
are always in the wrong ; for we do not find that
there is either debate, difference of opinion, or
protest on any question of law which the Lords
determine. If he does not consult them, why
are they paid ? It is well known that Mr. Burke's
brother lived very comfortably for six years on
the proceeds arising from this Impeachment ; and
the whole expence would pay and feed the
Prussian Army for two months of the present
campaign.

Again

Again it is to be considered, that Mr. Burke himself does not act in this case as a mere individual. When he declared, in the last Parliament, that Mr. Pitt and Mr. Dundas had, in one single instance, been guilty of an act of greater iniquity and corruption than had been committed by Nero, in the most heroic times of Roman iniquity; he only exposed himself, unless he established the truth of his assertion by proof. When Mr. Burke shocked every Gentleman who was a Member of the last Parliament, by the manner in which he spoke of his Majesty, at a time when every loyal subject offered prayers to Heaven for his health, he spoke merely as an individual: but far different is the case at present. He is now the Representative of the Commons, who represent the People of Great Britain. He spends a hundred pounds of their money every day the Court meets. Every evidence that he offers is the witness of the People. Either he takes no advice, or he has very bad advice. Day after day, month after month, and year after year, the trial is dragged on—yet the facts on which the Impeachment was first grounded were true or they were false; all the great points are passed by, and so little remains that we hope and trust the Lords willl take some steps to conclude a trial which, by its length, is become a grievance of a most
alarming

alarming nature. Little disposed as we are to agree with Mr. Burke in general, we fully concur with him in opinion, that let this trial end when it will, or how it will, " *infamy* must fall some-where."

―――――

ONE HUNDRED AND THIRTY-FIRST DAY. *May* 1.

Lord Kenyon sat this day for the Chancellor, and the Court met before two o'clock, when his Lordship informed the Managers, that the evidence last offered was inadmissible. Mr. Burke, as usual, said the Commons submitted, though they did not acquiesce, and lamented the inconveniences which the cause of the Commons sustained by the decision.

Mr. Burke then said he had some important evidence to offer, which he was confident was open to no sort of objection, and it was neceffary for him shortly to open the nature of it. He said, that Mr. Hastings in his defence had stated that the various sums of money which the Commons had in fact charged him with receiving, were really taken by him, and applied to the public

N N   service

service in times of great difficulty and distress, and he had given in a very great variety of evidence to prove the distressed state of the Company's affairs in the years 1779, 1780, 1781, 1782, and 1783. He had also given evidence to prove the great confederacy which was formed against the British Empire in India at those periods, and he loudly boasted of having preserved the British Empire entire in India, while her dominions were lost to her in America. Mr. Burke said, the Commons very readily admitted the distresses of the Company to be as great as Mr. Hastings stated them to be; but it then became necessary, by way of rebutting the defence made by Mr. Hastings, to go into the origin, progress, and termination of the Maratta War, in order to prove, that Mr. Hastings was the author of that war, which produced the confederacy against us, and excited France to use her utmost efforts for overturning the British Empire in India. He contended, that as the defence of Mr. Hastings was new matter, the Commons had a right to rebut it by new matter; and in this view they offered it, not stating the Maratta War to be criminal, but that Mr. Hastings was the author of the distresses which were brought upon the Company by that war. He therefore proposed to begin with the proceedings of the Governor and Council of

3

Bombay, in 1775, and so to go through the series
of measures pursued relative to the Marattas until
1783, a body of documents that would fill at the
least Seven Folio Volumes, and which could not
be gone through in Seven Years. Mr. Fox supported Mr. Burke, but very feebly. No other
Manager spoke.

Mr. Law, with great force, contended that in
no possible shape could this evidence be produced—That there was no point which had been
more disputed, than who was, or who was not
the author of the Maratta war. It was plain that
the late House of Commons did not believe Mr.
Hastings to be the author of the war, because
Mr. Burke had originally presented a charge, accusing Mr. Hastings as the author of it. That
nothing was ever done upon that charge; Mr.
Hastings boldly denied it, but claimed all the
merit of reftoring peace to India. How was the
fact as applied to the evidence? The Managers
had entered a letter from Mr. Hastings, in which
he said that he left Calcutta in July 1781, impressed with a belief that strong measures were
necessary to prevent the Company from sinking
under the accumulated difficulties that surrounded
them. The Managers had also entered a letter
from Sir Eyre Coote, dated in September 1781,
in order to prove that at that time no State ne-

cessity

cessity existed. To rebut this evidence, Mr. Law said the Counsel had given a variety of evidence to prove the actual state of distress at Madras, Bombay, and Bengal, in 1780, and the subsequent years—and now the Managers meant to repel it, by going into the history of the rise, progress, and termination of the Maratta war, a proceeding which he was confident their Lordships would not entertain for a moment.

Mr. Burke replied at very great length, and with very great violence, going over the same ground again.

Mr. Law, in reply, said, it would be an insult to their Lordships, and treachery to Mr. Hastings, were he to waste a moment in further observations on what had been said by the Managers.

Mr. Burke upon this grew exceedingly angry; and after much violent language, he said, that he rejoiced there were some persons amongst the audience of the day (the Turkish Ambassador and his suite were present) who did not understand English, as the *chicane* practised in this Court was of such a nature, that it would disgrace the proceedings of a Turkish Divan—or words very like it.

Lord Kenyon and several other Lords called to Order.

Mr.

Mr. Burke was visibly agitated, and qualified what he had said with an *if*.

The Bishop of Rochester repeated the words as he understood them---and that was, as a reflection upon the Court.

The Short-hand Writer was referred to; but Mr. Burke said, that Mr. Gurney could not read his own Short-hand Notes.

Lord Carnarvon got up and said, he did not conceive Mr. Burke meant to reflect upon the Court; and at last the Lords retired, to determine, whether it was competent to the Commons to go into the origin, progress, and termination of the Maratta war, in order to prove that Mr. Hastings was the author of that war, and could not there-fore plead the distresses and dangers of the Company as an excuse for receiving money privately, and carrying it to the public service, such diffi-culties being occasioned by that war, of which they charged Mr. Hastings to be the Author.

The Court adjourned.

ONE HUNDRED AND THIRTY-SECOND DAY. May 7.

WE have endeavoured through the whole of this long and tedious cause to present our readers

with

with a fair and impartial statement of the proceedings of each day; we shall preserve the same
spirit of truth, giving the abstraƈt of this day's
events, which, blessed be God, is the last of the
Trial, the speeches of the Managers excepted—a
circumstance so important, that we congratulate
the Lords, the Commons, the Country, and Mr.
Hastings, on its having taken place.

Lord Kenyon (when the Court assembled on
this day) informed the Managers, that the evidence they had offered could not be admitted.
Our readers will recolleƈt that this evidence did,
in faƈt, comprise the origin, progress, and termination of the Maratta war, including in it a period
of eight years, from 1775, to 1783, and filling at
the least six folio volumes of printed evidence.

Mr. Burke observed, that as the Court did not
state the grounds on which they rejeƈted the evidence, and as the Counsel had offered no argument, except that the admission of it would occasion delay, the Commons were utterly at a loss to
know why it was refused. Mr. Burke then said,
that this complaint of delay had been echoed from
one end of the kingdom to the other; that the
Managers were libelled, and their motives misrepresented. He then asked what one reason under
Heaven the Managers could have for wishing to
protraƈt this Trial, in which they had now been
                                        engaged

engaged above eight years, and he himself an Indian enquirer above fifteen years; that those who
were grown old, naturally wished for repose, and
the young to enjoy the pleasures of youth. The
prisoner was personally known to none of them,
to him they could have no enmity---he interfered
not in their polisical pursuits---it was therefore
impossible for any man, with any degree of justice,
to accuse them of delay. Here Mr. Hastings
started up, and said he did directly accuse the
Manager of delay; that every word he was now
uttering was irrelevant to the cause. He was proceeding further, when Lord Kenyon desired Mr.
Burke to proceed, and to go on with the evidence to which he supposed his remarks were pre-
liminary.

Mr. Burke then took a Newspaper from his
pocket, and said, that the same complaints which
Mr. Hastings made, he had met with in a paper
of this morning. After stating much more to the
same purpose, Mr. Burke proceeded to read the
paper, but was interrupted by Lord Kenyon, who
said, the Court could not receive any complaint
unless the Manager was prepared to support it by
legal evidence. That it was not the duty of the
Court to take notice of any matters which were
not brought regularly before them. That he
knew nothing of any Libels that had been pub-

lished,

lished, none of them having come under his inspection.

Mr. Burke again proceeded to state, in very
strong terms, the unwarrantable liberties taken
with the Managers and the Court in the reflections cast upon them. He was successively interrupted by Lord Caernarvon, Lord Thurlow, and
Lord Somers, who entreated the Manager to proceed with his evidence.

Lord Thurlow said, that no complaint could be
considered in the Court, unless from some circumstances immediately occurring. That the
Managers had it in their power to complain to
the House of Commons, who might either proceed themselves or by message to the Lords.

Lord Somers expressed his hope that the time
of the Court would no longer be consumed by
matter foreign to the cause. That the Lords
would take care of their own privileges.

Mr. Burke then insisted that they were an in-
tegral part of the Court, and he then read a long
protest against the decisions of the Court, and
denied that the Commons were to be looked upon
as common prosecutors.

The Lords declined to receive the protest.

Mr. Burke strongly declared that the Commons
were not the authors of the delay, and that it must
rest with the Court or Mr. Hastings.

The

The Earl of Coventry said, that as the Hon. Manager had taken infinite pains, and in a speech of considerable length, to prove that he neither wished for nor was the cause of delay, he trusted he would immediately produce his evidence, in order to convince the Court still more of the justice of his remarks.

This debate was ended about a quarter after three, when Mr. Fox and Mr. Taylor proceeded to deliver the evidence in reply, in the charge of presents and contracts.

After Mr. Taylor had concluded his evidence in reply on the contract charge, it was supposed that the whole business was over, but Mr. Burke said he had a new head of evidence to go through; that Mr. Hastings had entered a variety of testimonials from all ranks of people in India, expressing their fullest approbation of his conduct, and the sincerest affection for his person—that these testimonials were transmitted by Lord Cornwallis to the Company, and while the Commons of Great Britain were prosecuting Mr. Hastings in the name of the people of India, for practising every species of oppression upon them, that very people were telling the Commons that they were ignorant, uninformed, and deceived; he proposed, therefore, to enter Mr. Barlow's report of the Commerce of Benares, some letters from the

Naboh

Nabob Vizier and his Ministers, and some petitions from the Raja of Dinagapore and his Counsel. To save time, the Counsel said they admitted them all.

The last documents not being ready, Lord Kenyon said, that the Court had no blame to lay upon the Managers, yet they did think their Agents very reprehensible for not having the evidence at hand; and as it was understood all the evidence was to be closed on this day, the Court hoped there would be no longer delay, since it must be the wish of all parties to close this long depending Trial in this Session of Parliament.

Mr. Burke, with infinite solemnity in his manner, said to their Lordships—" As I have taken " the lead in this cause, it may be supposed that " I am better informed than my Fellow Mana- " gers, of the nature and tendency of the evi- " dence which is offered—that which I now mean " to produce, and I call God to witness to the " truth of what I assert, is of a nature so impor- " tant, that your Lordships cannot conscientiously " go to judgement, unless it is before you; it is " indeed of more consequence than any evidence " yet before you." At length the Books came, and Mr. Burke said, that one of the testimonials came from the Raja of Dinagapore, and his Ministers. He, therefore, proposed to rebut it by

giving

giving in the report of Mr. Paterson, on the cruelties supposed to have been exercised on some
inhabitants of Rungpore and Edracpore, in the
years 1781, and 1782.

Mr. Law objected to this evidence as utterly
inadmissible. He reminded the Lords that this
was a tale which he had pressed the Manager
years ago to bring forward as a charge, in a shape
in which it might be answered; the Manager declined to do so; and he trusted their Lordships
would not admit four folio volumes on the Minutes, to which the Defendant could not now
reply. Mr. Burke disclaimed every idea of
bringing the matter forward in this form, as a
criminal charge against Mr. Hastings; but the
Raja of Dinagapore, and his Ministers, having
stated the happiness every one enjoyed under the
Adminiftration of Mr. Hastings, they meant to
shew the miseries which the people sustained, and
which induced Mr. Hastings himself to order an
investigation of the conduct of Deby Sing, in the
year 1782. Mr. Fox supported Mr. Burke.—
Lord Stanhope, Lord Walsingham, and Lord
Kenyon spoke, and it being clearly the sense of
the Court that the evidence was inadmissible, Mr.
Burke at length gave it up.

But as this story has been once more, and we
believe now for the last time, alluded to, we owe

it

it in justice to Mr. Hastings to call the attention of our Readers to it. In 1788, in the third day of Mr. Burke's first Speech, he introduced this story, as applicable to the cause of Mr. Hastings. He detailed a variety of horrid cruelties, supposed to have been committed by, or by the orders of Deby Sing, and he said he would bring the charge home to Mr. Hastings. Lord Thurlow, who was then Lord Chancellor, said in the House of Lords, that the charges preferred by the Commons sunk to utter insignificance, when compared with this matter introduced by Mr. Burke in his opening speech, and that Mr. Burke would be a calumniator if he did not bring it forward in such a shape, as would enable Mr. Hastings to reply to it.

In 1789, Mr. Hastings prayed the Commons to introduce this matter in the form of an Article, or to give him satisfaction for the injury he sustained.

The Commons did not comply with his request.

In 1790, the Managers offered to introduce this report of Mr. Patterson, in order to shew what enormities might be committed without coming to the knowledge of an English Gentleman.

The Counsel rejected the evidence thus collaterally introduced; but said, that if preferred as a charge

charge they were ready and eager to refute it.—
The Lords voted, that it was inadmissible.

In 1791, Mr. Hastings complained loudly of
the injury he sustained by the introduction of so
atrocious a calumny, as this tale of Deby Sing
was. He stated what was strictly true, that in no
possible view could he be implicated in such
charges as were proved against Deby Sing, since
he had been most anxious to detect them, and to
punish the men if found guilty : that the cause did
not come to a conclusion in his Government, but
in the Administration of Lord Cornwallis, when
it fully appeared, that the guilt of Deby Sing was
trifling in a comparison with the magnitude of the
accusation, and that the most dreadful of these
cruelties, which Mr. Burke detailed with so much
effect in Westminster-Hall in 1788, never were
committed at all. Mr. Burke had it in his power
at any time, to lay before the Commons the grounds
on which he imputed criminality to Mr. Hastings
on this subject ; but this he declined to do, and
the whole tale has been buried in oblivion to this
day, when Mr. Burke endeavoured to get it on
the minutes of the trial ; not as a charge against
Mr. Hastings—not with the hope of obtaining redress for the people of India, but in order to
prove that the testimonials transmitted by Lord
Cornwallis from Dinagapore, in 1789, could not
be

be true, because great enormities which Mr. Hastings was most anxious to detect and to punish, were said to have been committed there in 1782.

The evidence being rejected, and the Managers declaring that they had totally closed their evidence, Mr. Law concluded the day by the following energetic address to the Court :

" The evidence on the part of the prosecution
" being now fully closed, we might avail ourselves
" of your Lordships indulgence in this stage of the
" proceedings, to observe at large upon the evi-
" dence adduced in reply, during the course of
" the present Sessions of Parliament. But my Lords,
" in pursuance of the same purpose which induced
" us in the last Sessions to forego a similar advan-
" tage, and to submit our evidence on one article of
" charge, the Contracts, to your Lordships consi-
" deration, unaccompanied by any prefatory or
" concluding comments whatsover, and to leave
" the evidence on another article, that of Presents,
" unenforced by such concluding observations, as
" in other circumstances, we might have been dis-
" posed to offer—

" In pursuance of that same purpose of accelera-
" tion and dispatch, which dictated our conduct in
" the instance I have alluded to, and with a view to
" the nearer and more immediate termination of this
" long

" long depending trial, we again relinquish an ad-
" vantage which can only be purchased at the in-
" tolerable price of further protraction and delay.
" All the attempts made in the present Session, to
" support the case of the prosecution, have ended
" in producing an effect directly contrary. We
" confidently trust, that the strong and important
" conclusions in favour of the defendant, which re-
" sult from the invaluable oral testimony lately
" given at your Lordships' Bar, cannot either have
" escaped your Lordships' penetration, or fail to
" have their due effect hereafter upon your Lord-
" ships' judgement.

" After returning to your Lordships our humble
" but grateful acknowledgements for the invariable
" patience and condescension with which our zea-
" lous but imperfect endeavours to discharge our
" bounden duty towards our client, have been at
" all times honoured during the course of so many
" years, it only remains for us, in the name and on
" the behalf of Mr. Hastings to implore, that so
" much of continued time may be yet allotted to
" this trial in the course of the present Sessions, as
" may be sufficient to bring it to an entire and ulti-
" mate conclusion. To that moment Mr. Hastings
" looks forward with impatient but fearless expec-
" tation—being as he is equally assured of his own
" innocence, and your Lordships' justice."

ONE

ONE HUNDRED AND THIRTY-THIRD DAY. *May* 8.

Mr. Grey, on this day summed up, in part, the evidence in reply, on the Benares article. Before we go into the particulars of his speech, we fhall recall to our readers' attention the circumstances under which this most singular of all transactions came to be preferred as a high crime against Mr. Hastings.

In 1786, Mr. Fox, who opened the charge in the House of Commons, argued, that Mr. Hastings had no right to demand military aid from Cheyt Sing, and that therefore all the acts which followed, and were consequent of it, were criminal. That the object of Mr. Hastings was to ruin Cheyt Sing, and that he was actuated against him by malice. In this opinion a large party followed Mr. Fox.

Mr. Pitt argued that Mr. Hastings had a right to tax Cheyt Sing, and that as all the acts which followed were justified by that right, they were not criminal. That there was not a shadow of evidence on which Mr. Hastings could be charged

with

with malice; but, said Mr. Pitt, Mr. Hastings was criminal in intending to commit an act which he did not commit; that is, to impose a fine of forty or fifty lacks of rupees upon Cheyt Sing for his contumacy. In this opinion too, Mr. Pitt was followed by a large party.

The resolution put to the vote was, that in the Benares Charge there was matter for crimination, and it was carried 119 against 79.

But though Mr. Pitt and his friends, on the one side, and Mr. Fox and his supporters on the other, thought Mr. Hastings was criminal, they fundamentally disagreed as to the point of criminality.

But seventy nine Members voted that there was no criminal matter in the charge. These, therefore, must have agreed with Mr. Pitt that Mr. Hastings had a right to tax Cheyt Sing, and with Mr. Fox, that it was not a crime in Mr. Hastings to intend to levy the fine, which, whether enormous or not, he did not levy. These seventy-nine Members formed a third party.

Now let us see how the case would have stood had the opinion of the House been taken *seriatim* on each allegation.

It cannot be known how many Members joined in opinion respectively with Mr. Pitt and Mr. Fox; but as the number was 119, it will be fair to state them as equal---that is, 60 on one side, and 60 on the other. We will suppose the question first to have been put by Mr. Fox, on the criminality of demanding a war subsidy from Cheyt Sing. Mr. Pitt and his Partizans would have voted that it was not criminal but meritorious; and to their number 60, the number of the third party, which is 79, being added, would have made 139 against 60, for rejecting the question.

If after this, the question of the criminality of the intention of finding had been put by Mr. Pitt, this too would in like manner have been rejected by 139 against 60, and the charge thus wholly dismissed; whereas, by blending two different propositions in one question, the charge was carried by the union of two parties, entertaining sentiments diametrically opposite in the same question.

The charge so voted in 1786, and reduced to the form of an article in 1787, was supported by the Managers in 1788, answered in 1792, and now in this year 1794, and on this day Mr. Grey replied to the evidence of the Counsel.

Mr. Grey took up a considerable time in replying to a charge brought against the Managers, of wilfully garbling and misrepresenting facts, both in the mode in which the article was drawn, and in the mode in which the Managers supported it.

He

He said the charge was serious, heavy, and that it was a charge against the House of Commons, whose Representatives they were. He then went through the different instances, with what success we do not presume to say, but a short relation of the main fact may help the public judgment.

In January 1775, Sujah Dowlah died. Mr. Hastings contended, that the Treaties subsisting between the States of Oude and Bengal did not cease by the death of the Sovereign of Oude.--- The majority, Messrs. Clavering, Monson, and Francis, voted, That they did cease and that they had a right to conclude a new Treaty, exacting the best terms they could for the Company. Being out voted, Mr. Hastings made a new proposition, which was, that Cheyt Sing should be made a Sovereign, subject only to the payment of a certain sum, half of which Bengal was to receive, and half the Sovereign of Oude. This proposition was also negatived.

Now, the charge brought against the Managers is this---that they applied the reasons offered by Mr. Hastings, to support a proposition that was negatived, to a proposition afterwards made, and which was accepted. The question is very simple: Upon what principle could the Managers reason in support of Rights, which Cheyt Sing really possessed? Not surely from any arguments

o o 2   urged

urged by Mr. Hastings to induce the majority to confer Sovereign Rights upon him, which they would not confer, but from the actual Rights conferred upon him by Treaty, not from any resolution they found in February, as to what should form an article in a Treaty not then executed, but from what was really contained in the Treaty itself when executed. We then come at last to this simple point---Was, or was not Cheyt Sing bound to afford Military assistance to his Sovereign the Company, in war? and Mr. Grey put it upon this issue---a point we again say (and lament it as a very great misfortune), that the Commons, to this hour, never did come to a specific vote upon.

Mr. Grey put this question upon its true ground, and he contended that Mr. Hastings had no right, under existing engagements, to demand a subsidy from Cheyt Sing in war. He very candidly admitted that Mr. Hastings had fairly refuted one allegation in the charge, that is, that he acted under the pretence of a war. Mr. Hastings having fully proved that he had received such information from Lord Stormont, (now Earl of Mansfield) as made it his duty to provide against the evils which might result from a war, to which Europe owed all the evils that it now experienced, and the greater with which she is threatened---meaning the

the American war, in which the late Monarch of France had the folly to take a part.

The remainder of Mr. Grey's speech was employed in the defence of Mr. Francis's conduct, in the course of which, he stated one fact, that totally exculpates Mr. Hastings even upon Mr. Grey's principles. It was this :—That when Mr. Hastings, in 1778, proposed to call on Cheyt Sing for a war subsidy, Mr. Francis expressed a doubt as to our right to make such a demand, though he acquiesced in its being made. That Mr. Hastings expressed his firm conviction of the right, adding that we were precluded by no engagements from increasing the power inherited in every State, of calling in all its subjects for extraordinary aids in times of extraordinary emergencies; but as Mr. Francis had doubts, he proposed to leave the Question of Right to be determined by the Court of Directors. We are at a loss to know how abilities, eloquence, or quibble, can get the better of this fact. Mr. Hastings acting under a delegated authority, acts according to his judgment. If he acted wrong the Directors were to set him right, which they could have done in one year. They received the benefit of the exaction; but we forbear to push this observation further, until we hear what Mr. Grey says, on Mr. Pitt's full acquiescence in Mr. Hastings's opinion of the

right,

right, and until we hear what he says, of this nation having benefited to the amount of six millions sterling by the expulsion of Cheyt Sing, and their renewing the Charter of the Company for twenty years, taking to itself two hundred thousand pounds a year from Benares, which is, in Mr. Grey's doctrine, a direct robbery.

Mr. Grey, as a fair and candid man, will not place the supposed occurrence of the House of Commons, in opposition to positive facts. He knows that this House never did give an opinion as to the right of taxing Cheyt Sing, and that that question never was specifically voted by the last Parliament.

At twenty minutes after three, Mr. Grey begged to retire, being ill and fatigued; at his desire the Court adjourned to Monday.

We are sorry that of twenty Managers, no one was ready to proceed, though the Commons this year sent a message to the Lords, to inform them that they were ready to proceed day by day if their Lordships thought proper.

ONE HUNDRED AND THIRTY-FOURTH DAY. May 12.

The Court met on this day before half-past twelve o'clock, being very thinly attended, though the

the auditors were numerous, when Mr. Grey immediately proceeded to close his summary evidence in reply on the first Article. He began by repeating the substance of his last speech, and very fairly admitted that the point of Right to demand assistance from Cheyt Sing in war, was the main point on which the innocence or guilt of Mr. Hastings must turn. He lamented that he could not be more amusing, but he said that the subject, though dry, was of the utmost importance.

Mr. Grey's speech, for the first hour, was chiefly a defence of the consistency of Mr. Francis, in which we say with deference that Mr. Grey completely failed---Not that it is of the least consequence in the decision of this cause, for we fully subscribe to the justice of a remark made by Mr. Grey, that to fix on the House of Commons the justice of the charge of inconsistency in not impeaching Mr. Francis, would by no means exculpate Mr. Hastings.

The plain and simple fact, stripped of oratory on both sides, is this—

That in July 1778, Mr. Hastings proposed to call upon Cheyt Sing to maintain three battalions of Sepoys during the war, of which they had then received intelligence.

That

That Mr. Francis concurred in the demand, though he expressed doubts as to the right.

That Mr. Hastings most clearly expressed his opinion as to that right; the Company, as Sovereigns, not being precluded by any existing engagements, from exercising the right inherent in all States, to call upon their subjects for extraordinary aids, in times of extraordinary emergency, and that Mr. Hastings expressly referred the question of right to be settled by the Court of Directors.

That on Cheyt Sing demurring to pay the Subsidy, Mr. Francis again expressed his doubts as to the right, and Mr. Hastings again expressed his clear conviction of the Company possessing the right.

In 1779, Mr. Hastings again proposed, that Cheyt Sing should pay five Lacks for that year, and that Mr. Francis concurred; but on Cheyt Sing demurring, Mr. Francis again expressed his doubts as to the right, and his opinion that Cheyt Sing had not the ability to oppose the compulsory measures which Mr. Hastings proposed to adopt.

That in 1780, Mr. Hastings again proposed to call upon Cheyt Sing for his subsidy. That Mr. Francis concurred; and on the usual delays being made, Mr. Francis also concurred in a proposition for marching troops to compel the payment; and

in

in a proposition for exacting a fine of one Lack of Rupees for his contumacy, the words of Mr. Francis were—" I acquiesce, though I hope the " threat will be sufficient." These are the Facts stripped of all ornament, and the world will draw their own conclusions.

After going through these points, Mr. Grey came to a further demand of cavalry, which Cheyt Sing was required to furnish. He admitted that Mr. Francis did concur in this demand; but he said, that finding opposition ineffectual, Mr. Francis was was then nearly about to quit Bengal, and did, in fact, embark for Europe the month after the demand was made.—Mr. Grey, in the fullest manner made that admission which the late House of Commons never would admit, namely, that rhe distress of the Company's affairs in November 1780, was to the full as great as the Council of Mr. Hastings had stated it to be. Mr. Grey imputed to Mr. Hastings the demand of cavalry from Cheyt Sing. The fact is as follows:

At the close of September, 1780, the Supreme Council of Bengal received advice of the defeat of Col. Baillie in the Carnatic, the retreat of Sir Hector Munro to Madras, and the expectation of a French armament.

In

In addition to this intelligence, 30,000 Maratta Horse were on the borders of Bengal, near Midnapore, and another body of Marattas was expected to invade Bahar. In this perilous state, Mr. Hastings proposed to send ample assistance to the Carnatic, and he requested Sir Eyre Coote himself to take the command of the army on the coast. He also requested Sir Eyre Coote, prior to his departure, to give the Supreme Council his ideas of the best mode of defending Bengal against the dangers that surrounded it. Sir Eyre Coote did so, and he proposed, as one measure, to form a camp in Bahar, to be composed of certain battalions, and as many cavalry as could be procured from Cheyt Sing. The Board (Mr. Francis concurring) requested Mr. Hastings to write to Cheyt Sing for Cavalry. Such is the origin of the demand for Cavalry, which Mr. Hastings is charged with having made, in order to harrass, oppress, and ruin Cheyt Sing.

After this, Mr. Grey came to the period of Mr. Hastings going to Benares, in July 1781 ; and here he made a pointed reference to the state of home Politics at this moment. He said Mr. Hastings went to Benares, intending to exact Five Hundred Thousand Pounds from Cheyt Sing, for his delinquencies, in aid of the Company's distresses. He reminded their Lordships, that

this

this nation was engaged at this moment in a war of the utmost difficulty and danger---a war which had brought great distress upon the country; and they had the melancholy prospect of that distress increasing considerably before they should meet again to give their judgment on this important cause. Suppose one of his Majesty's Ministers was to propose, if Mr. Hastings should be convicted, that a large fine should be exacted from him, in order to case the people of the burthens brought upon them by this necessary war. God forbid, said Mr. Grey, that such should be the law of this country. He wished their Lordships would reject so monstrous a doctrine. He said he fully concurred with the Counsel, that if the main and principal act were proper in Mr. Hastings, he meant exacting a War Subsidy, and if Cheyt Sing had been guilty of the contumacy with which he was charged, then the proposed fine of Five Hundred Thousand Pounds was not enormous; on the contrary, the expulsion of Cheyt Sing was a proper measure.

Mr. Grey, after commenting on the evidence, adverted to the remarks of the Counsel on the difference of opinion subsisting in the late House, as to the point of criminality in this charge. He did not think it quite decent in the Counsel to allude to it, but since they had, he would notice it.

it. It was perfectly true, that a Gentleman of great influence, and whose talents he admired, though he differed from him in politics, had given it as his clear and decided opinion, that Mr. Hastings was warranted in making the demands he did on Cheyt Sing—an opinion to which neither he (Mr. Grey) nor those who conducted this Impeachment could subscribe to; but that Mr. Pitt thought it criminal to intend to impose so large a fine upon him,

Mr. Grey did not pursue this to any conclusion; either he should not have alluded to this difference of opinion at all, or he ought to have stated all the points of difference.

Mr. Pitt not only most fully stated the right which Mr. Hastings had to make these several demands that are stated to be criminal in his articles; but that the prevarication and contumacy of Cheyt Sing was such, as justly to subject him to punishment. The offence of Mr. Hastings, in Mr. Pitt's idea, was the enormous amount of the intended fine. The complaint of Mr. Hastings is, and it is the first and great cause of the duration of the Trial—that the sense of the late House never was taken on the separate allegations in the Article.—Mr. Pitt also stated his clear opinion, that there was no evidence to warrant the conclusion, that Mr. Hastings was actuated by malice, yet he is charged,

charged with doing all that he did from malicious motives. Take away the charge of malice, and allow the right to demand a subsidy—what then becomes of Mr. Fox, and the Managers?

Mr. Grey at the close contended, that if the Lords adopted the opinion of the Managers, Mr. Hastings would merit a severe punishment. If they adopted the opinion of Mr. Pitt, he would deserve some punishment, because, though no fine had in fact been imposed, it was clear Mr. Hastings intended to impose one. He ran cursorily over the remaining part of the observations of the Counsel, and made no remarks on Mr. Dallas's conclusion on the nature of British justice.

The fact, however, is, that Cheyt Sing had been now expelled nearly thirteen years; in that period, the Nation has received six millions sterling, every shilling of which is a robbery and plunder from Cheyt Sing, if he were unjustly expelled, and the nation has consented to receive from Benares, for twenty years to come, two hundred thousand pounds a year more than they have a right to receive, provided his expulsion was unjust.

Mr. Grey concluded his summary by taking a ground totally different from that on which the charge was originally entertained, Mr. Grey seemed to feel the weakness of his case. It was first
brought

brought on and first argued in a manly way---
That Mr. Hastings had made demands contrary to
treaty---That his motive for making the demand
was ma'ice, and his object to ruin Cheyt Sing.----
At the close, Mr. Grey allowed that Mr. Pitt justified the right to make the demands, and scouted
the charge of malice. But Mr. Grey contended,
that if the Lords should concur with Mr. Pitt,
still the proposed punishment exceeded the actual
offence. Is there then an Englishman who will
not lament, that at the close of the seventh year
of a trial, it shou'd be a matter of doubt whether
the Commons, who voted to impeach Mr. Hastings, did vote upon the narrow ground Mr. Pitt
put the matter, or upon the broad ground on
which the Managers originally put it. Such is the
consequence of voting charges in a lump, and we
trust it will operate as an example in all future
impeachments.

The ground of the Benares charge is malice,
and the various demands made by Mr. Hastings
on Cheyt Sing, were stated to be made with a
view of harrassing, oppressing, and finally ruining
him, in order to gratify the malice that Mr. Hastings had conceived. The proof of the malice
Mr. Grey said, though not clear, was fairly to be
inferred from the circumstance of Mr. Hastings
having stated in his Narrative and Defence, that

it

it was highly indecent, and presumptuous in Cheyt Sing so far to interfere in the unfortunate political dispute of Bengal, as to send a Vakeel to congratulate General Clavering on his supposed accession to the Government of Bengal, at the time he attempted to seize it by violence. Mr. Pitt had treated such a proof with the utmost derision and contempt when it was offered to justify the charge in the House of Commons.

Another proof that Mr. Hastings was actuated by malice was this: that no demands had been made on the Zemindars of Bengal. It has already been stated, in reply to this observation, that the lands of Bengal were let, either at their utmost value, or which is the same, at an amouut which was supposed to be the utmost the lands would yield.

But the supposition, the most extraordinary in Mr. Grey's Speech was, that if Mr. Hastings should be convicted, one of the King's Ministers, on Mr. Hastings's principles, might propose to ease the burthens of the people, by imposing a large fine upon him. Let us bring this argument to the test of common sense: Suppose, as Mr. Grey did, that the Lords were to take up Mr. Pitt's idea, and to think that Mr. Hastings, by the Constitution of India, had a right to call upon

Cheyt

Cheyt Sing for extraordinary aids in time of extraordinary emergencies. Suppose them to reject,
as absurd and impossible, (as Mr. Pitt did), the
charge of malice, which is, in fact, the foundation
of the whole. Suppose them to think (as Mr.
Pitt professed to do) that the conduct of Cheyt
Sing was in the highest degree contumacious, and
merited severe punishment, and suppose them to
be of opinion, that the proposed fine of fifty
lacks did exceed the actual offence, then the question would be, whether upon the principles of
Mr. Hastings, one of the King's Ministers could
propose to relieve the public exigencies of this
country, by imposing a large fine upon him.

Mr. Hastings, in July 1781, was surrounded
with difficulties; he could not do as Mr. Pitt does;
he could not borrow as many millions as he wanted, and tax posterity with the interest of the debt.
He had, in fact, borrowed as much money as he
could get, before July 1781, and the Carnatic,
and Bombay, looked to him for the pay and subsistence of their armies.

Under such circumstances he intended to levy
a fine of forty or fifty lacks of rupees, from a man
who had been guilty of various acts of contumacy
and disobedience, and to employ that money in
relief of the pressing exigencies of the state over
which

which Mr. Hastings presided. He believed, and he thought right, that this sum did not exceed a third of the money in Cheyt Sing's possession. In pursuance of his plan, Cheyt Sing was put under an arrest. He was rescued, flew to arms, was victorious in the first instance, but in a month totally expelled from his Zemindary, carrying with him the principal part of his treasures. A new settlement was formed, by which the State gained an additional revenue of two hundred thousand pounds a year, which it has received from 1781, to this time, a period of nearly thirteen years.

Were the King's Minister to take up Mr. Grey's idea, we know not how it could apply to the case before us; Mr. Hastings intended merely to take four or five hundred thousand pounds from Cheyt Sing, a powerful and disaffected subject, but to leave him the remainder of his wealth, and the undisturbed possession of his Zemindary. His expulsion was the consequence of his resistance; and the State acquired an addition of 200,000l. a year, which, with principal and interest, added to the money taken at Bidjygur, makes about six millions sterling. If it were an enormous oppression to propose to take 4 or 500,000l. from Cheyt Sing, surely his expulsion is a greater act of violence, and calls loudly for redress.

Mark

Mark then what would be the consequence! The nation has spent One Hundred Thousand Pounds on this Trial: That money is lost and gone for ever. But even a part of it could not be recovered under the shape of a fine from Mr. Hastings, without the firmest conviction in the mind of every honest man, that Cheyt Sing ought instantly to be restored to Benares, and to receive from this country every rupee that has been unjustly taken from him. In this manner the Managers have invariably argued, and they have spoke the language of justice and common sense. The same Minister, therefore, who carries to the Exchequer the fine of Mr. Hastings, must drain the Exchequer of thirty-four millions, seven hundred and ten thousand pounds; for of that sum has Great Britain robbed India, through the agency of Mr. Hastings, provided there be truth in the language of the Gentlemen who have conducted the Impeachment. We think Mr. Grey argues fairly and seldom widely; but we have stated this instance, in order to shew that the ablest men will sometimes push an argument too far,

ONE

ONE HUNDRED AND THIRTY-FIFTH DAY. *May* 15.

————————

Mr. Sheridan performed his promise to the Lords, and finished what he had to offer in two hours and forty minutes. His speech was replete wit with and humour. The argumentative parts of his speech took up very little time, but he replied at considerable length to the animadversion of the Counsel of Mr. Hastings, on Mr. Sheridan's former speech. He justified himself from a very severe charge brought against him by Mr. Law, of having asked Mr. Middleton a question, and misleading him in his answer, by a paper that he put into his hand. He said it was the late Earl Camden who had asked the question which Mr. Law had supposed to come from the Manager.

He contended, that not one piece of evidence produced by the Managers had been disproved during the defence. He said, that much time had been taken by Counsel in their speeches, in order to prove points which he conceived of very

little

little importance to the cause. He ran very cursorily through the evidence, and said, though
it was very true that the belief of the disaffection
of the Begum obtained very generallry throughout India, it was rather a proof of the success of
Mr. Hastings's scheme, than any thing else. That
it was exceedingly improbable the Begum should
be concerned in rebellion, and said that the
evidence of two Nujeebs being taken in arms
at Pateeta, did not weigh in his mind. That
in this stage of the business he should think
all warm and intemperate expressions highly improper, and therefore should abstain from using
them.

In conclusion, Mr. Sheridan said, that the
Counsel had endeavoured to deter their Lordships from finding a verdict against Mr. Hastings,
by stating, that Six Hundred Thousand Pounds
had been taken from him for the public service
at a moment of great public exigency: that it
had all been employed in the public service, and
that the Nation, knowing of the transaction a few
months after it had taken place, had full opportunity of redressing the wrong nearly twelve years
ago. That it was impossible to vote that Mr.
Hastings had acted wrong, unless they were prepared to do full and complete justice to those who
had been injured.

Mr.

Mr. Sheridan said, he joined issue with the Counsel—he fully concurred with them: but such was his idea of the justice of their Lordships, that he was convinced they never would be deterred from doing justice from a dread of the consequences—Œconomical as the House of Commons was, he never could believe that they would deny justice to the people of India, because justice could not be done to them, without calling upon the people of England for a very heavy payment. For his own part, convinced as he was, that on this article Mr. Hastings was guilty of having taken from the Begum a large sum of money for the public, on a charge of rebellion, which was ill-founded, he was ready to avow, that it would be impossible to declare Mr. Hastings guilty, without giving to the Begum compleat restitution of all that had been taken from her, principal and interest. It was stated to amount to two millions sterling.

The Counsel had assumed, that the Benares Charge also was totally disproved; but they argued in the same manner, that if it were not disproved the Nation was bound to restore to Cheyt Sing, to call him from his present miserable situation, whether in a Maratta or a Mysore Camp, to pay back to him the Millions which had been brought into the Exchequer by his expulsion, and

to

to place him precisely in the state in which he stood when he was driven from Benares thirteen years ago. He would go further—every person injured by the acts of Mr. Hastings had a right to full retribution, or there was no justice in the prosecution of the Commons ; but he hoped their Lordships would not be deterred from their duty by such considerations. The Commons were not prosecuting for personal purposes. No. It was to do justice to India ; and to suppose that if it should appear the people of India were injured, this nation would merely stop at condemning the man who had injured them, while the nation received the advantages arising from his injustice, was a libel upon the country. Mr. Sheridan pursued this line of argument with infinite ability for some time, and concluded by thanking their Lordships for their indulgence, and by lamenting the length of this Trial, as a most heavy grievance, though he said he would not enter now into the cause of its protraction.

ONE HUNDRED AND THIRTY-SIXTH DAY. *May* 17.

Mr. Fox began soon after one, by stating that it was his duty, however harsh it may be, to enforce,

force, in the last stage of it, that charge which he had summed up many years ago. He proceeded to divide the subject of presents into two periods : the first, the sums alledged to have been received in 1772.

Mr. Fox, in considering this subject, said, that when Mr. Hastings removed Mahomed Reza Cawn, 1772, by order of the Court of Directors, the charge of the Commons was, that Mr. Hastings had virtually appointed Muny Begum to the office which Mahomed Reza Cawn had held ; which appointment was, the entire government of Bengal, and the entire conduct and management of its finances.

Mr. Dallas had contended, that Mr. Hastings had done no such thing. On the contrary, Mr. Hastings had totally abolished the office which Mahomed Reza Cawn held ; that he had taken upon himself and his Council the entire management of the revenues which Mahomed Reza Cawn had controuled ; and that in fact and truth, Muny Begum had no power, except in the household of the Nabob. This is a fact so clear, that no child who has been in India can dispute it.

Mr. Fox then said, that Muny Begum was the Step-mother of the Nabob, and therefore not so proper for the Guardianship as the Nabob's Mother. Mr. Fox, in this part of his argument, to-

tally

tally abandoned the assertion of the Commons, which was, in fact, that the Government of Bengal was delivered up to Muny Begum by Mr. Hastings.

After a long argument, Mr. Fox came to the real point of the charge, which was, that Mr. Hastings made the appointment for money ; Mr. Hastings admitted that one Lack and a half of Rupees had been received for entertainment, which sum the Manager contended was a bribe received by Mr. Hastings for an appointment to an important office.

Mr. Fox spent a considerable time in going into presumptions, as to the other sums charged to have been received ; but at last the whole turns upon this sum of one and a half lack of rupees, which Mr. Hastings confessed to have received, and which he never did deny having received.——Most fortunately, for the honour of Mr. Hastings, and for the cause of justice, Mr. Fox had the candour to bring forward a decisive piece of evidence in reply, which Mr. Hastings's Counsel had most anxiously wished to produce ; but it was not discovered while the defence was depending. It totally cuts up the whole argument of the bribe from Muny Begum.

Mr. Fox called Mr. Wright, the Auditor of India Accounts, and asked him :

Q. " From

Q. " From the time of Meer Jaffier to the ac-
" cession of Mr. Hastings, do there appear any
" allowances for the expences of an English Go-
" vernor on the accounts of the Company?

A. " Not in the accounts of the Company.---
" The book I have before me is called the Trea-
" sury Accounts with the Nizamut. There is an
" entry in the Belah Establishment for the month
" of Suffa Sun, 7th of the reign under the head
" of Morta Prucka. Paid charges of entertain-
" ing Lord Clive, 23,000 rupees. For the month
" of Suffa Sun, 8th of the reign. By the Hon.
" Harry Verelst paid him for his daily charges
" 2000 rupees a day, 96,000 rupees. These are
" all the entries prior to the accession of Mr.
" Hastings, for the expences of that kind."

Here, then, is proof positive that Mr. Hastings
did precisely what Mr. Verelst (described by Mr.
Burke as one of the honestest men in the world)
and Lord Clive had done before him. As long as
Mr. Hastings was at Moorshedabad in 1772, he
received, as Mr. Verelst had done in 1769, 2000
rupees a day, agreeably to established practices.---
It is self-evident, therefore, that whether Mr.
Hastings had appointed Muny Begum, or the Nabob's Mother, or any other person, to be guar-
dian of the Nabob, he would equally have received 2000 rupees a day, as long as he remained

at

at Moorshedabad. It could not, therefore, be a
bribe for an appointment to office; and to the honour of Mr. Fox be it said, that his justice induced him to make this point clear to the whole
world by his evidence. Upon all the other sums
charged to have been received, not one shadow
of evidence was adduced; and, indeed, Mr. Fox,
in 1790, gave up the whole, except the lack and
a half; and he has now put this transaction in so
fair and so clear a light, that malice herself can no
longer misrepresent it.

Mr. Fox argued on the presumption of Mr.
Hastings having been guilty, because upon the
death of General Clavering and Colonel Monson,
he re-appointed Muny Begum to that office, from
which that Gentleman, and Mr. Francis had removed her. He recapitulated his argument, and
proved very fully, that while Mr. Hastings was at
Moorshedabad. in 1772, he had received from the
Treasury of the Nizam, 2000 rupees a day for
entertainment, in the same manner that Lord
Clive and Mr. Verelst had done; of the bribes
there was no proof, and they rest upon certain
papers, which were submitted to the inspection
of the Company's Lawyers in 1776, who pronounced upon them, that the charges could not
be true.

Having concluded this part of his case, Mr.
Fox said he should now come to those presents
which

which Mr. Hastings had received, subsequent
to the Act of Parliament, the receipt of which
he publicly avowed, as well as his application of
them to the public service. He contended that
to receive presents after the Act of 1773, was
against law, and that Mr. Hastings must of course
be found guilty, though he received them with
the purest intentions, but that he should proceed
to state the circumstances under which they had
been taken, and the presumption that parts of
them at least were intended, at the time they were
taken, to increase the private fortune of Mr.
Hastings, though he afterwards changed that intention. Mr. Fox said, that Mr. Dallas by mis-
quoting the words in a clause of the Act of 1773,
had materially changed the sense of the passage,
he supposed that was accident, and not design; but
if the clause had been truly quoted, Mr. Fox
affirmed that it could not bear the sense put upon
it by Mr. Dallas.

As this was a subject of some length, if it was
agreeable to their Lordships, he would break off
here.

As the Court was rising, Mr. Hastings most
earnestly implored the Lords to consider the state
of the Sessions—that much time had lately been
lost, owing to the indisposition of the Managers,
and he dreaded the adjournment to another year.

That

That the illness of one Gentleman, Mr. Grey, was apparent, and another Hon. Manager had applied, as he understood, to postpone the Trial, on account of indisposition, from Friday last, to another day, though he had afterwards seen the Hon. Manager in the Park, on horseback. That he had been often ill during the Trial, and twice rose from his bed in a very high fever to attend in the Hall.

He prayed, therefore, that the Lords would go on so as to finish in this year; and then did not care how many days they sat.

Mr. Fox said, that in the situation of the Gentleman at the bar, he could well excuse any warmth of expression from him.—That it was true he had written to the Noble Lord who presided in the absence of the Chancellor, and said, that though he was ready to go on (as Friday last) yet if it would not occasion any material delay, he wished to postpone it, as he was indisposed. That it was true he did ride out, which might be rather imprudent for a person indisposed as he was ; but that, unless indisposed, he would not have expressed a distant wish for an alteration of the day.

Mr. Burke instantly rose, and said that Mr. Hastings was perpetually complaining, but that while the Managers were serving in this cause for
nothing,

nothing, the Criminal had Ninety Thousand Pounds of Nobkissin's money in his pocket.

ONE HUNDRED AND THIRTY-SEVENTH DAY. *May* 19.

THE Court met at a quarter before three, when Mr. Fox in a very handsome manner acknowledged that Mr. Dallas had not misquoted the Act, and that his argument was consequently fair; that the confusion arose from his (Mr. Fox) adverting to the 24th and not to the 23d clause of the Regugulating Act. Having done this full justice to Mr. Dallas, Mr. Fox proceeded to animadvert on the defence read by Mr. Hastings to the House of Lords in 1791. He said that Mr. Hastings in that defence had declared, that if he had mistaken the Act, every man with whom he had conversed or corresponded, had been in a similar error.— Mr. Fox lamented that the Counsel could not answer him, but he challenged the whole world to dispute his statement, and he added, that when Mr. Hastings took upon himself to state any thing as a fact, he was sure to be mistaken. Mr. Hastings had asserted in his defence in 1791, before the Lords, that if he was in an error in thinking that the Act of 1773, did preclude the receipt of presents even for the Company, every man with whom he conversed or corresponded, was in a similar

similar error. To prove that this assertion was not true, Mr. Fox read a partial selection from a debate at the Council Board at Calcutta, in October 1774; but if he had read the whole debate, it would have fixed the truth of Mr. Hastings's assertion beyond all doubt—The real statement we now give :—

Mr. Hastings brought on the 23d of October, 1774, two bags, one of gold and one of silver to the Council, being small presents that he had received since the regulation act had taken place in August—He left it to the Board to decide, whether he should continue *as* Governor General to receive those presents, and the following resolution passed instantly.

" Ordered, That the money be sent to the cash,
" and carried on account to the Company's cre-
" dit, under the head of Nuzzers, and that what-
" ever sums may be hereafter tendered by the
" Governor, be received and credited in the same
" manner" The question then is, Whether the argument of General Clavering and Mr. Francis which followed, applied to presents received by the Governor for his own use, or whether it meant to apply to an universal prohibition ? This is the whole point. The minutes prove that the subsequent debate turned upon what a Member might do under the law. General Clavering, and Mr. Francis said, that to receive presents was against law,

law, applying it to presents received by any man for his own use. They had previoufly determined the point of receiving them for the public.

Mr. Hastings insists upon it, that neither General Clavering nor Mr. Francis, nor the Directors, nor the King's Ministers, had ever expressed a doubt of its being competent to Mr. Hastings to receive money, if it were to be applied to the public service.

General Clavering and Mr. Francis agreed to receive the Rohilla prize-money, as a deposit for the Company, and to be disposed of hereafter as the Company chose. This was a present to the Army ; and in 1784, in Mr. Pitt's Administration, that money was given to the Army. When General Clavering sat in the Chair, in the absence of Mr. Hastings, he received a Nuzzer from the Zemindar of Burdwan, and sent it to the Treasury.

When Colonel Upton made the Mahratta Peace in 1776, he received a present, and was ordered to pay the amount of into the Treasury. When Mr. Hastings wrote to the Directors, in January 1784, that he had received a present of ten lacks of rupees from the Nabob Vizier, the Directors wrote to him in January 1783, with the concurrence of the King's Ministers, that the act precluded them from giving that present to him, if they were inclined to do so ; that the Act said, that all presents received should be construed to

be

be received to and for the sole use of the Com-. pany. That they approved of the intention of Mr. Hastings to appropriate the whole ten lacks to the public service, and directed him strictly to abide by the Act of Parliament. Now, if there is sense or meaning in language, it is clear that the Directors conceived Mr. Hastings might receive presents provided they were employed in the public service; but it does not stop even here.— The Directors in March 1784, when Mr. Pitt was the Minister, wrote to Mr. Hastings that they did not doubt his integrity; that after having received the several presents, they approved of his having paid them into the Treasury.

In no one Letter, is Mr. Hastings told, that to receive presents, and to apply them to the use of the Company is illegal. No such idea, from any act that was done, appears to be taken up any where;—and the fact undoubtedly is, that all men in India, and as far as we know from their acts, every man in England did believe prior to Mr. Pitt's Act, which is explicit and clear as to the future, that it was not illegal for a Governor to receive presents, and to apply them to the Public Service.

Mr. Hastings is, therefore, completely warranted in asserting, that neither in conversation, nor in correspondence, did he ever hear it doubted, that the Governor General, though precluded

from

from receiving presents for his own use or behalf, might receive them for the Company. If further proofs were wanting, what shall we say to the Aſts of the King's Ministers, who knowing as early as July 1782, that Mr. Hastings had received and applied more than 200,000l. as presents for their service, have kept the money from that time to this----when the amount, principal and interest, is more than 600,000l.

Having stated that Mr. Hastings must be convicted for receiving presents against law, it being a crime to receive presents, even though they were applied to the public service ; he entered into a very long and ingenious train of reason, in order to shew the presumption to be, that when Mr. Hastings received these several sums, or at least a part of them, he did really intend to apply them to his own use. The great argument was, that Mr. Hastings had appealed to Mr. Larkins, as being privy to the whole process of the receipt of these several presents, whereas it appeared, on the examination, that he was not acquainted with these transaſtions until the 22d of May, 1782.----We are confident that the same honourable and fair sentiments which pervaded the mind of Mr. Fox, when he produced evidence in reply, that totally exculpated Mr. Hastings from having received 2000 rupees a day from Muny Begum as

Q Q   a bribe,

a bribe, still have their influence over him, and that he will rejoice to be informed from undoubted evidence, that his whole arguments rested on a fallacy which will be apparent to him and the whole World, when fairly stated.

In May 1782, Mr. Hastings wrote to the Directors, that he had received and applied to their service 200,000l. presents made to himself; that these sums were received for their use, at a time the Company much needed them, and that if they wished for further information, he was ready to answer upon honour, or upon oath, to any questions the Court might put to him.

This Letter reached England in May 1782, when Mr. Fox was the Minister. No sort of notice was taken of it until March 1784, when Mr. Pitt was the Minister, Mr. Fox having been thrown out on the failure of his India Bill.

The Directors, with the concurrence of Mr. Pitt, wrote to Bengal, that they had received the letter of Mr. Hastings, stating the amount of the presents he had received---that they did not mean to express a doubt of his integrity; on the contrary, after having received these presents they cannot avoid expressing their approbation of his conduct in bringing them to the credit of the Company; yet the statement appears so unintelligible

telligible, that they desire Mr. Hastings to answer three questions. He having voluntarily offered to answer any questions they might put to him.

These questions were :

1st. At what period was each sum received?

2d. What were the motives of Mr. Hastings for concealing the knowledge of these receipts from the Council?

3d. Why were bonds taken for part of those sums, and others entered as deposits?

To this Letter Mr. Hastings replied from Cheltenham. The two latter questions he replied to. The first he answered as well as he could, by saying, that he believed the sums were received nearly at the time they were paid into the Treasury, but that he would refer them to Mr. Larkins for a more particular answer to that first question, or for any investigation respecting the particulars of this transaction, as Mr. Larkins, was privy to every process of it, and possessed, as Mr. Hastings believed, the only memorandum which he ever kept on the subject.

Mr. Fox contended, that the words every process of it, meant the trasaction from first to last, a conclusion which no man living will draw who reads the letter of the Directors to which the

letter

letter of Mr. Hasting is an answer. The fallacy that the subject is taken up piecemeal. The letter of Mr. Hastingss from Cheltenham, and the letter of Mr. Larkins from Bengal, are applied as an answer to an accusation of the Commons, with which it has nothing to do ; and Mr. Larkins, in Westminster Hall, said, that his letter was merely an answer to a letter from Mr. Hastings, and consequently, confined to the subject of that letter. The most cruel part of the business, as it respects Mr. Hastings, is this, that his answer to the letter of the Directors, has been read in Westminster-hall, as it were an answer to the Charge of the the House of Commons.

Mr. Fox contended, that the expression in the letter from Cheltenham, and in Mr. Hastings's defence, conveyed this meaning, that from the first Mr. Larkins was privy to the money transactions of Mr. Hastings, whereas Mr. Larkins swears that he knew nothing of them until the 22d of May 1780, according to his recollection; but Mr. Fox omitted to relate another part of Mr. Larkin's testimony, which puts the matter in a very different view—for Mr. Larkins swore, that though he did not recollect being told by Mr. Hastings prior to the 22d of May 1780, that the bonds were the property of the Company, he must have had some information on the subject, or he should

should have received, on account of Mr. Hastings, the interests due upon these Bonds as it became due; whereas, in point of fact, he had never
received any interest upon them. Every thing
that genius and ingenuity could do, was done by
Mr. Fox, in order to convince the Lords that
Mr. Hastings did intend at one time to apply part
of these presents to his own use. He lamented that
the Council could not speak after him, and gave so
fair a challenge to all the world to refute his reasoning, that we shall proceed with our observations, as
we state the several parts of his speech—Mr. Fox's
argument, was intended to shew, that tho' Mr.
Hastings had ultimately paid into the Treasury all the money that he received, there was the
strongest reason to believe, that for a time, at
least, he intended to appropriate a part of these
sums to his own use, which was a substantial
crime, as it most undoubtedly is; if the evidence is clear upon this point, the Lords
must pronounce Mr. Hastings guilty. The proof
he contended, was clear from the false and contradictory accounts that Mr. Hastings had given
of these money transactions, and that these accounts were false and contradictory, appeared from the evidence of Mr. Larkins, which Mr.
Fox quoted. The question then is, did Mr. Fox
quote Mr. Larkins's evidence fairly? That he

meant

meant so to do, we are confident ; but he omitted the most material part of it. It turns altogether upon Three Bonds, which were taken by Mr. Hastings, in his own name. One dated in November, 1780; and the other two in October, 1780.

These bonds were for four Lacks and six thousand Rupees, or 40,000 l. and were apparently the property of Mr. Hastings from the 5th of January 1781 to the 22d of May 1782 —It is clear from the Evidence, that he never meant to apply *any Part* of the remaining £. 160,000 to his own use. The *whole Sum* received and accounted for was £. 200,000 independent of Nobkissen's present. On the 22d of May 1782, Mr. Hastings wrote to the Directors, that the Bonds were not his property. An inference might be drawn, that from the year 1780, and until the end of May 1782, Mr. Hastings really intended to convert this money to his own use ; but to obviate this inference, Mr. Hastings *had said*, that Mr. Larkins knew from the first, that the bonds were not his property ; and further, that prior to his going to Benares in July 1781, he had written on the back of each bond, that they were not his property, and that he left the bonds with Mr. Larkins. Mr. Fox said that this account was *false*, for though the bonds were left
with

with Mr. Larkins, the date of the indorfement was not prior to July 1781, as Mr. Hastings had asserted, but on the 29th of May 1782.

The first material question is, by what means was this falsehood, as Mr. Fox calls it, detected; Not by the Managers; but by the *eagerness* of Mr. Hastings to put the *truth* of his assertion *beyond a doubt*. This induced him first to search the India Houfe for the bonds, and on their not being found, he desired Mr. Larkins in Bengal, would make a public application *to Lord Corn-wallis*, that the Bonds might be fearched for, and, if found, that they might be sent to the Company, which they were, and, as his Lordship states, at the desire of Mr. Hastings. The bonds arrived, and on the indorfement being adverted to, it appeared most clearly that they were not dated prior to July 1782, but on the 29th of May, 1782.

We admit that the mistake *is clear*; how far the epithet *false* can be applied to the Act, *is another point*; for we think the justice of the following reflection must strike every honest man. Mr. Hastings in his speech to the Lords in May 1791 ; after expressing his surprize at his own mistakes when writing on matters of accont, without having a single paper or document of any sort near him, adds, after stating that he was *himself* the person who desired the Bonds might be searched

Q Q 4

for

for and sent to Englnd, " Had my instructions
" for the purpose intended by the indorsement
" of the Bonds been invented for the pur-
" pose of deception, I should have stopped when
" I had assigned it. Instead of this, I sought,
" and with a diligence which it is not likely that I
" should have employed to detect myself in a false-
" hood, first for authentic copies of the Indorsed
" Bonds, at the India-houfe, and afterwards, for
" the originals at Calcutta. These being found,
" proved that I had erred in my account of the
" transaction; but it also demonstratively proved
" that I had given that account, believing it to
" be true, and presumptively, that my intention,
" and consequent instructions to Mr. Larkins
" were, that the Bonds, in the event of my death,
" should be cancelled by him."

But the most material part, and which would
afford a very strong presumption indeed against
Mr. Hastings, if the evidence were as Mr. Fox
stated it, is now to be mentioned. After stating that the mistake as to the date of the Bonds
was difcovered by Mr. Hastings himself, not by
his Accufers, he faid,

" My Lords, after this I should be almost
" afraid to hazard a fuppofition; but as the Bonds
" were left with Mr. Larkins, as my Attorney,
" and as Mr. Larkins knew from the first that
they

" they were not my property, I concluded, that
" I told him, that in the event of my decease, he
" was to deliver them to the Council, which I
" confounded with the Act, of having endorsed
" them."

. Mr. Fox affirms, that Mr. Larkins positively
fwore, he did not know until the 22d of May,
1782, that the Bonds were not the Property of
Mr. Hastings. If he did so swear, the inference
would be fair, that between the receipt of Bonds
in January 1781, and May 1782, it might be presumed, that Mr. Hastings intended to take this
40,000l. to himfelf, but still we shall be *puzzled*
to know *why* Mr. Hastings was fo anxious to have
the Bonds produced.

Mr. Fox dismisses all the conclusions and all
the fuppositons, and meets the fact fully. Mr.
Hastings asserts most confidently, that Mr. Larkins knew from the first, that the Bonds were not
his property. The question then is, does Mr.
Larkins, or does he not swear, *in the manner that*
Mr. Fox stated him to swear?

We will endeavour to give his Evidenc *most*
correctly.

Mr. Larkins fwears that he does not recollect
being told, until the 2d of May, 1782, that thefe
Bonds were not the property of Mr. Hastings;
that he does not recollect having been instructed
by

by Mr. Hastings in 1781, to deliver up those Bonds, in the event of his decease, to the Company, that he hopes he is not expected to swear that he might not have forgotten it; that he certainly does not recollect it; that he certainly thinks it would have made an impression upon his memory: but he cannot undertake to swear positively that Mr. Hastings did not give such an instruction, but if he did, he had forgotten it. Here is the substance of Mr. Larkins's evidence, which Mr. Fox stated fairly up to this point. It is not positive but Mr. Fox had a right to argue upon it as he did.

But on the farther examination of Mr. Larkins, he swore, that those Bonds *never made part of Mr. Hastings's private Property, that they were never entered on his books.* That the money *never made part* of *his* private *cash*, but was carried *immediately into the Treasury.* That *no interest ever was received upon those Bonds*; and then to a farther question, Mr. Larkins answered, page 2760.

" I do not recollect what instructions I had re-
" ceived from Mr. Hastings, between the month
" of January, 1782, when they were first applied
" for, and the 22d of May, 1782, when I be-
." same completely acquainted with the transaction.
Q. " Whether he gave you any explanation
" upon

" upon the fubjeft. Answer, I have already said,
" that I must have received some information
" from Mr. Hastings, which induced me to con-
" sider thefe Bonds, though apparently his pro-
" perty, not fo; otherwife, one year after their
" date, I should have applied to the Treasury
" for the annual interest which then became pay-
" able upon them. I did not do so; but I
" do know that Mr. Hastings ever told me be-
" fore the 22d of May 1782, any thing that could
" have led me to suppose from whom that money
" was obtained!"

This is a fair and complete abstraft of all the
Evidence to this great and essential point. The
interest due upon these Bonds in November
1781, was 3200l. Mr. Hastings was then at
Benares, and Mr. Larkins had the Bonds at
Calcutta. Is it, or is it not fair to believe, that
the reafon which induced Mr. Larkins not to
receive the interest was, Mr. Hastings having
told him, that the Bonds were not his property.
Every Gentleman will draw his own conclufion,
but if it had been true, as Mr. Fox stated, that Mr.
Larkins swore positively, that he had no communication prior to the 22d of May, 1782, it would
be clear that Mr. Hastings had asserted a falsehood; and it would be fair to prefume, he had
fome nefarious purpofe to answer in having so
done;

done ; as the Evidence *really stands*, is it not rather more fair to conclude that Mr. Haftings remembered rightly ?

We repeat it, that Mr. Fox himself, very much to his honour, produced a piece of evidence which Mr. Hastings for many years had searched for in vain, and which totally exculpated him *from the first charge*, that is, of having applied to his own use a sum of One Lack and a half of Rupees, in 1772, given as a bribe for an appointment to office.

The whole argument on which Mr. Fox rests to criminate Mr. Hastings, is so unworthy of him, that he would not have used it we are sure, had he fairly considered the evidence. When Mr. Hastings declared, that Mr. Larkins was privy to every process of his money transaction, it was in July 1785, before he was impeached, and it is impossible for any man who reads the Letter to the Court of Directors from whence this expression is taken, to apply the sense and meaning, which Mr. Fox applies to it, provided he first reads the Letter from the Directors, to which this is a reply. He is asked three questions by the Directors, and without book or account with him, he answers those three questions, and says, that if the Directors wish for further information, or for the means of making any investigation, he refers them to

Mr.

Mr. Larkins, who was privy to every process. What process is it he alludes to ? The process that had a reference to the questions put to him by the Directors. But as Mr. Fox in his hurry stated it, every Gentleman must have supposed, that this Letter was a defence of some accusation of the Commons, and not a reply to three specific questions put to him by the Directors.

What follows? Mr. Hastings says, perhaps, you will think what I now tell you, sufficient for any purpose you may have to answer; if not apply to Mr. Larkins. The Directors were satisfied— The Board of Controul was satisfied—for they never inquired further about the matter. But Mr. Hastings was not satisfied. He had been asked at what period the several sums composing the 200,000l. was received?—He answered, that he believed, nearly at the time they were paid into the Treasury ; that he had no memorandum, but would write to Mr. Larkins, to send the original memorandum if he had it, to the Directors. Mr. Hastings did so ; Mr. Larkins did send it, with a letter ; and this letter of Mr. Larkins, and this memorandum have been argued upon, as if they were presented by Mr. Hastings, as *a complete* answer to the charge preferred against him by the House of Commons. This is a fallacy. If there is any thing false in the letter, or in the account,

Mr.

Mr. Fox has full right to say so, and to make the most of it ; but his candour, had he considered the subject, would have prevented him from stating the letter, so as to impress his auditors with a belief, *that it was a reply to a charge of the House of Commons.*

Having thus cleared the ground, we come to consider what Mr. Hastings did say, when his conduct was viewed in a different light.

The Directors and the King's Ministers in June 1785, returned him their thanks for his long, faithful, and able services. They did not accuse him of breaking the law, by accepting and paying into their Treasury 200,000l. On the contrary, they approved what he had done, and merely wanted to know why he took Bonds for some of the sums, and entered others as deposits—why he concealed the receipt from his Counsel and the Directors, and at what period the several sums were received. The answer was confined to the questions asked. But the House of Commons charged him with breaking the law, in accepting the presents at all ; and they charged him with receiving them with a corrupt intention of applying them to his own use. Let any Gentleman read the answer of Mr. Hastings to these charges---let him read Mr. Larkins's evidence, and then

we

we affirm, that he will find no contradiction whatever in the accounts.

In the defence made by Mr. Hastings in the
House of Commons, there is not one syllable
from which an inference can be drawn, that Mr.
Hastings meant to impress the House with a belief
that Mr. Larkins knew from whom any one of
the sums was received, further than appears by
the account sent home in May 1782. This is so
material a part in the case, that if we repeat our
arguments in some measure, the *importance* of
the subject will excuse us.

In the defence made by Mr. Hastings in the
House of Lords, there is not one single syllable
from whence it can be inferred that Mr. Larkins
knew either the persons from whom the several
sums were taken, nor the periods at which they
were taken, further than appears in the account
of the 22d of May 1782.

But in the defence before the Lords, there is
this remarkable expression :

" As the bonds were left with Mr. Larkins, as
" my Attorney, and as Mr. Larkins from the first
" knew that they were not my property, I con-
" cluded that I told him in 1781, that in the event
" of my decease he was to deliver them to the
" Council, which I confounded with the act of
" having indorsed them."

This

This is the true and only point of the least consequence. Here is a positive assertion made by
Mr. Hastings, that Mr. Larkins knew from the
first that the Bonds were not the property of Mr.
Hastings; and Mr. Fox says, that Mr. Larkins
positively swears to the contrary. If he really
did so, then Mr. Fox would have a sound argument. Mr. Fox, we are confident, is incapable
of making the assertion he did, unless he thought
it was true. It happens, however, that Mr. Larkins swears that he cannot, at the distance of twelve
years, recollect that Mr. Hastings told him the
Bonds were not his property, or that he desired
him to deliver them up on the event of his death.
He thinks such a circumstance was not likely to
escape him, but he also swears, that on these
Bonds no interest ever was received, and that
unless he had had some intimation from Mr. Hastings, which at this distance of time he cannot
recollect, he certainly should have received
the interest on those Bonds, which he never
did.

One would conceive it impossible for any evidence short of positive recollection to justify Mr.
Hastings more fully. What motive can be assigned for Mr. Larkins's neglecting to receive the
interest upon these Bonds, amounting in October
and November 1781 to Thirty-two Thousand
Rupees,

Rupees, or 3000l. but the one Mr. Larkins assigns, that he must have had some communication from Mr. Hastings, though he cannot recollect at this distance of time what it was; where presumption is to determine guilt or innocence, the man who undertakes to state what an evidence has proved, should state it fairly and in toto; and we are confident Mr. Fox would have done so, if it had occurred to him.—He would not allow for a moment, a few years ago, that the 2000 Rupees a day received by Mr. Hastings in 1772, was other than a bribe for an appointment to office. This year Mr. Fox very honourably produced evidence himself, which removed all doubts, by shewing, that all Governors, when at Moorshedabad, received the same allowance.

In his first day's speech he brought a serious accusation against Mr. Dallas: That having misquoted the Clause of an Act, the argument founded upon it fell to the ground. On the second day he acknowledged that he, and not Mr. Dallas had misquoted the clause.

The Lords, who have all the evidence before them, will naturally look to that, and to that alone. No remarks that do not apply to the whole evidence can have weight with them; but the Public who heard Mr. Fox's speech have a right to know, that, from haste, *he did not state the whole*

R R *of*

of Mr. Larkins's evidence on this most important point.

We have already proved that there is no evidence on this article, except the voluntary confession of Mr. Hastings himfelf—We have already shewn that a letter, written by Mr. Hastings in July 1785, to the Directors, was alluded to by Mr. Fox, as if it were an anfwer to the charge of the House of Commons, but that on this fallacy being detected, and when the letter is considered as it ought to be, with a reference to that letter, to which it is an anfwer, no contradiction of any kind will appear in it; we shall therefore proceed with Mr. Fox's arguments.

He observed, that it appeared by the Paper which Mr. Larkins tranfmitted to the Court of Directors, that upon the Cabooleats or engagements for money granted to Mr. Hastings, there was a balance of forty thoufand pounds due: That of this sum ten thousand was received, and has never been paid to the Company: That though the Paper states the remaining thirty to be in balance, it is even now a matter of doubt where it is, and that Mr. Haftings may have that money in his pocket at this moment, or Gunga Govind Sing may have it, but that, in fact, Mr. Haftings has never given the Company any satisfaction on this point.

Here

Here again Mr. Hastings has very just ground to complain that Mr. Fox, professing a fair summary of the evidence, has, in his hurry, most materially misrepresented it. *This Paper has nothing to do with the charge of the House of Commons.* The Directors desired to know from Mr. Hastings, in March 1784, at what periods the several sums which he had carried to their credit were received? Mr. Hastings in answer, in July 1785, says, he believes he can affirm with certainty that they were received near the time that they were paid into the Treasury, but if the Directors wish for further information, he refers them to Mr. Larkins, who was privy to every process of the transaction, and possesses as, he believes, the only memorandum that he, Mr. Hastings, ever kept of the transaction. He says also, that this will be a channel for making *any further investigation they please.* The Directors and the Board of Controul enquire no further; but Mr. Hastings himself writes to Mr. Larkins, and desires him to send that memorandum to the Directors. Mr. Larkins does so.—Surely *from the moment* the Directors possess the Paper, they are the persons to enquire. Mr. Hastings had assured them that he had paid into their Treasury *all the money he received.* If, from the information which that Paper afforded, it appeared either

to

to the Directors, or to the Board of Controul, that there was a balance *in Gunga Govind Sing's hands*, or a ballance *upon the Cabooleats uncollected*, they, and not Mr. Hastings, were the persons to order an enquiry in Bengal. Mr. Hastings fays, " I will afford you the means of mak- " ing any investigation—apply to Mr. Larkins." The Directors made no investigation, and Mr. Hastings is now accused for a neglect, which, *if it be one at all*, must be accounted for by the Board of Controul. When we say *accused*, we do not *mean* that he is legally accused, for though the Commons were in *possession* of the Paper, by which it appeared that there was a balance of a Lack of Rupees in the hands of Gunga Govind Sing, and that Forty thousand Pounds were uncollected, they have neither charged Mr. Hastings with *criminality* nor *neglect*, for not enforcing the paymont of those several balances; and therefore every thing faid by Mr. Fox on these points, is foreign to the charge. Mr. Fox connected with the receipt of this money *the character of Gunga Govind Sing*, of whom he faid there was *but one opinion*, and that a very bad one. Here again Mr. Fox did not quote the evidence by any means correctly. The substance of all the evidence relative to Gunga Govind Sing is as follows—

Mr.

Mr. Young fwore, that he bore a very bad charaΏer among the natives and Europeans.

Mr. Peter Moore fwoɼe, that he was a man of very bad charaΏer, and considered as a general oppressor of every native he had to deal with; that by the Europeans he was detested, and by the natives he was dreaded.

Mr. Harwood fwore, that he has heard Gunga Govind Sing was very arbitrary and oppressive in his public employment, and that that was his general charaΏer.

Mr. Anderfon swore, that he did not recolleΏ any official complaints, nor indeed any complaints, against Gunga Govind Sing: that he did not think he had generally a bad charaΏer; on the contrary, he thought he generally had a good charaΏer, but at the fame time there might be persons found in Bengal who would give him a bad charaΏer; there were perfons who had taken opposite fides of a party, which will have an effeΏ upon the minds of people, and persons who had suffered by his appointment, who were his competitors.

Sir John Shore swore, that he did not believe Gunga Govind Sing was deficient either in skill or ability: That he was acquainted with him for a great number of years: That he knew no native fit for the appointment he held: That he

certainly

certainly should not have selected him by choice but cannot recollect at present whether he could have pitched on any other perfon in preference: That he did not find Gunga Goving Sing so active and zealous as he wished him to be: That he believed any native in the situation in which Gunga Govind Sing was placed, would use his influence for his own advantage, and he had no doubt Gunga Govind Sing did so: That when detached to Dacca and Bahar, Sir John, by his own choice, took with him, as his Executive Officer, the fon of Gunga Govind Sing.

But the most fingular circumftance attending this man, is contained in the evidence produced by Mr. Burke in reply, and it ought to operate most forcibly upon the mind of every candid man —general abuse should go for nothing.

Mr. Stables, after Mr. Haftings had quitted Bengal moved in council, " That Gunga Govind Sing, his son, and all his dependants, be removed from their offices"—and he fays, " The cries and complaints of the natives in general, shew how unworthy he has been of his trust."

Sir John Macpherson, the Governor General, opposes this motion, and fays, " Gunga Govind Sing is not himself defirous to be continued in office—he fees that he has lost the confidence of a majority of Government, and he knows that he

has

has no dependance to place upon my support beyond the moment that either past or present misconduct is proved against him.

" I think there can be little fear, after the
accusations that have already come forward
against him, but the natives will make complaints. The danger is on the other side, and
should make us cautious not to admit general
charges without proof against him. The precedent is a bad one *in any country*, but espe-
cially in Bengal. The outstanding balances, and
their magnitude since the management of Gunga
Govind Sing, would make a very heavy charge
against him ; but on the other hand, if he can
prove that a greater revenue has been realized
from the provinces during his service as Dewan,
than in any preceding period of the administration of the revenue, he has a substantial claim to
justice."

The Directors were so struck with the injustice of the mode in which it was proposed to
proceed against Gunga Govind Sing, that they
wrote to Bengal in August, 1788, as follows,
after very fairly and fully stating the case.

" Although we feel no predilection for Gunga
Govind Sing, we must fairly acknowledge that we
do not think sufficient ground was laid to justify
his removal from office."

R R 4   " Another

" Another ground for his removal was the expectation that complaints would come which were kept back by his continuance in office. In the early periods of our territorial possessions, when the whole Administration of the country, provincial and superior, was in the hands of one person, (Mahomed Reza Cawn) such an apprehension might be allowed to prevail. But we think it would now greatly impeach both the vigour and justice of our Government in Bengal, to suppose that any considerable act of injustice could be committed by any individual whatsoever, without the means of complaint and reparation being open to the aggrieved."

Such is the opinion of the Directors and of the Board of Controul; and against this, Gunga Govind Sing, described by Mr. Burke " as a man at the sound of whose name all India grew pale," nothing criminal has yet been proved, though he resigned his office in May 1787, and from that period has been a private inhabitant of Calcutta; and the only complaint preferred against him came to a solemn hearing in the Supreme Court of Judicators, where Gunga Govind Sing was honourably cleared, and his accusers committed to prison, both for perjury and forgery. It will not be said, that the influence of Mr. Hastings protected him; for from the moment he left Bengal, the Supreme

preme Council were adverse to Gunga Govind
Sing, and Lord Cornwallis will not be suspected
either of protecting, or of oppressing him. No
Gentleman can believe from the evidence which
have we given *fairly on both sides*, that Gunga
Govind Sing *is* such a man as Mr. Fox describes
him to be.

We have already gone through the most material parts of this celebrated Speech. There
were some points which we did not expect from
so fair a reasoner as Mr. Fox. He said, that
Mr. Hastings having given the whole power of
Bengal to Gunga Govind Sing in 1781, might have
received many considerable sums, of which nothing was yet known. After a seven years Trial, and
with incontrovertible evidence before the Court,
that Bengal had been progressively improving in
Agriculture, Population, and Commerce, during
the Administration of Mr. Hastings; after the
opinion of India on the character and conduct of
Mr. Hastings was so well known, it was not to be
expected, that so fair a man as Mr. Fox, would
have wandered from what did appear in the evidence, into surmises, as to what Mr. Hastings
might have done, which has not been discovered.

Mr. Fox, in stating the several presents, did not
endeavour to connect with them any corrupt act
done by Mr. Hastings in favour of those who
gave

gave money; nor was there any thing stated by
way of aggravation, except in the case of the
present received from the Nabob of Oude,
amounting to 100,000l. which was accepted, Mr.
Fox said, at a time when the Nabob was compelled to rob his Mother.   Here again Mr. Hastings
has every reason to complain of the hard treatment he has met with; and *we* may a little admire
the nature of British Justice.

This present was accepted in September 1781,
and compleatly paid in February 1782.   As fast
as the money was received, Mr. Hastings expended it in the public service, a great part being
advanced to the army, in a period of the greatest
public distress.   The propriety of this present, it
remained with the Directors to determine.   They
might have taken it for the Company, or given it to
Mr. Hastings, or have applied it in liquidation of
the Nabob's debt; for after taking credit for
these ten lacks of rupees, and after taking the fifty-
five lacks from the Begum, there was still a
considerable balance due from the Nabob to
the Company.

The Directors, with the approbation of the
King's Ministers determined to keep these ten
lacks to themselves in January 1783; and it is
surely rather too much to hear Mr. Hastings accused in May 1794, of receiving these ten lacks, and

to

to hear it asserted to be an aggravation of the offence, that he had taken it from the Nabob about
the time that a part of the Treasures of the Begum were seized, in order to discharge a part of
the debt due from the Nabob to the East-India
Company.

This observation will indeed apply to every act
done by Mr. Hastings—nothing that he did, if he
acted wrong, would have been a permanent evil.
In twelve, or at the utmost, in eighteen months, any
any one act of his might have been reversed, but
all his acts have been confirmed, and the advantage accruing to the nation by confirming them
all, is thirty-four millions seven hundred and ten
thousand pounds, while Mr. Hastings has been
seven years arraigned as a Culprit, for what he has
done. After this, and after his having received
the thanks of the King's Ministers, and the Directors, for his long, faithful, and able services, we
may surely say, *that nothing in politics is certain.*

In the preceding remarks we have shewn, that
of all the sums which Mr. Hastings admitted he
had received, he is not accused of having ultimately applied one rupee to his own use.

The accusation is, that for some time he intended to appropriate to his own use the one fifth
part of the sums that he received—We have fairly
stated

stated the evidence, and the World will draw it own conclusions.

The present received from Nobkissen, resting upon Mr. Hastings's declaration alone, and it being in proof, that it was applied to the payment of certain charges, which are admitted to have been incurred for public services, we shall proceed to remark on what Mr. Fox said relative to the Mahratta and to the money given by Mr. Hastings to purchase the neutrality, and the assistance also, of Moodajee Borsla, in the course of the last general war. Though it be clear that Mr. Hastings was not the author of the Mahratta War, we shall argue the point without considering whether he was or was not the author of it, and we shall look to the actual situation in which the British Government stood in India at the commencement of the year 1781.

Hyder Ally had totally defeated Colonel Baillie, and had compelled Sir Hector Munro to retreat to Fort St. George. The Marattas in Guzzerat kept General Goddard at bay. Madajee Sindia was advancing from Malwa, and Moodajee Boosla had sent his son Chimnajee Boosla, at the head of thirty thousand horse, to invade Bengal in her richest quarter. The Nizam of the Decan, who had formed the confederacy against us, was threatening to take the field, and to attack the Northern

thern Circars. Nuzeph Cawn, who possessed the person of the Emperor, was hostile to us. A superior French fleet arrived upon the Coast in January 1781, and was expected to return with land forces, as soon as the season would admit.

In this desperate state, though Mr. Hastings knew that Moodagee Boosla was unwillingly drawn into the confederacy against us, it surely became necessary to take some means to rid our western frontier of so powerful a body of men, as a thousand accidents might provoke hostilities. Nor was this all; Colonel Pearse, who was going to reinforce Sir Eyre Coote with five regiments of Sepoys, could not march through Cuttack, while 30,000 Maratta horse remained there.— Chimnajee Boosla, very frankly said that, dragged as his father was, against his will, into the confederacy, his army was reduced to such as state of distress, that it actually required assistance from Bengal, or it could not be kept in order.

In Nov. 1780, Mr. Hastings privately sent Chimnajee three lacks of rupees, and in April he concluded a Treaty with him, by which he gave him thirteen, and lent him ten lacks more, which have never been repaid. In return for this sum of 260,000l. a free passage was secured for Col. Pearse's army through the Maratta Province of Cuttack;

Cuttack; two thousand Maratta horse were to join the Colonel; he was to be well supplied with provisions, and the Maratta army of 30,000 horse was to return to Berar. These conditions were most honourably performed, though the Maratta horse came too late, and returned from Gaujam.

The consequences of this arrangement were most beneficial—From that moment one great Member of the Confederacy withdrew himself, and the other parts of the Confederacy distrusted each other. But before the *confequences* of this Treaty *could be known*, Mr. Dundas proposed a resolution, which the House voted, that Mr. Hastings had concluded a precarious Treaty, on most extravagant and dishonourable conditions, one party who made it having no authority so to do: But we believe Mr. Dundas very materially changed his opinion, when he knew that every good consequence which Mr. Hastings predicted, actually happened. No further effort was made against us by the Berar Mahrattas during the war; on the contrary, the most perfect amity subsisted between them and the English. A peace with Sindia followed in October 1781; a truce with all the Mahrattas in January 1782; and a general peace with them in May 1782; and we got ultimately out of the war in India, without the loss

of

of an inch of territory; on the contrary, Lord Lansdowne was enabled to save a West India Island, by restoring to the French, the settlements we had taken from them in Bengal, and in the Carnatic. Mr. Dundas fairly confessed, in 1786, that the man who did not see in Mr. Hastings the features of a great Statesman, must be blinded by prejudice.

Now let us see what Mr. Pitt and Mr. Dundas have done in a situation not very dissimilar from that of Mr. Hastings. It is of no consequence to shew, if it could be done, that the war might have been avoided, in which we are now engaged. The discussion of the question would be as useless now, as it was in 1781, to enquire whether the Directors, the Government of Bombay, or Mr. Hastings, was the author of the Mahratta war. If Mr. Pitt brings us as honourably out of this, as Mr. Hastings brought us out of the Mahratta war, *his important services,* will be the more gratefully acknowledged than those of Mr. Hastings have been. The fact is, that though Spain, Austria, Prussia, the Germanic Body, Great Britain, and Holland, are united against France, her numbers, and her situation, and the enthusiasm of the people have enabled those who direct her armies, to baffle all our efforts on the Continent.

The

The King of Prussia, though the first to en-
gage against France, professes his inability to continue the war. This nation, which was the last
engaged in the contest, consents to give him One
Million Four Hundred Thousand Pounds, and
uses her influence with Holland to give him Four
Hundred Thousand Pounds more, for the service
of a body of troops during the present campaign.
The Treaty is warmly approved by the House of
Commons.

But tho' a confiderable sum has been sent in
advance, the king of Prussia has totally ruined
us in the Netherlands, by not complying with the
terms of the treaty. We lament the situation in
which this breach of Faith has placed Mr. Pitt;
but we do not blame him.

The treaty by which Mr. Hastings gave 260,000l.
to Moodagee Boosla, produced the most decisive
and immediate good confequences, yet that treaty
is branded on the Journals of Parliament, with the
epithets " precarious," " unwarrantable," " ex-
" travagant," " impolitic," and " dishonourable."

None of the reasoning *now used* in favour of
Mr. Pitt, *could be heard* in defence of Mr. Hastings; the House of Commons fees, and wisely
sees, in the case of Mr. Pitt, the danger of en-
couraging, abstract discussions at this perilous
moment, and therefore every attempt to prove

that

that the war might have been avoided is discovered. The calamity *is at our door*, and as Mr.
Hastings well said, when Hyder had overrun the
Carnatic, " This is the season for action, not for
" debate :" But in the *last general war*, when the
American contest armed the world against Great
Britain; Gentlemen of the most opposite parties
in Parliament, forgot their personal animosities,
and though in daily habits of accusing each other
as the authors of the calamities which England
then sustained, joined most cordially in *condemning* the measures of those in India, who were
bravely struggling through every difficulty; and
who, instead of receiving from time to time, as
Lord North did *then*, and as Mr. Pitt does *now*,
all the support that Parliament could give, had to
contend with every species of counteraction,
which the folly, or the prejudice, or the ignorance,
of persons who then guided the National Councils, could throw in their way—But though all
men of enlightened minds, must now see the
errors they then committed, one man, and but
one man has the manliness to step forward and
acknowledge his mistake.—We mean Mr. Dundas, who professing to think in 1782, that the
removal of Mr. Hastings was a wise and necessary measure, did in that year, move his recal in
the House of Commons. But in 1784, he vo-

s s   luntarily

luntarily stepped forth, and then expressed to the House *his joy*, that the proprietors of India Stock, had successfully opposed his motion, being *convinced* that by continuing Mr. Hastings in India, they had performed a very effential public fervice.

As Mr. Fox slightly touched upon the Marratta war and the Marratta Peace, we have offered the preceding remarks to our readers.

We have been particular in our observations on Mr. Fox's Speech, because it applied to the great and important article on which the Impeachment *now* refts.

It is indeed charged by the Commons, that the *objeEt* of Mr. Hastings in all his aEts, were " to " acquire *for himself, and his dependants, exor-* " *bitant wealth.*"

He is charged therefore with giving 18,000l. a year to Sir Eyre Coote—a bullock contraEt to Mr. Coftes—an Opium contraEt to Mr. Sulivan— one agency to Mr. Auriol—a second to Mr. Belli—and a third to Sir Charles Blunt.—

These are *all the accusations*, though his prosecutors had to review his dispofal of a great patronage during a Government of *thirteen years*— If for argument sake, it were to be admitted, that the profits arising to the individuals on these contraEts and agencies were as large as the managers

state

state them to be, the aggregate amount would be trifling, when compared to the profit, *on a single loan*, in England, in the late war.

Mr. Hastings was charged with taking very large bribes, betwen the years 1772 and 1774, and concealing the receipt of them—and with receiving large bribes, between the years 1780 and 1784; the receipt of which he discovered—His view in receiving these several sums was said to be, *to acquire for himself exorbitant wealth.*

The subject, though apparently extensive, does in fact lie in a very narrow compass.

All the charges *in the first period*, that is from from 1772 to 1774, are unsupported by a tittle of evidence, except that which applies to the sum of Two thousand Rupees a day, received by Mr. Hastings in the year 1772, when he was at Morshadabad, agreeably to the practice of his predecessors. Whether it was right in Lord Clive, in Mr. Verelst, and in Mr. Hastings, to receive that allowance for entertainment, is not the question— But it is clearly *proved*, that it was not that which the Commons charged it to be — a bribe for the appointment of Muny Begum to a public office — consequently the charge falls to the ground.

The presents received by Mr. Hastings between 1780 and 1784, are distinguished by Mr. Fox, under the name of the " avowed presents." That is, presents of which there is not a tittle

to

of evidence as to the receipt of them, beyond the voluntary information given *by Mr. Hastings himself.* — It was firſt contended by Mr. Fox, to receive these presents subsequent to the aſt of 1773, was *a breach of the law.* It was next contended that Mr. Hastings did *for a time,* intend to apply a part of these presents *to his own use*—These are the important questions to be considered. Mr. Fox said every thing that man could say upon both, and we admit, that his arguments would have the greatest weight, provided he had reasoned *upon the evidence*—The faſt is, that he only took *a part of the evidence,* and omitted that part which placed the matter in a very opposite point of view.

.ONE HUNDRED AND THIRTY-EIGHTH DAY. *May* 23.

The Court met to-day at half past two, when Mr. Taylor replied on the Contraſts.

ONE HUNDRED AND THIRTY-NINTH DAY *May* 27.

Mr. Taylor concluded his summary of the contraſts.

ONE

Mr. Burke's 1st Day.

ONE HUNDRED AND FORTIETH DAY, *May* 28.

———

Of Mr. Burke's fpeech, on this day, it is ab
folutely impossible to convey an adequate idea to
thofe who did not hear it. Every term of abuse
which the Englifh language affords, he applied
to Mr. Hastings; but not one word had the least
conneftion with the Evidence which has been
in the trial. As we wish at all times to do justice to Mr. Burke, we fhall transcribe two passages from a speech printed by Mr. Burke himfelf in the year 1785, when Mr. Pitt and Mr.
Dundas were as much the objefts of his detesta-
tion, as Mr. Hastings appears to be now; and
we desire our readers to believe, that, if possible, he abused Mr. Hastings this day in grosser
language, than he then did His Majesty's present
First Lord of the Treafury and Secretary of State.

" Let no man hereafter talk of the decaying
" energies of nature, all the Afts and Monu-
" ments in the records of Peculation, the con-
" folidated corruption of ages, the patterns of
" exemplary plunder in the heroic times of

s s 3   " Roman

" Roman iniquity, never equalled the gigantic
" corruption of this single act.

" Your Ministers knew, when they signed the
" Death Warrant of the Carnatic, that the Na-
" bob would not only turn all the unfortunate
" Farmers out of employment, but that he has
" denounced his severest vengeance against them
" for acting under British authority. With a
" knowledge of this disposition, a British Chan-
" cellor of the Exchequer, (Mr. Pitt) and Trea-
" surer of the Navy, (Mr. Dundas) incited by
" no public advantage, impelled by no public
" necessity, in a strain of the most wanton per-
" fidy, which has ever stained the annals of man-
" kind, have delivered over to plunder, impri-
" sonment, exile and death itself, according to
" the Mercy of such execrable Tyrants as the
" unhappy and deluded souls, who, untaught by
" uniform example, were still weak enough to
" put their trust in English Faith."

If the imagination of our readers can suppose
it possible for abuse on an individual to be more
virulent than that which we have quoted here,
Mr. Burke on this day abused Mr. Hastings with
more virulence than he abused Mr. Pitt on the
28th of February 1785. We think it necessary
again to remark, that this abuse of Mr. Pitt, is
taken

taken from a speech published by Mr. Burke himself.

———————

Mr. Burke's 2d *Day.*

ONE HUNDRED AND FORTY-FIFTH DAY, *May* 30.

Mr. Burke began, on this day, by restating what he had faid yesterday, that Mr. Hastings, instead of appearing in a humble and decent manner, had dared to accufe the Houfe of Commons of the bafeft ingratitude, that he had given them Impeachment for Impeachment.

After Mr. Burke had spent a considerable time in repeating what he had before said on this fubjeƌ, he went to the next head that he had dwelt upon on the laſt day, and contended that Mr. Hastings was not founded in asserting that the Government of India was not arbitrary.

It will be fufficient to fay, that Lord Cornwallis, in one of the minutes alluded to by Mr. Burke, expressly fays, that every thing of Law, of Police, and of Regulation, tending to meliorate the condition of the people of Bengal, it owes to the British Government. Every

s s 4   thing

thing depending, prior to the British Adminiſ-
tration, on caprice, and the pleasure of the Sovereign, or the perſon to whom he delegated his
power.   In Lord Cornwallis's evidence there is
the following queſtion and anſwer.

" Q. What is the general mode of proceeding
" againſt refractory Zemindars according to the
" Laws and Cuſtoms of Hindoſtan ?'"

" A. It is difficult to deſcribe the regular mode
" of proceeding in a deſpotic Government, but
" they are frequently confined and dispoſſeſed."
This is the compleateſt poſſible anſwer to three
fourths of Mr. Burke's ſpeech.

Mr. Burke alſo repeated what he had before
ſaid of the inſolence of Mr. Haſtings in accuſing
the Houſe of Commons of the baſeſt ingratitude.
He ſaid he had impeached the Body who had impeached him.   That until this time, every man
who had been impeached by ſo great a Body as
the Commons, ſeemed ſenſible of their misfortune; but different was the caſe with Mr. Haſtings.   He boaſted his merits, while he aſſerted
his innocence.   The facts alluded to are theſe, and
the impartial part of mankind may think there is
more of Truth than Inſolence in what Mr. Haſtings ſaid to the Lords in 1792.   Mr. Haſtings affirmed to their Lordſhips, that the Commons had
impeached him for acts which the King's Ministers

ters had fully approved. That while the Managers were declaring in Westminfter-Hall, that Mr. Hastings had desolated the Provinces of Bengal, the India Minister was proclaiming to the House of Commons, that Bengal had been the best governed, and the most flourishing Country in Indostan under the British Administration. That while the Managers were declaring, that the refources of the Company were diminished under the Administration of Mr. Hastings, Mr. Dundas was proving to the Houfe of Commons, by the evidence in figures, that under the administration of Mr. Hastings, they had increased two millions sterling a year; that is, that in 1772, when he came to the Government, they were three millions; and in 1785, when he left it, they were five millions sterling a year.

After stating thefe facts in the boldest but in the clearest language. Mr. Hastings adds, addressing the Commons. " I gave you all, and " you have rewarded me with confiscation, dis- " grace, and a life of impeachment."

If the above assertions were not strictly true, then indeed Mr. Hastings would be the most insolent man alive. But the whole world knows, that each assertion is true, and until Mr. Burke spoke, we believe no man living thought of applying the word Insolence for Truth.

Mr.

Mr. Burke spoke from a quarter before Two till a quarter after Five, and went through a part of Benares, tho' he professed his intention to be, not to go into any of the articles which had been so fully detailed before. The greatest number of Lords present was Nineteen, they were reduced to Thirteen before Mr. Burke had finished. The audience was numerous, and of course the epithets used by Mr. Burke, which were of the coarsest kind, carried even beyond his former abuse of Mr. Pitt, would be circulated very generally.

―――――

Mr. Burke's 3d Day.

ONE HUNDRED AND FORTY-SECOND DAY. *June* 3.

The court met at two o'clock to-day, and Mr. Burke proceeded to sum up the remainder of the Benares Charge. The account of it stands thus:―
It was opened by Mr. Fox and Mr. Grey in two days. It was closed by Mr. Anstruther in a speech

of

of one day. The evidence in reply was closed by Mr. Grey in a speech of two, and by Mr. Burke in a speech three days, fo that eight days have been employed by the Managers in Speeches on the Benares article, independent of what Mr. Burke said in his first opening fpeech: and after so much time, and after fo much money spent, the evidence proves, that when Cheyt Sing was expelled in 1781, Mr. Hastings raised the public revenue of Benares from 230,000l. to 400,000l. a year: that this increased revenue has been regularly paid from 1780 to 1793, and that there is no sort of doubt of this increafed revenue being regularly paid in future; that the country has flourished eminently fince the expulsion of Cheyt Sing; that Benares has considerably increased in building and in population fince the expulsion of Cheyt Sing ; that the Police, establifhed by Mr. Hastings, in Benares, has rendered that city the first in India. To this clear, decided, and undoubted evidence, Mr. Burke opposed a Letter, written by Mr. Hastings in 1784, in which he stated, that by the bad management, of the Aumil after a very heavy drought, the country had been greatly oppressed, and that in the line through which he marched, from Buxal to the extremity of the Benares Province, the natives had

had desrted their villages, owing to the neglect of the Aumil.

The next was a report from Mr. Duncan, in 1788, who fays, that fome Pergunnahs had fallen off since the expulsion of Cheyt Sing.

Now Mr. Burke rejects all evidence from Gentlemen of all descriptions; rejects the solemn assertions of the People themfelves; rejects the Public accounts; rejects all that his Friend Mr. Dundas has faid of the flourishing state of Benares; and insists upon it, that Mr. Hastings and Mr. Duncan have proved, that the Country is utterly ruined. And with this, at last, the Benares Caufe is ended, until the Lords shall decide, whether the six millions sterling, which this Nation has received from Benares shall be restored to Cheyt Sing.

The fame mode of stating facts which distinguished Mr. Burke, when he told what passed in a large company, when the late Lord Dover was present, distinguished him in relating passages from the Letters of Mr. Duncan and Mr. Hastings. He read what the former Gentleman said of the state of some trifling Pergunnahs; and from that partial statement, he argued, that the whole Province of Benares was ruined inevitably; that Province from which the Company has received 400,000l. a year, from 1782 to this day.

He

He read parts, or rather he desired Mr. Wyndham, to read part of a letter from Mr. Hastings,
in which he reprefented the confequences of an
alarming drought, and the bad conduct of the
Aumil when joined together for one year: but
when Mr. Wyndham came to the following parts
of the fame letter, Mr. Burke desired him to stop;
we fhall therefore infert it in this place.

" I have the happiness to find all men satisfied
" and happy in the excellent administration of the
" city of Benares, and have experienced what few
" men of the first station have known in the inter-
" courfe with the natives of India, if of any other
" country, the voice of adulation, divested even
" in my own presence, from myself, in the eager-
" nefs of bestowing a better merited praise upon
" another. Such is the tribute which the wisdom
" and integrity of Ally Ibraham Caun have extort-
" ed from the hearts of thofe who have been
" fubjection to his jurisdict."

At half past four, Mr. Burke complained that
he was tired, and the Court adjourned, having sat
only two hours and a half, though the Commons
had fent a meffage that they were ready to proceed day by day until the Trial was clofed; but
no Manager was ready to proceed to clofe this
everlasting Caufe; and yet the Managers formed
a Com-

a Committee, instructed to inquire into the causes of the duration of the Trial.

The court meets again on Thursday, when it is hoped, tho' hardly expected, that Mr. Burke will close. Nothing new has been said: from 1788 to 1794, the same remarks have been repeated.

———

Mr. Burke's 4th Day.

ONE HUNDRED AND FORTY-THIRD DAY, *June 5.*

The Court, on this day, betrayed strong symptoms of being fatigued by the great length and small advance made by Mr. Burke in his closing Speech. The audience was thinned considerably, the Commons were few in number, no Managers, and only twelve Lords present. Mr. Wyndham afterwards arrived. Mr. Burke began at two, by restating, that Mr. Hastings, by expelling Cheyt Sing, and by his own subsequent regulations, had utterly ruined Benares.

In justice to the British nation, we wish to remark that from the letter, of which Mr. Burke read a part, and from the answer of Lord Cornwallis, it is clear that the revenue of 400,000l. a year which Mr. Hastings had fixed as a proper sum

sum for the British nation to receive, was a sum which the Country could well pay, leaving the Rajah a sum amply sufficient for his dignity. and expence.

The country did pay this Revenue under Mr. Hastings, under Sir John Macpherson, and under Lord Cornwallis. It continues to pay it under Sir John Shore, yet with all this Evidence before him, with the Evidence of the public accounts; did Mr. Burke insult common sense on this day, by repeating again that Benares had been utterly ruined by Mr. Hastings.

Mr. Burke then went into the complete history of Oude, though the whole has been abandoned by the Commons, and read extracts from Minutes, which do not apply in the least to any matter depending on this impeachment. Mr. Burke said he charged Mr. Hastings with treason and rebellion, that is the Commons did so, for not laying his Persian correspondence before the Council.

From ten minutes past two, until the Court rose a quarter before five, not a syllable said by Mr. Burke, had the least reference to any matter in charge against Mr. Hastings.

The whole Speech applied to those Articles, which the House of Commons have abandoned. By the last House, they were voted without being

i   ing

ing read, and this Houſe precluded the Managers from going into them at all. Consequently, this was a day totally lost; and the Lords
ſeemed to think so, for the number Twelve, which
the court conſiſted of, when it aſſembled, was reduced to Nine before Mr. Burke had done.

When the Lords retired, a Petition was pre-
ſented from Mr. Hastings to the Lords, in which
he reminded their Lordſhips, that when the Reply
was postponed last year, it was stated that in faƈt
it would be no loss of time, as the Court might sit
day by day, so as to finish it and come to judgement early in this Sessions; that except the short
delay by the examination of Lord Cornwallis, the
whole of this year had been taken up by the Managers in reply.

That he could not help being alarmed at the
advanced state of the Session, compared with the
progress made by the Managers in the Reply;
and, therefore, he most earnestly intreated, that
their Lordship swould take his unparallelled case
into conſideration; and that they would be sui-
tors to His Majesty not to prorogue this Sessions,
until the Speech in reply was finished; and until nothing but the Judgement should remain. The
Lords, after this Petition was read, determined to
meet again on Saturday.

As this was a day wholly lost, no man could
form

form an idea of the time Mr. Burke will take—
Ten guineas have been given to receive a guinea
for every fpeaking day that Mr. Burke shall yet
take; but it is very singular, that though the
Commons sent a message to the Lords, that they
were ready to proceed day by day, Mr. Burke
himself desires the Lords to indulge him with a
day's recess. It was at his request that the Court
did not meet last Saturday, and it was at his earnest desire that the Trial was put 'off from this
day to Saturday. We trust, however, that the
time will come, when every circumstance attending this unparalleled Trial will be fully explained.

In such a season of calamity and danger, that
instead of evidence, epithets disgusting to all who
hear them, should be fo lavishly bestowed upon
a man who has done as much to serve his country, as any British subject now living, is indeed
a very ferious evil. Nobody desires to stop Mr.
Burke.

If the Commons, in whose name he speaks,
think it right to keep all that Mr. Hastings procured for them, and to boast of the amount,
value, and importance of his acquisitions.

If the King's Ministers thinks it right to hold
a language in the Houfe of Commons so totally
different from what Mr. Burke holds in West-

T T   minster-

minster-Hall, still there can be no reason why some period should not be put to such contradictions. Let us therefore hope, that his Majesty will be addressed not to prorogue Parliament until Mr. Burke has done. The Lords who assembled to hear the opening Speech of Mr. Burke, to the number of one hundred and sixty-eight, are now reduced to ten.

The Managers, Mr. Wyndham excepted, have deserted Mr. Hastings, and the whole world anxiously await the day of judgment.

Mr. Burke's 5th Day.

ONE HUNDRED AND FORTY-FOURTH DAY, *June* 7.

The Court met at two, twelve Lords present. Mr. Burke began by complaining in very strong terms, both of the Court and Mr. Hastings; of the latter, for writing a most audacious Libel, under the name of a Petition? and of the former, for having received it upon their Journals. What the House of Commons would do, in consequence of this insult, he could not tell, as he had not yet had an opportunity of consulting the House upon it; he should therefore proceed as if no such Libel had been written.

What

What Mr. Burke calls a Libel, is the Petition presented by Lord Hardwicke to the Lords, in which Mr. Hastings states truths that certainly do no credit to the Managers. The fact is, that in the last year the Lords wanted the Commons to begin and to finish their reply. Mr. Burke and the Managers persuaded the Commons to desire the Lords to put off the Trial to this year; and it was said in the Commons, that it would be no real loss of time, because the reply could not be finished in the last year, but by deferring it to this year, the House might meet day by day, and actually conclude it very early in this Session.

To this promise, and to the breach of it, Mr. Hastings did very strongly allude in his Petition to the Lords; for it was impossible for him not to be apprehensive, that instead of pronouncing Judgement in this year, Mr. Burke's speech would not be finished, unless their Lordships interceeded with his Majesty, to keep Parliament sitting some time longer. It is equally certain, that the Commons did send a message to the Lords, that they were ready to proceed day by day. Mr. Burke applies continually to the Lords, and desires them not to sit two days together.

Is it possible for Mr. Hastings not to feel? and has he not a right to complain? Mr. Burke says, no other person has ever dared to complain as Mr.

Hastings

Hastings has done. It may be so, but it is equally true, that no Englishman before this day, has been seven years on his trial, or impeached for the measures which he took to bring thirty-four millions sterling into the Public Exchequer, and to add two millions sterling a year to the annual Revenue of England. If the language of Mr. Hastings is bold, let it be considered, that his services and their importance are universally acknowledged.

Mr. Burke then recapitulated the material points of his last day's speech, not one of which had the least reference to any one of the four articles, on which Mr. Burke himself admits the impeachment depends; but as the result of all was said to be, that the dominions of the Nabob of Oude were utterly ruined by Mr. Hastings, we shall, as in the case of Benares, appeal to facts, in order to prove that the ruin consists only in the imagination of Mr. Burke.

In January 1775, Sujah Dowlah, Nabob of Oude, died, and was succeeded by his son, the present Nabob. It was determined by the Government of Bengal, in opposition to the opinion of Mr. Hastings, that the Treaties subsisting between Bengal and Oude expired with Sujah Dowlah. They, therefore, compelled the Nabob either to give up all connections with Bengal, or to consent

sent to increase the Subsidy which he paid for a Brigade of British Troops, from 21, to 26,000l. a month; and also, to cede for ever to the Company, the Province of Benares.

Mr. Burke defended this act; though Mr. Dundas described it, as it certainly was, a most flagrant breach of a Solemn Treaty. The Directors concurred in opinion with Mr. Hastings, that the Treaty with Sujah Dowlah did not expire at his death; but they were well pleased by the increase of the Subsidy, and the acquisition of Benares, both of which resulted from the intimate connection formed by Mr. Hastings with Sujah Dowlah, in the year 1773.

At the latter end of the year 1775, such was the distress of the Nabob, and such the confusion in his country, owing to the Begum withholding his father's treasures, which left an army of one hundred thousand men many months in arrears, that the Nabob was persuaded by Mr. Bristow, to apply for British officers to command his forces. The request was complied with, and a number of officers were sent to Oude upon emoluments and allowances, infinitely beyond any that were enjoyed by the Bengal army. Mr. Burke misrepresents this matter so completely, that any person who heard him, must have supposed that Mr. Hastings formed this arrangement, whereas it was in

fact

fact done by the majority, Messrs. Clavering, Monson, and Francis.

Two of the officers first appointed were Major Webber, Aid-de-Camp to General Clavering, who was not in the Company's Service, and Major Marsack. It is no reflection upon Major Webber, who is a very worthy and honourable man, to say that he made a handsome fortune in the Nabob's service in four yers. It is well known that Major Marsack has purchased the fine Seat and Park of Lord Cadogan, at Caversham. Many other officers appointed by General Clavering in 1775, have returned with easy and independent fortunes. This Nabob had Aid-de-Camps, Secretaries, Adjutant, and Quarter-Master-General, Pay-master, and Commissaries, with their Deputies.

Mr. Bristow, who was the Chief, is supposed, upon good grounds, to possess the largest fortune that ever was made in India. We do not mention this as invidious very far from it, but in order to shew that the system under which so many fortunes were made in Oude, was not formed by Mr. Hastings, as Mr. Burke so erroneously states, but by General Clavering, Colonel Monson, and Mr. Francis.

The Nabob had no money, and was unable to pay these new military and civil establishments, or to discharge what was then owing to the Company.

Company. He therefore assigned certain districts to Mr. Bristow, who, in concert with the
Minister, was in truth the Sovereign of Oude, a
fact stated by Captain Edwards, who swore that
the Nabob was in a state of subordination to all
the residents alike. In other words, and in another passage, he said, that the Nabob's Minister,
who was under the influence of the resident, entirely governed the country. Such was the system
established in 1775 by the majority, and this system continued under Mr. Bristow first, then under
Mr. Middleton, or Mr. Purling, until September,
1781, when it was in some degree altered.

In 1784, Mr. Hastings made an arrangement
with the Nabob, by which it was agreed that if,
the Nabob discharged the debt then due to the
Company; and if in future he regularly paid the
subsidy due for the British Troops, no resident
should have the slightest interference in his dominions. This arrangement, which Mr. Burke
has quarrelled with, as he does with every thing,
was very fully approved by the King's Ministers,
and was ordered by them, to be invariably ad-
hered to. It has been so, but still we exercise a
superintending power in Oude, precisely similar
to that which was exercised by Mr. Hastings.
Lord Cornwallis, who, on all occasions speaks
and acts as a man of honour, was unwilling that

his

his countrymen should undergo the scandal of being the authors of disorders with which they had
nothing to do, and wrote to the Directors, " That
" the Disorders in Oude are to be traced in the
" character of the Prince," whom he describes as
very extravagant, and utterly averse to business
of any kind. His Lordship therefore protected
the Minister, Hyder Big Khan, against the Nabob, and as often as the Nabob seemed disinclined
to act agreeable to the wishes of the Minister,
Lord Cornwallis has remonstrated, and the evil
was redressed. When this Minister died in 1792,
the Nabob waited to know the pleasure of Lord
Cornwallis, before he appointed a successor.

From 1773, when Mr. Hastings formed the
first arrangement with Sujah Dowlah, to this time,
we have received above seventeen millions sterling from Oude. Oude has, in fact, paid above
one third of the annual expence of the Bengal
army, independent of the large sums in bullion,
remitted to the Treasury, in Calcutta, which enabled us to preserve India, in the last general
war.

• We have proved, by a reference to facts, which
are of general notoriety, that the system which led
to our first interference in the internal Government of Oude, was not the system of Mr. Hastings, but of General Clavering, Colonel Monson,

and

and Mr. Francis. Justice to those Gentlemen induces us to declare, that no such mischievous confequences as Mr. Burke states, did result from that interference.

The Military Farmers General, as Mr. Burke calls them, guarded the extreme Provinces of the Nabob's Dominions, countries which Mr. Bristow described, before these officers were appointed, as in such a state of anarchy and rebellion, that they could hardly be said to make part of the Nabob's dominions ; under these Military Farmers General, the countries were much better governed than they had been before or since, and revenues were collected, and brought into the Treasury at Lucknow, from districts which before those Officers were appointed, had paid nothing to the Nabob.

That the assumption of the Government of Oude, by the British resident Mr. Bristow, in 1775, and the continuance of the same power under Mr. Middleton, was a serious evil, and that the employment of British officers to collect revenues, was liable to every objection stated by Mr. Hastings, is most certain; but it was an evil, as it affected our own service, not as it injured the Nabob's subjects. Is there a man so weak, or foolish as to believe, that Oude is better governed now, than it was either by Mr. Bristow or Mr. Middleton?

ton? Certainly it is not; but as the Nabob has discharged all his debts to the company, and as he now regularly pays the subsidy, we have no right, or pretence for interfering with him in his government, except by advice, which has been equivalent to command to this day.

Even the removal of every species of interference in the internal affairs of Oude, was made criminal in Mr. Hastings, by one of those thirteen articles, which the Commons passed without reading, though the King's Ministers expressed their fullest approbation of the conduct of Mr. Hastings in forming that arrangement.

We have gone through this subject. It is true that it has nothing to do with any matter in charge, but it will serve to shew with what ingenuity Mr. Burke can turn acts of merit into crimes.

From this country of Oude, so compleatly and irretrieveably ruined, this nation has received above 17 millions sterling since 1773. It is to receive in future years half a million sterling each year, and it is completely protected by the British forces from Foreign invasion. It is absurd, ridiculous, contrary to fact, and to common sense, to state a country as ruined, which is enabled for twenty years together, to pay such sums to a Foreign State, merely for military assistance.

ONE

ONE HUNDRED AND FORTY-FIFTH DAY, *June* 11.

Mr. Burke's 6th Day.

The Court this day assembled at two o'clock; twelve Lords being present, and Mr. Wyndham with Mr. Burke. The Manager recapitulated what he had said the last day, and then went into a very strong and pointed attack upon the testimony and conduct of Sir Elijah Impey, a Member of the House of Commons, and upon the several Gentlemen who had been employed in Oude. He went through the Begum charge in part, contended that it was impossible they should have been in rebellion in the year 1781, that the whole was a story invented by Mr. Hastings, as a plea for seizing her treasures; and offered, as a proof of it, that the Directors had sent the most positive orders for instituting a particular enquiry into the truth of the accusation against the Begum, which orders the colleagues of Mr. Hastings would have carried into execution, had not they been over-ruled by Mr. Hastings.

This subject occupied Mr. Burke for a considerable time; and in the course of this speech, he applied so many coarse epithets to Mr. Hastings, that at length he started up, and declared,

that

that the Directors had sent no orders for instituting the inquiry mentioned by Mr. Burke; and
that Human Nature must at last be exhausted by
hearing such gross falsehoods so often repeated.

Mr. Burke appeared a little confounded, but
recovering himself said, he hoped the Court would
not permit that wicked wretch—that scourge of
India—that criminal, to insult the House of Commons.   After some time Mr. Wyndham said,
the best way would be, to read again the orders
of the Directors, for the enquiry alluded to by
Mr. Burke.   As this is a matter of a most delicate
nature, we shall merely state the Facts, to which
the orders of the Directors applied; the orders
themselves, the minutes that followed them, of
which parts only were read by Mr. Wyndham,
and leave the world to form their own conclusions.

In July 1782, the Directors were informed
that in consequence of the support given to Cheyt
Sing, the Guarantee of the Company had been
withdrawn from the Begum; that Mr. Hastings
had strenuously encouraged and supported the Nabob in resuming the Jaghire, and in seizing the
treasure of the Begum, they were informed that
all the treasure taken, amounting to 500,000l. had
been applied to the discharge of the debt due by
the Nabob to the East-India Company.   The Benares

nares narrative, and the affidavits, were sent home
by the fame conveyance, and arrived in July
1782. The Directors answered these advices on
the 14th of February 1783.

The Managers gave the answer in evidence
in 1788, and prefaced it with these words—
" Then the Managers acquainted the House they
" would next proceed to shew that the Directors
" did order an Enquiry to be made in India into
" the conduct of the Begum, that all the world
" might know the real truth of the case; and that
" Mr. Hastings did stifle that Enquiry. The
" letter is then entered by the Managers in page
" 920, and the answer in these words.

" If it should hereafter be found that the Begum
" did not take that hostile part against the Com-
" pany which has been represented, as well in the
" Governor General's Narrative as in the several
" documents therein referred to, and as it no where
" appears from the papers at present in our posses-
" sion, that they excited any commotion previous
" to the insurrection of Cheyt Sing, but only arm-
" ed themselves in consequence of that transaction,
" and as it is probable that such a conduct pro-
" ceeded entirely from motives of self-defence, un-
" der an apprehension that they themselves might
" likewise be laid under unwarrantable contribu-
" tions, we direct that you use your influence with
" the

" the Vizier that their Jaghires may be restored to
" them."

Here is the order; and the point in dispute is,
whether this be an order for enquiring into the
truth of the Rebellion of the Begums, or whether it be an order to use the influence of the
Bengal Government to restore to her her Jaghire; as to the treasures, the Directors are totally
silent on that subject; yet it is obvious, that if an
enquiry was ordered, and if in the result of that
enquiry she should prove to have been falsely accused, on what principle of justice, or common
sense, could the Directors have passed over the
Treasures.

The Government consisted of Mr. Hastings,
Mr. Wheeler, Mr. Stables, and Sir John Macpherson. After the Letter of the Directors had
been read, Mr. Wheeler stated his wish always to
conform implicitly to the orders of the Directors;
that those then before them were entirely provi-
sional; that he was fully convinced, not only from
the report of Mr. Hastings, but from the opinions
of many individuals totally unconcerned on the
subject, that the Begums at Fyzabad did take a
hostile part against the Company during the dis-
turbances at Benares; but as the Directors appeared to be of a different opinion, and conceived
that there ought to be stronger proofs of the de-
fection

fection of the Begums than had been laid before them, he thought, that before they decided on these orders, the late and present Residents should collect all the information they could upon the subject.

If there be sense or meaning in language, Mr. Wheeler said, before I consent to intercede with the Nabob, for the restoration of their Jaghires, I desire to know, what has been their past and present conduct.

Mr. Hastings replies, that he thinks Mr. Wheeler has mistaken the intention of the Directors—that he sees nothing like an Order expressed or implied, for such an enquiry as Mr. Wheeler proposes. Here the matter drops until the 22d of September, when a Minute from Mr. Staples is read, in which he says, that the Directors seem not to be satisfied—that the disaffection of the Begums is sufficiently proved,

He therefore thinks, that the late and present Resident, should be called upon to collect what further information they can, and the Commanding Officers who were at the time in the Vizier's country.

If there be any meaning in language, this motion was not made in compliance with an Order, but because Mr. Stables conceived that the Directors

rectors seemed not to be satisfied with the information before them.

Mr. Hastings appealed to the letter. He says it does not order an enquiry, but adds, if evidence is to be collected, it should be collected from all persons capable of giving it, and not confined to official characters.

To this Minute Mr. Staples makes no reply.

Sir John Macpherson, (whose Minute Mr. Wyndham did not read, (though it follows in the next page,) says, " I have read the letter of the " Directors with attention. When it was first " read in Council, I understood that the para- " graphs about the Begums, as directing an in- " vestigation, &c.

" On a close attention to the words and spirit " of the different paragraphs upon the subject, I " do not think we are directed to commence any " new investigation of Evidence. Indeed I do " not see how any new investigation of Evidence " could be regularly undertaken, or what salu- " tary purpose it could answer.

" There has been no appeal from the Begums " to this Government, and there certainly was " sufficient proof, at the time, that those who had " the management of their concerns during the " troubles of Benares, were no friends, but real " enemies to the cause of the English."

Here

Here is all the evidence to this point; Mr. Burke contends that an enquiry was ordered, that the colleagues of Mr. Hastings thought so, and that Mr. Hastings to screen himself refused it. If Mr. Burke had read all the evidence as it is on the Minutes, Mr. Hastings would have been unpardonable in interrupting him. It would have been seen, had the whole been read, that neither Mr. Wheeler, nor Mr. Stables, proposed an enquiry, because it was ordered, but because Mr. Stables thought the Directors seemed not to be satisfied, and because Mr. Wheeler would not apply for the restoration of her Jaghire, until he knew her past and present disposition.

Sir John Macpherson was clearly of opinion, that there was no order for an enquiry. Why did Mr. Wyndham omit Sir John Macpherson's evidence? Why did the Managers, when they called Mr. Stables to this point in 1788, not call Sir John Macpherson, who was also in England? These are questions which may fairly be asked by those who wish really to know the truth.

We do not mean to excuse Mr. Hastings, however, on any ground but this. Mr. Burke set out, by saying, that he would read the evidence, to shew that Mr. Hastings had disobeyed the orders of the Directors. He gave the book to Mr. Wyndham,

U u   who

who read a garbled account, and Mr. Burke argued, as if the whole had been read.

―――――――――

ONE HUNDRED AND FORTY-SIXTH DAY, *June* 12.

Mr. Burke's 7th Day.

This day produced nothing new from Mr. Burke, or worth recording. He desired Mr. Wyndham to read the account transmitted by Major Gilpin and Captain Jacques to the British Resident at Lucknow, of the distresses suffered by the Women of the Khord Mahl, or Concubines of Sujah Dowlah, in 1782; but he totally omitted a reference to the evidence of those Gentlemen, by which it appears, that no British subject, much less Mr. Hastings, who never heard of their distresses, could be accountable for them; that they had no sort of connection with the Begum, and that no measures pursued against her, could in any respect add to or diminish the distresses of these unhappy women, who had a very small allowance from the Nabob, and that small allowance was irregularly paid.

By reading the description of these distresses, and

and omitting the evidence of the cause of them, Mr. Burke made out a very piteous tale; and with this, and other matters, which had no connection with Mr. Hastings, he continued until near six o'clock, when the Court adjourned, and meet again on Saturday, on which day Mr. Burke, it is said, is to make an end of his Speech.

There were two very curious points in this day's Speech, on which we shall make a few observations.

The first was where Mr. Burke said, that this country had a particular interest in the good Government of India, since the Public were to receive from the surplus revenues of India in future five hundred thousand pounds a year. How Mr. Burke could venture to allude to this law, is indeed astonishing.

It passed in the last Session; and though Mr. Burke had solemnly pledged himself to oppose with his utmost force, every attempt to perpetuate the present oppressive and corrupt system by which India is governed: he actually absented himself as often as that Bill was under discussion in the House. It has passed, and it is grounded upon data, which are death's blows to the Impeachment; for it is assumed, that we have a right to all we possess in India; and it is assumed, that the revenues in future will be equal to what they now produce. If

Mr.

Mr. Hastings has been justly impeached, heavy indeed are the demands which the Princes of India have upon England, for the public robberies of Mr. Hastings; and very considerable must be the annual deductions from the future revenues of India.

The second is a point, which tho' not immediately respecting Mr. Hastings, proves, that Mr. Burke has omitted no means to obtain information, and as he has procured none, it establishes most clearly the assertions of Colonel Duff, that India is united in his favour.

Mr. Burke said, he had received a letter from Mr. Bristow, in which that Gentleman affirmed, that one of the Eunuchs of the Begum had suffered corporal punishment at Lucknow. It is proved in evidence, that Mr. Hastings neither directly nor indirectly authorized such a punishment, nor was he ever acquainted with this circumstance. The fact undoubtedly is, that if the British Resident had not interfered to prevent it, the Nabob would have put these Eunuchs to death; Mr. Hastings knew nothing about them. The material question, and the only one in which he is concerned is this;—" Was it right or wrong " in him to withdraw the Guarantee of the British " nation from the Begum, and to advise the Na- " bob, to take from her certain sums of money, " for

" for the purpose of liquidating the Public Debt,
" which he owed to the company ?"

The supposed cruelties to the Eunuchs, the supposed distress of the concubines in the Khord
Mahl, Mr. Hastings, connot be responsible for;
Major Gilpin and Captain Jacques have fully
proved, that he neither knew of the one or the
other. But the curious point is this, that though
Mr. Burke has let it out, that he has been carrying on a secret correspondence in Bengal, he has not
been able to excite the Begum, or her Eunuchs,
or any human being to complain of the tyranny,
oppression, injustice, or cruelty of Mr. Hastings.

ONE HUNDRED AND FORTY-SEVENTH DAY, *June* 14.

Mr. Burke's 8th day.

Mr. Burke on this day began by stating, that
Mr. Hastings had despoiled the Nabob of Bengal,
like an ancient knight, of all his armour—his hel-
met—his hawbeck—and at last cut off his spurs—
that he afterwards restored him to all his privileges, for the purpose of again bringing into power

that

that infamous, corrupting, and corrupted prostitute, Munny Begum; that he made her Chief Justice, and the country was again given up to murderers and robbers —that he set up the country gentlemen to auction, and put his own domestics in possession of the estates of the Nobles of the country.

This part of Mr. Burke's speech was unconnected with any matter in charge; equally irregular was it to state, that Mr. Hastings had been a bullock contractor—Mr. Burke then went very slightly through the contracts; the abolition of the provincial Councils and Gunga Govind Sing,— he then went back to Oude, and came back again to Bengal, to what he called the bribe of the entertainment—that is, the sum of two thousand Rupees a day, paid to Mr. Hastings, while he was at Moorshedabad in 1772.—Mr. Burke then said, that if the Lords would attend him one hour on Monday, he would finally close; upon which the court adjourned.

ONE HUNDRED AND FORTY-EIGHTH DAY, *June* 16.

Mr. Burke's 9th and last Day's Speech.

Mr. Burke began by an allusion to a speech of one of the council, whom he accused of taking improper liberties, and he then mentioned an epigram*, of which the same gentleman was the supposed author.

As it is in proof, that the sum of 2000 Rupees a day received by Mr. Hastings in 1772, was for entertainment, agreeably to established custom, and not a bribe, as charged by the late House for an appointment to office, Mr. Burke took up quite *a new ground* — He affirmed that the covenants were made precisely to prevent this sort of abuse — Here again Mr. Burke fails — for both Lord Clive and Mr. Verelst subscribed the covenants, as well as Mr. Hastings; both those Governors took the two thousand Rupees a day for entertainment, without conceiving it to be, as it certainly was not, a breach of their covenants—Mr. Burke then re-

---

* Oft have I wondered that on Irish ground,
No poisonous reptiles ever yet were found ;
Reveal'd the secret stands of Nature's work,
She sav'd her venom, to create a Burke.

u u 4   turned

turned to Kobkessin's present, which he affirmed
to be worse than any act of Verres, and applied
the epithets, rogue, common cheat, swindler, to
Mr. Hastings, for having taken that present for
the Company.

Mr. Burke then came to Lord Cornwallis's evidence, which he insisted proved Bengal to be ruined
—He then read the 39th section of the Act of the
24th of his present Majesty, to prove the oppressions of Mr. Hastings, — The Act of Parliament,
he said, had declared the oppressions and the oppressor, and addressing himself to the Lords, he
said, You must repeal this Act of Parliament, you
must declare the Legislature *a Liar*, before you
can acquit Warren Hastings.

Mr. Burke then said, that Mr. Hastings had
pleaded his merits, which was no answer to a criminal charge, but in fact, every act which he stated to be meritorious, had been condemned by a
former Parliament, Mr. Dundas having moved
forty-five resolutions, each of which condemned
some act done by Mr. Hastings. Every one of
those, said Mr. Burke, not excepting one of
them, were all censured by the House of Commons.

Mr. Hastings admits this statement to be true,
and told the House of Commens he did so, at the
same time that he complained of the cruel injuries
he

he suffered, by that body having censured and prosecuted him in one chara&er, for a&s which in another they had very fully approved, and of which they continued to enjoy all the benefit — Mr. Burke next affirmed, that Mr. Hastings was the author of the Maratta war, and that he concluded it, by a dishonourable peace.

At last Mr. Burke came to his close, which was the strongest mixture of the sublime and beautiful in language, but weak and silly in argument, that we ever remember to have heard. — He alluded to the miserable state of France at the present moment — to the murder of the best of Kings, and the most glorious of Queens, and to the destru&ion of the Parliament of Paris, a court almost as dignified as that which he was then addressing, and uniformly pure in its legal decisions — to the destru&ion of all ranks and orders in society; and after praying that heaven would avert from us the miseries that have desolated France, he said, that if it should be their Lordships lot to submit to the axe of the Guillotine, on any future and dreadful convulsion, their last hours would be more tranquil from a refle&ion, that in the great cause before them they had decided by the rules of equity and justice. With a peroration of which this is the substance, Mr. Burke concluded this long trial; and as he quitted Parliament

in

in the course of the Session, we shall here give the debate that took place on the motion of thanks to the managers, when it was brought forward by Mr. Pitt.

HOUSE OF COMMONS,

28th June. 1794.

MR. PITT said, he rose to make his promised Motion, for the Thanks of that House to the Managers for their conduct in the Impeachment against Warren Hastings, Esq. When first he intended taking this step, he had considered it as a matter of course, to which he thought no possible objection could have been offered from any quarter of the House; but when he had postponed his motion, upon intimation that it was intended to be opposed, he had set himself to consider what objections could be made to such a measure generally, or to this one in particular. The Impeachment itself had been voted, not only from a conviction that there was sufficient ground to put the party accused upon his trial, but as a terror to
those

those placed in a similar situation in the government of our distant provinces; nor was there any
exercise of their power in which the House
shewed themselves more majestic than in that pro-
tection which they thus shewed themselves determined to afford those parts of the British empire,
which, by being thus far removed from their immediate inspection, might be supposed most liable
to oppression and plunder. When he looked at
the magnitude of the task which they had thus
imposed upon their Managers, he could not avoid
feeling every thing in their favour, and a business
of such extent, and executed so ably, covered
every error they might have lapsed into, if such
could be really imputed to them, and that no ex-
ception ought to be taken to it, unless a total failure or miscarriage could be imputed to them.
Where, he asked, could such a charge be stated?
Perhaps the length to which the trial had been
protracted might be objected; this was a presumption naturally to be looked for, if we looked either
at the nature of the transaction itself, the charges
exhibited upon the occasion, or the evidence ne-
cessarily produced in support of those charges.
Was there any thing in all these which could be
fairly imputed to their managers? On the contrary, it formed the peculiar privilege and advantage of trial by impeachment, over the ordinary
proceedings

proceedings in the courts of justice, that delinquencies beyond their reach were to be brought,
if deserving, to punishment without the interven-
tion of those legal shackles which frequently arrest
the avenging hand of the law in the ordinary forms.
This, however, which, instead of an objection, was
an argument in favour of impeachments generally,
was unnecessary to be urged in the present instance, if Gentlemen, instead of computing the
years, took the trouble of analyzing the trial by
the number of days, and the few hours occupied
in each day, which it had taken up. The next
point to be considered was, that of this time, whether more or less, how much of it had been occupied by the managers, and how much by the defendant in the several replies, and still further,
what additional delay given by the latter, by un-
ceasing and unwearied objections taken on his
part to almost every thing offered on the part of
the prosecution. To prove this disposition to objecting to evidence, Gentlemen had but to look
to the Report made by their Committee on the
causes of delay, they would find it fully proved.
It was in the next place to be recollected, that
their Managers had to discuss questions in the
course of Mr. Hastings's Trial, which they could
not tamely relinquish without abandoning the privileges of the Commons, as contradistinguished
from

from the ordinary courts of law. Upon all these grounds he, and he trusted the House with him, would by no means be inclined to admit, either that there were any grounds for imputing any delay whatever, or even if there were, that their Managers were to be censured for it. But these objections, true or false, came in the present stage too late. If they were well founded, better they had been made in time, when the correction of them, as they arose, might have prevented two acts of injustice; rendering the Defendant an object of persecution, and their Managers of delusion, in going on with measures in themselves wrong, but which the silence of that House seemed to sanction. Under all these circumstances, he could see no possible ground of objection to the present motion; those who were of opinion from the beginning, that the prosecution was a just and necessary one, should not now object to its conclusion; those who were originally of a contrary opinion, and adverse to the instituting any proceedings whatever, he appealed to their candour, whether being in a minority throughout, they ought to expect the House to act in the sequel, as they wished in vain to persuade them to act at the commencement; but rather allow the House to act as was usual in similar cases. Did they wish for the acquital of Mr. Hastings? That was an
event

event no longer in their hands, but rested in another place; how then could that wish operate, either as a motive or reason for with-holding the usual thanks? Any thing now done in the House of Commons could have no effect upon the Lords —Mr. Hastings must be acquitted or condemned upon legal evidence and legal evidence alone. It was not a question now, what the House would do if the Impeachment was now to be voted. The whole business was concluded as far as depended upon the House; and not to thank the Managers, would be to depart from usual practice on similar occasions. It was certainly true, that such Gentlemen as had uniformly, throughout the course of the trial, shewn themselves adverse to the Managers, could not add any thing to the eclat of the Managers, by joining in the vote of thanks: on the contrary, their dissent would prove it not a business of course, but rather of discrimination; still, however, he could not help expressing a wish that on this, as on another occasion, hereafter to be submitted (the vote of thanks to Lord Hood), the vote of that house might be unanimous. He concluded with moving, " That the thanks of that House be given to the Managers appointed by them to conduct the prosecution against Warren Hastings, Esq. for the faithful Management in the discharge of the important trust reposed in them."

Mr.

Mr. DUNDAS seconded the motion.

Mr. SUMNER said, he could not avoid expressing his surprise, that a motion such as that he had just heard read, should be considered as a matter of course. He said, that he rose with considerable diffidence to oppose a motion which had been made by the Right Honourable Gentle.man, with whom it was generally his good fortune to agree. The Right Honourable Gentleman had supported the motion with all his talents and with all his influence, but he must add, he had not displayed any degree of candour in the course of his speech, when he presupposed the objections which would be made from a certain description of Gentlemen in that House, one of whom he had infinite pride and pleasure in declaring himself to be. Mr. Sumner said, he was happy to avow himself a very great admirer of Mr. Hastings; that he looked up to him with every sentiment of regard and affection; but his objections to the present motion arose from circumstances utterly independent of Mr. Hastings. The Right Honourable Gentleman had said, that Mr. Hastings could not in any shape be affected now by any motion that could be made in this House ;— that the decison was before a competent Court, which could only determine by evidence. Admitting

mitting this to be the fact, as he did, still a vote of thanks was, in a certain degree, a vote of approbation of the Managers conduct. Surely the period was too short for the House to determine upon the conduct of their Managers. Seven years had the trial lasted, and it had been attended with circumstances new and extraordinary. It was true, that on former occasions thanks had been voted, and as the Speaker had informed him from the chair, before the judgement was pronounced, but certainly not until the verdict was known. In this instance the thanks would be voted many months before the judgement, and though any thing that could be construed into an approbation of the Commons, would not affect the judgement, there was an indecency in the proceedings which led him to oppose it in the first instance by the previous question.

Mr. Sumner said, that if the time were not improper, he certainly would not oppose a vote of thanks to the Managers, one *excepted*, who had faithfully discharged the trust imposed on them, by supporting the specific charges, voted by the last House of Commons. Mr. Sumner said, that he retained the same opinion which he had so often professed of the charges, which he thought to be ill founded; but it was the duty of the Managers to support them, and he never would

refuse

be fo illiberal as to objeƈt to their receiving the
thanks of that House at a proper time, provided
they could be given without their bestowing their
thanks at the same time on the leading Manager,
who, he contended, by his conduƈt, had disgraced and degraded the House of Commons,
and had dared, in their name, to vilify every
Gentleman who had had the honour and good fortune to serve his country in India; including in
his abuse, all their conneƈtions of every defcrip-
tion, and applying the odious epithet *gang* to this
body of men. The Speaker calling out order,
Mr. Sumner said, that if he could find more mea-
fured expressions to convey to the Houfe his fenfe
of the misconduƈt of Mr. Burke, and of the disgrace he had brought upon the House, he would
use them; but he would proceed to explain of
what nature the Manager's conduƈt had been, in
the hope that it would be as much reprobated by
the House, as he knew it was *by all descriptions of
persons out of doors.* The faƈts that he fhould detail, the Members in general were ignorant of, for
very few indeed had attended; and of all Members of the Houfe, the Right Honourable Gentleman below him was the last man who was competent to decide on the conduƈt of the Managers,
his various avocations making his absence from
the trial an aƈt of necessity. He had too high an
opinion of the Minister to think it *possible* for

x x   him

him to have made the motion before them, had he ever heard the leading Manager in Westminster Hall. Mr. Sumner said, in the light he viewed a vote of thanks, he cou'd not possibly assent to it. Did the House know that Mr. Burke had folemnly affirmed, that Captain Williams had murdered Raja Mustapha Cawn with his own hands? He would ask, what authority had the House given to Mr. Burke to make such a charge? Was it decent or honourable in the House to suffer such language to be uttered against any Gentleman, and yet deny to him the means of defending himself? All that man could do was done by Captain Williams to bring this outrageous calumny to a fair trial;—he petitioned the House upon it five years ago, the House would not bring a charge that he could reply to; and is the Manager to receive thanks for daring to charge an English Gentleman with murder in a speech, and there to leave it?—Is this British justice!

The last House voted twenty articles of impeachment against Mr Hastings; three were gone through in the last Parliament—Benares, the Begum, and the Presents. This House, by a formal vote, precluded the Managers from going into any other articles, except the Contracts; and the prosecution was finally closed in the first session of this Parliament. Does the House know, that in contempt and defiance of this resolution, the Manager insisted on his right to go into the other

articles,

articles, and expressly told the Lords, that the Commons had not abandoned them, nor ever would abandon any one of them? Will the House thank the Manager for this contempt of their authority? Does the House know, that the language used by the leading Manager to the Court was in the highest degree disgraceful? That he had the presumption to tell the Court, whether with a view to intimidation, or from the wildness of the moment, that the Commons had not only prosecuted, but they had found Mr. Hastings guilty when they impeached him; that the Lords could not acquit him without proving the legislature a *liar?*—Is such language to be borne? Is this British justice? Will an English House of Commons approve of such sentiments? What is a solemn trial by impeachment but a mockery, a farce, if such language is not scouted by every man who hears it? The leading Manager find ng the general sentiments of Gentlemen who have served in India to be strongly in favour of Mr. Hastings, and, in order to invalidate the testimony of the witnesses, has attempted to blacken and to blast the character of every Gentleman who has breathed the air of Asia. Was this universal abuse necessary in order to convict Mr. Hastings? Is the character and fame of every man to be torn in pieces without a hearing? Is this to be done by the authority of the House of

X X 2   Com-

Commons? Are they prepared to adopt at once the extravagant and indecorous substitution of the slang of Billingsgate for the strong energetic language of truth and justice? Will they confer on Mr. Hastings, by this vote, the minor titles of swindler, thief, rogue, sharper, cheat, or the more daring descriptions, tyrant, oppressor, and murderer? " I charge him," said the Manager, " as " a *tyrant, oppressor,* and *murderer in the largest* " *sense of the word.*" Does the House know, that though Mr. Burke was reprimanded for accusing Mr. Hastings of murder, he repeated the charge on the very next day, and again repeated it a few days ago, as he says himself, *in the largest sense of the word?* Instead of thanks, does he not deserve the resentment and the reprobation of the House? Has the House ever charged Mr. Hastings with murder? On the contrary, has it not reprimanded the Manager for using such foul language? In his last and closing speech he has dared to say, that he charged Mr. Hastings with murder in the largest sense of the word, and this at a period when he could make no new charge of any kind without a positive disobedience of the orders of the House. Shall we return him thanks for abusing so grossly the confidence which the House reposed in him?

Did the House mean to impeach every man who had served his country in India when they put

Mr.

Mr. Hastings on his trial ?—The violence of the Manager had spared neither the dead nor the living. Hear, said Mr. Sumner, what he says in his closing speech :

" This cruel tyrant, Hannay, a substitute for a
" still more cruel and bloody tyrant, Warren
" Hastings—Hastings says to Hannay, you have
" sucked blood enough for yourself, now suck
" blood for your neighbours."

Does this House authorize such language? Colonel Hannay is dead. No part of his conduct is implicated in the articles on which the cause rests.

Speaking of another Gentleman, the Manager says, " This Balfour, the writer of this extraordi-
" nary letter, one of the military farmers general
" employed under Hannay in desolating the coun-
" try." Is such language to be countenanced or endured? What is there in the charge that applies in the smallest degree to Major Balfour ?

Speaking of Major Osborne, the Manager said,
" Major Osborne had been dismissed. A court-
" martial removed him, justly or unjustly I care
" not, from his situation. There he sits in that
" box. Who sent him to Oude, to suck the blood
" the military had spared?

What is there, said Mr. Sumner in the articles on which the Commons rest their case that applies

to

to Major Osborne? The House is degraded and disgraced by the misconduct of the Manager.

" His supple, worn-down, beaten, cowed, and " I am afraid, bribed colleague, Mr. Wheler." Is this justtfiable language to be applied to a man who is no more, when there is no evidence that can warrant such an insinuation? In any stage of the trial, said Mr. Sumner, such language would be highly improper; but in the last stage of it, after evidence was closed on both sides, to make such remarks was in fact to betray the cause entrusted to him; for he excited no sentiments but those of indignation and contempt, either in the Court or in the audience, by such general and illiberal abuse.

In the same indecent terms that the Manager had mentioned every Gentleman almost who had given evidence on the trial, did he address the Court. Does the House know, that in offering a piece of evidence which the Court unanimously rejected, the Manager told them that he was addressing an assembly of nobles, that they would not do so foul a thing as to reject the evidence he offered; for if they did, they would act like thieves in a night cellar?

Mr. Sumner said, he could continue to quote passages from the last speech of the Manager so very offensive to decency, so degrading to the character

character of the House of Commons, as would
shock the ears of every Gentleman who reflected,
that as a Member he shared in the disgrace brought
upon them all by the Manager; but he trusted he
had laid sufficient grounds for the motion which
he meant to conclude with, and would therefore
move the previous question?

Mr WIGLEY said, he rose to second the motion, and very fully concurred in all the observations of his Honourable Friend. But there was
another reason which also weighed most forcibly
with him; the House was sensible of the clamour
which had been raised out of doors, and justly
raised on account of the unprecedented duration
of this trial. The House felt it, and had ordered
a Committee to report the causes of the duration
of it. The House had good reasons, he presumed, though they did not occur to him, for appointing the Managers to be members of that
Committee. It struck him, that they were made
judges in their own cause, for the fault must be
with the Managers, the Counsel of Mr. Hastings,
or the Lords. In the close of that Report another
was promised. Was it decent to thank the Managers before any motion was even made upon the
first, or before the second Report, though promised so long ago, was delivered? No precedent

of

of former thanks applied in any degree to this case.
The trial had lasted seven years, and would not be
finally terminated until the next session. Let
Gentlemen consider the nature of their Managers'
conduct before they came forward with a vote of
approbation. If the trial had been finished in the
first year, the House would have been competent
to form an opinion, but the Members had deserted
the Hall, and even the Managers very few had
lately attended. At all events, Mr. Wigley conceived the present to be a very improper time to
vote thanks to the Managers.

Mr. ROBINSON said, he had been present in
Westminster Hall when the leading Manager had,
in his opinion, treated the Court with very great
indecency. The security of the constitution depended upon each branch of the legislature being
kept perfectly distinct, on its being treated with
every degree of respect. As the leading Manager
had not acted towards the Court in a manner that
became him to act, he should certainly oppose his
receiving the thanks of the House.

Mr. WINDHAM said, that although at first intending not to speak, as being in some degree a
party in the question, yet he felt himself relieved
from this, by the distinction taken between Mr.
Burke

Burke and the other Managers; although he was convinced there was not one of them but would be proud to be connected with him in the fame and honour of the transaction. Declaring himself as competent to decide upon what had passed at the trial as any other person whatever, from his constant attendance, he affirmed, that in every instance quoted by the Member who opposed the motion, he had been completely mistaken; in many instances attributing to Mr. Burke words never uttered by him, and in others the expressions were so garbled as not to be understood. He, for one, had never conceived, that in speaking upon what the Managers looked upon as crimes of the deepest dye, they were to observe the courtly language of a drawing-room.

Mr. FRANCIS said, that his intention in addressing the House on the present occasion, was to give his testimony as a witness to certain points of fact. That having attended the trial with the greatest diligence, and more constantly, he believed, than any other Member of the House, he was at least a competent witness upon every thing that passed, and that he did not mean to assume any other character in this debate. That, without questioning the Honourable Gentleman's veracity, he did and must dispute the exactness of his recollection

lection on many points; and that even the Ho
nourable Gentleman himself had not trusted entirely to his own memory, having been obliged to
refresh it by recurring to a newspaper, to which
Mr. Francis well knew that no confidence ought
to be given. That he thought the Honourable
Gentleman had greatly overstated, and given a
very harsh and strained costruction, in every instance, to the language used in the pleadings by his
Right Honourable Friend;—but that, in some
very material particulars, he took upon him to affirm, that the Honourable Gentleman had been
grossly mistaken or misinformed. For example,
the expression of *Spider of Hell* was never applied by his Right Honourable Friend to Mr.
Hastings; it was a quotation from a speech of Sir
Edward Coke against Sir Walter Raleigh, and Mr.
Burke, when he mentioned it, had spoken of it as
a weak and foolish expression; that the words, *a
Judge of Hell*, were nothing but a quotation from
Virgil,

Castigatque auditque dolos, subigitque fateri,

which the Honourable Gentleman had thought fit
to translate into very vulgar English, and then
fixed his own English words upon Mr. Burke.
There was another instance, more material than
all

all the rest, on which he could aver with positive
certainty, and would be ready to do so, in a court
of justice, if it were necessary, on which the Honourable Gentleman was most competently mistaken, namely, when he asserted that his Right
Honourable Friend had treated a vote of this
House (in which some expression he had used relative to Sir Elijah Impey had been disavowed
and disapproved of) with levity and disrespect.
This charge, Mr. Francis affirmed, was not true,
and that there was not the smallest ground or pretence for it : that, on the contrary, when his Right
Honourable Friend mentioned this vote in Westminster Hall, he did it in terms of the greatest deference and respect, and with a most singular
choice and propriety of language ; for the truth of
which Mr. Francis appealed to Mr. Fox.

Mr. Francis then observed, that Gentlemen who
laid such mighty stress on casual expressions, or
other little circumstances not essential to the conduct of so heavy and so labourious a business as
the Impeachment, should have been particularly
cautious in stating the facts with the utmost accu-
racy;—and finally, that even if it had been true,
that any inconsiderate or even passionate expression had escaped any of the Managers, which he
was far from admitting, it would be no objection
to the vote of thanks now proposed. That this
vote

vote expressed nothing but to thank the Managers *for their faithful management in their discharge of the trust reposed in them,* and neither did nor could be supposed to bind the House to adopt every individual word used by the Managers in their pleadings; and that therefore, unless it could be stated and proved, that their management had been *unfaithful,* which had not been attempted, nor even pretended, the House could not justly refuse their assent to the resolution as it stood proposed.

Mr. FOX, contrary to his intention, found himself obliged to say a few words. He disclaimed all separation between the rest of the Managers, and the Right Honourable Member, so eminently qualified, not only by nature, but likewise by his particular study and attention to be, as he was termed, their leader in this business, and with whom it was their boast and glory to be identified. As to the imputation of using harsh terms, he did not conceive, that the Managers were chosen for their capabilities in courtly phrases; and as to persisting to think the fate of Nundcomar a murder, if there was any blame in it, it was his, for it was he and not Mr. Burke who had so expressed himself before the Lords, subsequent to the censure passed upon Mr. Burke by the House, and he was yet to learn, how any vote of that, or any other

House,

House, however it might controul his words or
actions, was to shackle his thoughts or opinions.

Mr. LAW rose after Mr. Fox and said, that it
was unnecessary for him to say much more than to
confirm the statement of his two honourable friends,
Mr. Sumner and Mr. Wigley, which he did most
completely; nor could he suppress his surprize
and astonishment at the conduct of gentlemen of
character, whose talents he revered, in attempting
to excuse the leading Manager, by asserting, that
in some instances, his expressions had been misrepresented. Mr. Law solemnly affirmed that they
were not; that the English language did not afford expressions more gross, violent, abusive, and
indecent than those which the Manager had used.
If any passage in his speech could be called sublime and beautiful, it was at best but sublime and
beautiful nonsense; at other times his expressions
were so vulgar and illiberal, that the lowest black-
guard in a bear garden, would have been ashamed
to utter them. He was indeed surprised that a
Right Hon. Gentleman (Mr. Fox) should conde-
scend to mix his character with that of the leading
Manager. Mr. Law said, he had been a very constant attendant upon the trial, and he had often
seen the Right Hon. Gentleman exert his great
abilities in support of the cause assigned to him,
and

and as often excited in order to correct the follies, and the intemperance of the leading Manager. Whatever his abilities might be, he was totally unfit to conduct a public trial. His violence, his passion, and his obstinacy were unconquerable; and as for his supposed information, he was really astonished that a man who had been twenty-two years employed in Indian inquiries should still be so very ignorant of India. His prejudices had totally warped his judgment. The feeling of the public, Mr. Law said, would not, and coulld not be changed by a vote of that House. Many thousand persons of both sexes had heard the closing speech of the Honourable Manager, which had lasted nine days. His expressions could not be mistaken; and he was confident, that if the minutes of the short-hand writers were called for, it would appear that the terms he used, instead of being less, were more illiberal, outrageous, and offensive than his honourable friends had represented them to be. They were universally reprobated from the first characters amongst the numerous audience that heard them, down to the messengers, door-keepers, and guards. In that House, Mr. Law said, Gentlemen would not speak out; but he knew that they condemned the conduct of the leading Manager as much as he did; but observed, that he was not to be controuled;

and

and that opposition only made him the more violent. Mr. Law said, the Manager had treated the
Court as ill as he had done Mr. Hastings. To
the truth of the various quotations, one excepted,
which was of an old date, he bore the fullest testimony. The expressions were used in this year,
and all of them within a month. The context in
no instance could take away from the grossness
or illiberality of the expressions. It was disgraceful to the House, and scandalous to the cause
of justice, that the most atrocious libels fhould be
uttered against Gentlemen whose conduct was not
in question, and who consequently could not
defend themselves. Amongst the Gentlemen with
whose characters the Manager had made free, there
was a very old and intimate friend of his own,
Major Osborne, a Gentleman of as fair and ho·
nourable a character as any in England, and a
man who knew how to defend himself. It was
highly unjust in the House, and highly impolitic,
to afford their sanction in the slightest degree to
any of the abominable calumnies that were uttered. It involved them in injustice, inconsistency,
and absurdity. It degraded the national character
most unjustly throughout Europe. Barrere in the
National Convention had the other day detailed
as a fact, an infamous falsehod, which party malice
had invented many years ago;—he meant the accusation,

accusation, that the English were the authors of
the dreadful famine that raged so fatally in Bengal
in the year 1770. At that time, Mr. Law said, he
was in Bengal, and he affirmed most solemnly that
every exertion was made by the British government to lessen the shocking miseries which the
people sustained, not from any mismanagement of
the government, which was then in the hands of
Mahomed RezaÇawn, but from a failure in the pe-
riodical rains; that every civil servant of the Company, every British Officer at every military station,
and every Englishman throughout Bengal, exerted
himself to alleviate the distresses of the people.
The most liberal subscriptions were entered into,
and every personal exertion used, to procure grain
wherever it could be found; yet some modern
historians had represented the English as the cause
of that famine, and as insensible of the miseries
it brought upon the people.

In the same style of misrepresentation did the
leading Manager, in the first year of this trial, introduce a story which resounded through Europe,
to the disgrace and scandal of this nation; he
meant the story of Deby Sing. Mr. Law said,
that on its being told, he affirmed that it could not
be true. He knew that cruelty was no part of an
Englishman's charaƈter in any country, and as
little so in India as any part of the world. This
justice

justice he was sure the noble Marquis would do
to his countrymen ; for he was too high and too
honourable a character to conceal the truth, because men of great consideration in this country
had been misled.   The noble Marquis had shewn
himself to be superior to those follies and prejudices which had distinguished so many persons in
England.

The leading Manager had implicated a very intimate friend of his in the story of Deby Sing ; he
meant Sir John Shore, whom the Minister had selected to govern Bengal.   He had described that
Gentleman as an accomplice in the crimes of Mr.
Hastings, and had gone so far in folly as to re-
monstrate to the Directors on their appointing him
Governor General of Bengal.

Mr. Law said, that when he heard the Manager
tell this story with so much confidence in Westminster Hall, he was sure from his own knowledge
of the country that the story could not be true ;
but his regard for Sir John Shore, and his zeal for
the honour of his country, induced him to sift the
business to the bottom.   He went most carefully
and attentively through all those volumes which
the Manager had in his possession also, and he
boldly challenged the most inventive malice of
the most malicious man that ever existed, to affix
blame either upon Mr. Hastings or Sir John

y y   Shore

Shore for any concern they had in that transaction. The fact was shortly this; a district was rented for two years to a man of the name of Deby Sing, and let out again by him to under-farmers. This man had for years been employed in the revenue line, and was much esteemed both by Sir John Shore and Mr. Anderson.

The first year the rents were regularly paid; in the second there were complaints of great severities having been used in the collection of the revenue. The first and the only act done by Mr. Hastings throughout the whole business, was to order Deby Sing to be removed, and that in so hasty a manner, as to expose himself to the charge of having acted with too much severity to him. A Gentleman was deputed to receive the complaints of the natives, Mr. Paterson, of whom the world has heard so much, and who was so little pleased with the extravagant encomiums of the leading Manager, that he has publicly disavowed him, and has publicly expressed concern that his reports should have been tortured into evidence against Mr. Hastings, who had no sort of concern in the business; but was most anxious to detect the enormities of Deby Sing, and to punish him.

Mr. Paterson transmitted to Calcutta all the complaints he had received, and amongst them were statements of cruelties practised upon certain

tain of the natives, too shocking to be repeated. These complaints arrived when Mr. Hastings was absent, and the Board appointed a Committee of Company's servants (all senior to Mr. Paterson, and not junior, as the Manager stated) to sift this business to the bottom. The Commissioners were sworn, and the examinations were taken upon oath. Their commission did not terminate until long after Mr. Hastings was in England; and the result of the fullest examination was, that the most dreadful of the cruelties charged never were committed at all, and that for such severities as were exercised, no possible blame could attach upon any English gentleman. Such, Mr. Law affirmed, was the true state of the case; and it was a disgrace to the House of Commons that the leading Manager should have travelled out of his indictment, in order to utter his calumnies against Sir John Shore, and the public servants employed in the revenue line.

Mr. Law lamented exceedingly that so superior a man as Mr. Fox, since he had accepted the office of a Manager, had not condescended to examine and to judge for himself before he spoke. Had he ever himself looked into the history of Deby Sing, he never could have justified for a moment the conduct of the leading Manager.

Nor

Nor was this, said Mr. Law, the only instance in
which the leading Manager had quitted the articles entrusted to him, in order to indulge the malignity of his own disposition. He had lately described Mr. Hastings as a man of a low, vulgar,
and obscure origin, whose occupations had been
base, mean and sordid. If it were of any consequence in this free country, and at this period, for
a man to value himself upon the accidental circumstance of family, Mr. Hastings might have as
fair grounds to boast of his family as any Gentleman in the House. Such topics are ridiculous;
but that from such a man as the Manager a
word should be uttered on the subject of low,
mean, and obscure origin, was indeed most extraordinary, the Manager of all men living ought to
have avoided such a topic. Mr. Hastings, the
Manager said, had been a fraudulent bullock
contractor in the year 1761. This is downright
calumny. Where is the charge voted by the
House, or where the evidence, that entitled him
to make such an assertion? Indeed, said Mr.
Law, the Manager, in his closing speech of nine
days, wasted five of them upon points that had
not the most distant relation to the cause entrusted
to him by this House; and the more he considered his conduct, the more he was convinced, that
from 1788 to this day, he had systematically, for
some

some purpose or other, delayed the close of the trial to as late a period as he possibly could, to the abuse of public jnstice, at a most ·enormous expence to the nation, and to the manifest inconvenience of all ranks of people.   Every thing he had done was for the purpose of delay.   The House collectively had not attended, and therefore could not judge; but such Gentlemen as had heard the Manager examining witnesses, keeping some of them four days together, asking questions that had no relation to the points in issue, or putting the same questions over and over again, must be convinced that delay, and delay alone was his object.   No words, Mr. Law said, could convey to Gentlemen who had not heard his closing speech an adequate idea of it—it lasted nine days—two were employed in going thro' the Benares, and two in going over the Begum article.   A most indecent procceding Mr. Law said, in his opinion, and a very poor compliment to the Managers, who had well and ably performed their duties; a proceeding that could have no other effect than to weaken the force of their observations.   Such was the universal remark.   Another day was wasted in part by remarks on the article, which the Right Hon. Gentlemen (Mr. Fox) had enforced by every argument that talents, eloquence, and ingenuity could bring forward, and which well merited the

most

most serious attention of every man. Mr. Law. said, though he differed in opinion with Mr. Fox, yet he must do him the justice to say, that all that man could do to support the cause, he had done. But here again the leading Manager must interfere; he must destroy as far as he could the effect produced by Mr. Fox's speech: he went over the ground again, until listlessness, fatigue, and disgust were apparent in every countenance. The remaining four days were wasted by the Manager upon points that had no sort of relation to the charge, improper at any time to have been agitated, but when dwelt upon in a speech in reply, which ought to be confined to remarks upon evidence before the Court, in the highest degree indecent and irregular. Part of the time was wasted in reading papers that are not in evidence, and in blackening the characters of Gentlemen who cannot defend themselves. What, then, could the Manager mean, but to scatter his calumnies as wide as he could, and to continue the trial to the latest possible moment he could? Mr. Law said, and it was well known, that he had no sort of connection with Mr. Hastings, and that he had in India disapproved of some some of his political measures; beyond this he had never gone, as an Honourable Member (Mr. Francis) well knew. On political subjects he had differed with Mr.

Hastings,

Hastings, but never upon any one of the four points on which this impeachment rests. On those points he never had but one opinion; and he believed the mind of every fair and impartial man in the kingdom was made up as to Mr. Hastings. He was confident that Mr. Hastings in no one act of his public life, had been warped by interested or malicious motives. One good effect this trial would have—it would convince his countrymen how grossly they had been imposed upon, and they would be less liable to imposition in future.

Mr. Law concluded by saying, that as he thought the conduct of the leading Manager throughout the trial, had entailed shame and disgrace upon the House of Commons, he should vote most heartily for the previous question.

Mr. FOX, in explanation said, that what he had said on the topic alluded to, was the result of a full consideration of the subject, and not from the hearsay of any person whatever; and what, were the same occasions to occur, he should not hesitate to say again; but if it was from hearsay only that he had his information, he wondered how the Honourable Member came to know that circumstance: but he could tell him the fact was quite the reverse.

Mr.

Mr. ANSTRUTHER supported the conduct of Mr. Burke, and said, that though the leading Manager originally had told the story of Deby Sing, yet it was another Right Hon. Gentleman (Mr. Fox) and himself who proposed to give evidence upon it, thinking they might make Mr. Hastings responsible for the acts of Deby Sing. It was true the Court had unanimously rejected the evidence ; but he still retained his own opinion on that, and on other points of evidence which had been rejected.

Mr. SUMNER spoke in explanation ; he wished, if any one Gentleman doubted his veracity, to refer to the minutes of the short-hand writer, as the only criterion by which they could determine who was right in the statement of the language used by the Right Honourable Manager ; and upon this point he declared himself willing to meet any of those Gentlemen who considered it in a different point of view from him.

Mr. SHERIDAN supported the conduct of Mr. Burke ; he said, that if the question was merely whether the Managers merited the thanks of the House or not, that he should not vote on the occasion, but the motion for the previous question on the ground on which it was moved,

i   viz.

viz. for the purpose of throwing a reflection on the conduct of one of the Committee, changed its nature entirely, and he therefore should feel it his duty to remain in the House with those who oppose it.

The question was then put, when there appeared,

For the previous question	21
Noes —	55
Majority	34

The question of thanks was then put, when there appeared,

Ayes	50
Noes	21
Majority	29

The usual motion, that the Speaker do give the thanks of the House to the Managers in their places, was then put and carried; and the SPEAKER addressed the Managers in the following speech:

Gentlemen,

IT is my duty to communicate to you the thanks of this House, for the manner in which you have discharged a most arduous trust, on an

occasion

occasion highly interesting to the honour and justice of the nation.

The subject, to which your attention has been directed, was intricate and extensive beyond example : You have proved, that it was well suited to your industry and eloquence, the exertions of which have conferred honour, not on yourselves only, but on this House, whose credit is intimately connected with your own. A forcible admonition has been given on this occasion, to all persons in situations of high and important national trust, that they can neither be removed by distance, or sheltered by power, from the vigilance and authority of this House, which is possessed of no privilege more important than that by which it is enabled to bring public delinquents to the bar of public justice, and thus to preserve or rescue from dishonour, the *British* name and character.

But in addressing you on this occasion, and in considering the beneficial consequences to be expected from this proceeding, it is impossible. not to advert to the increased security which the constitution has derived in the course of it, from the recognition and full confirmation of the principle, that an impeachment is not discontinued by a dissolution of Parliament; a principle essential to the privileges of this House, and to the independent and effectual administration of public justice.

Under

Under these impressions, suggested by the nature and importance of your trust, and by the
manner in which you have discharged it, I obey,
with the utmost satisfaction, the commands of this
House, by stating to you their resolution

" That the Thanks of this House be given to
" the Members, who were appointed the Mana-
" gers of the Impeachment against *Warren Has-*
" *tings,* Esq. for their faithful management in their
" discharge of the trust reposed in them."

Mr. PITT moved, that the Speaker do print
his speech.

Mr. BURKE said, that by the orders of the
House, when the Thanks were given, he and his
brother Managers were tongue-tyed, and had no
means whereby to express their gratitude but by
their submission to those orders. But he thought
he should be wanting in gratitude if he did not,
the moment the penalty of silence was removed,
seize the first opportunity to express his own satisfaction, and that of his fellow Managers, on the
occasion. They had laboured to discharge their
duty, they had completed the task, and they were
paid by the Thanks of that House, the first reward
men could receive. Next to the Thanks he must
notice the very dignified and elegant manner in
which

which the Speaker had discharged that task, in which he consulted not only the grandeur and dignity of that House, but at the same time politeness and attention to them. He then entered into a short defence of the conduct of the Impeachment. He assured the House, that no asperity of remark should provoke him to say a word, that prejudices arising from personal friendship, or from a sense of personal obligations, were too laudable for him to be discomposed at: he would only assure the House, that he had thrown no general reflections on the Company's servants, having merely repeated what Mr. Hastings himself had said of the troops serving in Oude; and it would be found by referring to the 12th and 13th articles, that the House had marked their opinion of the officers serving in Oude, in the very terms that he had used; and as for the other expressions, they had been very much misrepresented.

Mr. LAW, in reply to Mr. Burke, said, that he desired not to be included amongst those Gentlemen, if any such there were, which he did not believe, who acted either from early prejudices, or from a sense of favours received; he was as independent of Mr. Hastings as of the two Right Honourable Gentlemen who were united in the

present

present question; and he gave his vote from
the firmest conviction that he was right, and that
instead of thanks, the leading Manager merited
the reprobation of every man who had the honour of the House and of the country at heart:
he was, indeed, sorry to see the Right Honourable Gentleman (Mr. Fox), whom he much respected, acting in the present instance under such
a leader. He knew what the sense of the country was, and no vote of that House, though supported by all the influence both of the Minister
and of the Opposition, could change the public
mind, or convince the people of the propriety
of the conduct of the leading Manager. With
regard to his having misrepresented any one expression used by the leading Manager in Westminster Hall, he was confident he had not,
and that if the minutes of the short-hand writer
were referred to, it would be found, that he
had been infinitely more abusive and violent
than he had been represented in the quotations that
were made. Mr. Law repeated, that no contradiction, let it come from what quarter it
would, could have the slightest effect in this
case; it was impossible to mistate what so many
thousands had heard, what so many thousands
had reprobated, and which, as he said before, excited no other sentiments than those of contempt

and

and indignation in the minds of the auditors, from persons of the highest rank down to the door-keepers, guards, and porters, attending in and about Westminster Hall.

APPENDIX.

APPENDIX.

IT may possibly be deemed more satisfactory to our Readers, if we cite at length the authorities for the several assertions made in the course of the debate.

The vote alluded to by Mr. Sumner, which precluded the Managers from going into any further articles except contracts, passed the 14th of February, 1791, and is in the following words:

" That in consideration of the length of time " which has already elapsed since the carrying up " the impeachment now depending against Warren " Hastings, Esq. *it appears to this House to be pro-* " *per,* for the purpose of obtaining substantial " justice, *with as little further delay as possible, to* " *proceed to no other parts of the said impeachment* " than those *on which the Managers have already* " *closed their evidence,* excepting *only such parts* as " relate *to contracts, pensions,* and *allowances.*"

Upon

Upon this motion a division took place, Mr. Ryder proposing, that the prosecution should be *instantly closed;* the numbers were 161 to 79, so that it was carried to go on as far as the contracts, but no further.

It is to be observed, that in obedience to the letter and the spirit of this vote, that the Managers brought forward the article of contracts, and *then* entirely *closed* the prosecution in May 1791; that is, in *four sitting days* after this resolution of the House was voted. The impeachment then rested upon four articles—The Benares, the Begum, the Presents, and the Contracts. The defence was confined to these four articles; and the evidence *in reply,* was also *confined* to them; the Lords rejecting every thing offered that was not strictly evidence *in reply to these four articles.* Mr. Fox, Mr. Grey, Mr. Sheridan, and Mr. Taylor, who summed up these four articles, confined themselves most correctly to the matter contained in each; but Mr. Burke contended, that the Commons had not abandoned one of the twenty articles; and when stopped by the Court, retired to consult with Mr. Windham before he would give up the point.

The proof that Mr. Burke attacked the characters of the civil and military servants of the Company collectively, will be found in the quotations that we shall give from his speeches in four several years.

years. Mr. Burke denies this charge, and says, he merely repeated the reflections that Mr. Hastings had cast upon the Company's servants; yet in various passages of his speech, he has accused Mr. Hastings of making common cause with them. In his last speech he accused Mr. Hastings of disobeying an order transmitted to him for enquiring into past abuses; commented on the excuse offered by Mr. Hastings, which was, that any irregular acts committed were owing to a want of a system of law and policy, and did not originate in the habits of licentiousness in the Company's servants. Forgetting *all that he had said*, Mr. Burke seriously told the House, that it was not he, but Mr. Hastings, who had calumniated the Company's servants. Mr. Burke added, that the House, in the 12th and 13th articles, had given their sentiments of the officers serving in Oude. It is not now of moment to state, though the fact is true, that the last House voted the 12th and 13th articles without reading one line of them; but had they been voted after the fullest enquiry, they were totally abandoned *by a vote of this House*; the *only* step this House ever took being totally to abandon all that the last House had voted, *four* charges excepted; and into the *truth* or the *falsehood* of those four charges it never enquired. We do not say this with a view of diminishing the

z z

importance

importance which may be fairly due to those four charges; but as this House of Commons has, by *an express law*, appropriated *to the public service*, the *proceeds*, to use a mercantile phrase, which arose from the acts that are charged to the criminal in those charges, it is fair to say, that they were not *voted* by this House of Commons, and that this House *cannot believe them to be true.*

In the very sensible and energetic speech addressed by Mr. Speaker to the Managers, he truly says, that the House possesses no privilege more important than that by which it is enabled to bring public delinquents to the bar of public justice, and thus to *preserve or rescue from dishonour the British name and character.*—A noble sentiment, and most eloquently expressed. There never was an occasion on which the House of Commons acted so disinterestedly. In the *original charge* it was affirmed, that the various measures pursued by Mr. Hastings, by which thirty-four millions sterling were acquired for Great Britain, and an additional revenue of two millions sterling a year, were flagrant violations of public faith, or acts of outrageous tyranny, plunder, and oppression.

The charge is now *curtailed*, but in its present state is of great importance. Mr. Sheridan, speaking *in the name* and on the behalf *of the Commons*, said, that if Mr. Hastings were found *guilty* on the

Benares

Benares, the Begum, and the Presents, œconomical as the House was, it would be *impossible* not to give the *parties* aggrieved *full* and *complete restitution;* that is, to take *from the public six millions sterling,* the principal and interest of the money taken from Cheyt Sing; two millions sterling, the principal and interest of the money taken from the Begum; and eight hundred thousand pounds, the principal and interest of the presents taken by Mr. Hastings, and paid into the public treasury : to this sum of *eight millions eight hundred thousand pounds,* which must be paid in money, is to be added, a deduction of two hundred thousand pounds a year from the future revenue of Benares. By no other means *can the British nation be rescued from dishonour,* provided Mr. Hastings be guilty. No Gentleman, therefore, who considers the speech of the Speaker, or the speech of the Minister, which contained *the same sentiment,* can withhold his approbation, not unmixed *with wonder,* at the very great disinterestedness expressed *by both.* Any other nation than Great Britain, when involved in an expensive and calamitous war, the fatal effects of which we daily experience, and after having paid so largely for foreign aid, would be contented to enjoy the advantages that were procured for them thirteen years ago without further investigation, until India called for redress. But

though

though the Minister of India has unequivocally declared, that an empire in the East has been *well governed;* though he presented, and the legislature passed a bill, by which the public participates to a great amount in the advantages obtained by Mr. Hastings; though from various accidents the Company were unable to pay half a million *in this year to the public,* until the Legislature gave them leave to *borrow the money;* such is the sacred regard which the Minister professes for the *honour* of the nation, that *for seven years* he had allowed that party which was once called *the Opposition,* to exert every talent they possess in order to prove, that without fixing *everlasting disgrace on the British name and character,* Mr. Dundas must not continue *to impose upon the world* by boasting of the importance and value of our Indian territories. Our opinion is, that the Managers have been completely mistaken; an opinion we may be allowed to give, as we are not judges in the cause, and as all the evidence is closed; but if the Managers are right, the nation must pay to India *eight millions eight hundred thousand pounds,* and we must take off two hundred thousand pounds a year from our India revenue in future, or the nation must undergo the double disgrace of *having proved,* that it has *robbed* and *plundered* to an *enormous amount,* and of putting into its own

1   pocket

pocket all that was obtained by that *robbery* and *plunder.*

The following passages are selected from Mr. Burke's speeches in the several years:

MR. BURKE, IN 1788.

" MY LORDS.

" The Gentlemen who have it in command to support the impeachment against Mr. Hastings, late Governor General of Bengal, have directed me to open *a general view* of the *grounds* upon which the Commons have proceeded in their charges against him : to open a general view of the *extent*, the *magnitude*, the *nature*, the *tendency*, and *effect* of the *crimes* with which they have charged him.

" *What the greatest interests of the nation has be-gun, its highest tribunal will accomplish. Justice will be done to India.*

" It is not *solely*, whether the prisoner at the bar be found *innocent* or *guilty*, but whether *millions* of *mankind* should be *miserable* or *happy.*

" My Lords, It is not only the subjects of this great empire who are concerned, *but the credit and honour of the British nation will itself be decided by this decision.*

" We

" We know that as we are to be served by men, that the persons who serve us *must* be tried *as men*, and that there is a very large allowance indeed due to human infirmity and human error. This we know, *and have weighed before we came to your Lordships bar.* But the crimes *we charge* are not the *causes* and *effects* of *common human frailty*, such as we *know* and *feel*, and *can allow for ;* but they are *crimes* which have their rise in *the wicked dispositions of men*—they are crimes which have their rise in *avarice, rapacity, pride, cruelty, ferocity, malignity of temper, haughtiness, insolence ;* in short, every thing that manifests a *heart blackened to the very blackest—a heart dyed deep in blackness—a heart gangreened to the very core.*

" We have not chosen to bring before you *a poor, trembling delinquent.*

" We have brought before you *the head, the chief, a captain general of iniquity*—one in whom all the fraud, *all the tyranny of India are embodied, disciplined, and arrayed.*

" You have now a *boundless object*—it is not *from this county, or that parish,* but *whole climes,* and *differing nations.*

" Knowing your Lordships to be possessed, along with all other judicial virtues, with that of *patience,* I hope, and trust, you will not grudge *a few short hours* to the explanation of *that,* which

has

has cost *the Commons* near fourteen years of assi-
duous application—that you will not refuse *a few
hours* to what has cost the *people of India upwards
of thirty years* of their *innate inveterate patience to
endure.*

" The first of his acts was the most bold and extraordinary that I believe entered into the head of
any man, *I will say, of any tyrant, which was nothing less than a general exceptionless confiscation of
the property of Bengal.* He put it up to a pretended public, but in reality to a private and corrupt auction.

" I shall say nothing either of the circumstances of the purchase, or of the right of the people
to their property, or to the nature and mode of
detection, *until that great question, the greatest of
all* which we shall bring, shall be brought before
your Lordships, *particularly as an article of
charge.*

" And here I come to the beginning of a
great notorious system of government, which
consists of many abuses, branched out into such
a variety of ways, *and has so much affected the
kingdom,* that I may venture to say, *it will make
one of the greatest and most weighty parts of the
charges.*

" I charge him with having taken away *the lands
of orphans,* with having alienated *the fortunes of wi-*

dows

dows—with having *wasted the country and destroyed the* inhabitants, after cruelly *harassing* and *distressing them.* I charge him *with having tortured their persons, and dishonoured their religion, thro'* his *wicked agents,* who were at the bottom and root of his villainy.

" I charge him *in the name of the Commons of England.*

" Now, my Lords, what is it we want? We want to have the cause of *oppressed princes*—of *undone women* of the first rank, redressed—of *desolated provinces* and *wasted kingdoms, redressed.*— Do *you* want *a criminal,* my Lords? When was there *so much iniquity* charged against any one? —No, my Lords, you must not look to India to furnish one, for Mr. Hastings has not left in India *substance enough* to furnish *such another delinquent.*

" I impeach Warren Hastings in the name of the people of India, whose *laws, rights,* and *liberties he has subverted.* I impeach him in the name of the people of India, *whose country he has destroyed*—I impeach him in the name of *human nature, which he has cruelly injured and oppressed in both sexes.*

N R.

MR. BURKE IN 1789.

" Eminent for the *pillage* and *destruction of provinces.*

" Crimes of *great enormity,* the *ruin* and *expulsion of illustrious families,* the *total ruin of villages,* the total expulsion *of the first houses in Asia.*

" A *man* who, in *his own person,* has done more *mischief* than all those persons whose evil practices had produced *all those laws,* those regulations, and even *his own appointment.*

" A corrupt, shocking arrangement was made, and Bengal saw *a dancing girl administer its laws.*

" He has *murdered* that man by the hands of Sir Elijah Impey.

" He gorged his *ravenous maw* with an allowance of 200l. a day. He is not satisfied *without sucking the blood of* 1400 nobles. He is never *corrupt* without he is *cruel.* He never *dines without creating a famine.* He feeds on the *indigent,* the *decaying,* and the *ruined,* and them he depresses together; not like the generous eagle, who *preys* on a *living, reluctant, equal prey :* No; he is like the *ravenous vulture,* who feeds on the *dead,* and the *enfeebled,* who destroys and incapacitates *nature* in the destruction *of its object,* while devouring the

carcases

carcases of the dead, and then prides himself in his ignominious security, and his *cruelty* is beyond his *corruption*; at the same time, there is in his *hypocrisy* something more *terrible* than his *cruelty*. For at the same time that he exercises a *proscription* that sweeps off the bread *of thousands of the nobility*, he turns the precious balm that flows from wounded humanity into *deadly, rancorous, and mortal* poison *to the human race*.

" Mr. Hastings feasts in the dark alone; *like a wild beast he groans in a corner over the dead and dying*; and like the tyger of that country, he wishes to withdraw it to a cavern, to indulge with unobserved enjoyment in all the wanton caprices of his appetite.

" He comes a *heavy calamity* to the nation, as we say a country is visited by *famine* and *pestilence*.

" His *crimes* are so *multiplied*, that all the contrivances of ingenuity to cover them are *abortive*.

" If the language had furnished me, under the impression of those feelings, a word sufficient to convey the complicated atrocity of that act, as it stood in my mind, I should certainly not have used the word *murder*; but having no other, I was obliged to use that word.

MR.

MR. BURKE IN 1791.

" One cannot conceive a *crime* that defames
human nature, of which this man is not charged in
the articles of impeachment that are given before
your Lordships; and with respect to the Commons
of Great Britain, when human nature is stirred
with rage against his crimes; when it is the *sympa-
thy* which God has planted in us, and *horror* of
those crimes, that has called the Commons to your
Lordships' bar. When they hear of *murders*—
when they hear *of women torn from their houses*—
when they hear *of the most cruel racks and tortures
that can be inflicted, and* all this *from the avarice
of the man who is at your Lordships' bar.*

Every drop of blood that was spilt in consequence of his acts, *was murder.* We charge him
with robberies—we charge him *with tortures*—we
charge him *with cruelty.*

" The *unfortunate people of England,* for *fourteen years have suffered these things.* It is *they* that
have had *patience.*

" The Commons wish at this moment to close
the charge, and to proceed *no further* in any of
the articles now before you, than those on which
they have already delivered their evidence. My
Lords, *the Commons* rejoice at the approach of a
day

day, by them *so long wished*, a day which is to vindicate and give glory, or to obscure *for ever*, the justice of this kingdom. The Commons have approached it with a manly confidence, but at the same time, with an anxious solicitude for the greatest stake any nation ever did, or ever could have, namely, whether its highest bodies on judicial proceedings; whether its highest tribunals shall vindicate that justice, without which no government can stand; whether they shall vindicate the dispensations of Providence, that has committed so great an empire in so distant a country to Great Britain; whether this country has energy and ability *to protect them*; whether we should retain a country so remote and distant, notwithstanding all the difficulties that nature has thrown in our way. My Lords, I venture to say, *this day* is a day most justly desired by the House of Commons.

MR. BURKE IN 1794.

" This swindling MÆCENAS—swindling of glory, and obtaining honour under false pretences—a bad scribbler of absurd papers, who could never put two sentences of sense together.

" A frau-

" A fraudulent Bullock Contractor—his ex-amples are of persons who have become rebels to their sovereigns.

" A traiterous and rebellious assumption of the power which belongs only to the King, as Sove-reign, with both Houses of Parliament.

" If you allow such doctrines, your Lordships are as wild, savage, and unprincipled as the pri-soner who stands at your bar.

" His supple, worn-down, beaten, cowed, and I am afraid, bribed colleague, Mr. Wheler.

" Hear what Lord Coke says of a passage in Virgil—

Castigatque, auditque dolos, subegitque fateri.

" Such are the damned and damnable proceed-ings of a Judge in Hell, and such a judge was Warren Hastings.

" We charge him as a tyrant, an oppressor, and murderer, in the largest sense of the word.

" A man whose origin was low, obscure, and vulgar, and bred in vulgar and ignoble habits—more proud than persons born under canopies of state, and swaddled in purple.

" The indecency, the rancour, the pride, and the insolence of the Dows, the Hastings's, and their adherents.

" You

"You have seen the atrocious insolence, the tyrannical pride, with which he reproaches us.

This cruel tyrant HANNAY, a substitute to a still more cruel and bloody tyrant, WARREN HASTINGS—HASTINGS says to HANNAY, you have sucked blood enough for yourself, now suck blood for your neighbours.

" Captain Williams murdered Rajah Mustapha Cawn with his own hand.

" No man is a tyrant, who is not, when he can be, a rebel.

" God forbid that I should praise that Committee in any respect—I know it was a *committee of robbers.*

" A species of account, which, in a night cellar amongst thieves, could hardly be attempted.

" I wore a suit of fine cloaths as Jew bail—they all will burn for your gang.

" Here is a watch—I wore it as long as I chose, and now I give it up to the gang.

" As to house-rent for aid-de-camps, he may say, I have found lodgings in St. Giles's *for some of the gang.*

" A sink not only of filth and excrement to shock the natural senses, but of filth and excrement to shock the moral sense of every visitor.

" Vindicating

" Vindicating himself by the founding of a col-
lege for thieves, pickpockets, felons, and house-
breakers.

" In the swindling account, swindle upon swindle—and Mr. LARKING keeping the private as he
kept the public account, has swindled a whole
year in his account of this transaction.

" A common-place dog-trot fraud, of the
meanest of mankind.

" You must repeal the Act of Parliament, if
you acquit Mr. HASTINGS—you must pronounce
the Legislature a liar.

" Major OSBORNE had been dismissed. A
court martial had removed him—I care not whether justly or unjustly; there he sits in that box.
Who sent him to Oude to suck the blood the military had spared? A wild beast when his belly is
full may be pleased and lick your hand. You might
have a serene day under such a beast, but can you
under that man HASTINGS?

" He is a captain general of iniquity—thief—
tyrant—robber—cheat—sharper—swindler. We
call him all these names, and are sorry that the
English language does not afford terms adequate
to the enormity of his offences.

" Revenge is a sort of wild justice—it is the
test of heroic virtue—we will continue to the end

to

to persecute. I vow, that we bear immortal ha-
tred against this scum, filth, and pollution of Indian guilt; if the Commons do not, I take it all
to myself.

"Sir WALTER RALEIGH was called a spider
of hell. This was foolish, indecent, in Lord
COKE. Had he been a Manager on this trial, he
would have been guilty of a neglect of duty, had
he not called the prisoner a spider of hell.

"I tremble for the event, because, if the prisoner is innocent, the Commons are guilty.

"Nothing but the malice of the House of
Commons could have instigated them to institute
this prosecution, if they had not been sure of his
guilt—Nothing but a great party formed by his
wealth could support him.

"We reduced this cause into a smaller compass,
into *four charges*, because of the long protraction
of it—those we left being as bad as the rest.

"What! compare this man, a bullock driver,
with TAMERLANE and those conquerors?—When
GOD punished PHARAOH and Egypt, he did not
send armies, but lice and locusts, to lay the land
waste.

"This *arbitrary creature—ignorant—stupid—*
from a blind presumption, overturned the whole
system, and ruined the trade of the country. By
his

his own conduct, he set all vigilance asleep: by his bullock contracts he corrupted his coadjutor.

" When he comes before you, you find him possessed of no one quality fit for any business whatever.

" Sometimes God has made wickedness mad.

" I ask and scrutinize what was latent in a tyger's heart—what was in a tyger's breast to do—and that he did.

" He formed all these infernal plots in his mind, uncertain which he would execute.

" At the same time that he had the rapacity of a vulture, he had not the talons or the beak of a vulture—he lost his prey.

F I N I S.